D1715292

CURRICULUM IN CONFLICT:

Social Visions, Educational Agendas, and Progressive School Reform

CURRICULUM IN CONFLICT:
Social Visions, Educational Agendas, and Progressive School Reform

LANDON E. BEYER
DANIEL P. LISTON

Teachers College, Columbia University
New York and London

Published by Teachers College Press, 1234 Amsterdam Avenue, New York, NY 10027

Chapter 5 is adapted from "Discourse or Moral Action? A Critique of Postmodernism," by Landon E. Beyer, in *Educational Theory*, volume 42, number 4, 1992, pp. 371–393. Reprinted by permission.

Library of Congress Cataloging-in-Publication Data

Beyer, Landon E., 1949–
    Curriculum in conflict : social visions, educational agendas, and
progressive school reform / Landon E. Beyer, Daniel P. Liston.
        p.   cm.
    Includes bibliographical references and index.
    ISBN 0-8077-3529-9. — ISBN 0-8077-3528-0 (pbk.)
    1. Education—United States—Curricula.   2. Curriculum planning—
Social aspects—United States.   3. Postmodernism and education—
United States.   I. Liston, Daniel Patrick.   II. Title.
    LB1570.B466   1996
    374'.00973—dc20   95-26770

ISBN 0-8077-3528-0   (paper)
ISBN 0-8077-3529-9   (cloth)
Printed on acid-free paper
Manufactured in the United States of America
01 00 99 98 97 96   8 7 6 5 4 3 2 1

To our children:

Nate, Leah, and Emma

Ira and Matthew

Contents

Acknowledgments

First, we want to thank the people who read and gave us feedback on various chapter drafts: Roy Andersen, Nicholas C. Burbules, Michael Dale, Scott Fletcher, Jo Anne Pagano, and Steven Selden. We would also like to thank the anonymous readers, employed by Teachers College Press, who reviewed the manuscript. While we take responsibility for the views in this work, we are grateful for the comments and suggestions made by others.

Second, we would like to thank Sarah Biondello and Carol Chambers Collins of Teachers College Press who have been supportive and encouraging throughout the project. In their efforts they have been consistently thoughtful and gracious.

Third, Lanny Beyer completed a significant amount of work on his portion of the book as part of a sabbatical leave during the 1992–1993 academic year while he was a resident of Friday Harbor Laboratories at Friday Harbor, Washington. The staff and researchers at Friday Harbor were generous in providing library research assistance, access to relevant resources, and intellectual and moral support. He is especially grateful to Dennis Willows, Director of Friday Harbor Labs. Dennis's progressive orientation to the day to day activities of the lab itself, and to the social relations it engendered, contributed to a quality of life that was instrumental to completing the work associated with this project.

Finally, Dan did not receive a sabbatical and had to work long extra hours in order to keep up with Lanny, who read, wrote, and fished at Friday Harbor. He would like to thank his colleagues in the School of Education at the University of Colorado at Boulder who humored him in the process, especially Ofelia Miramontes, Phil Distefano, and his wife, Michele Seipp, for her patience and love.

Introduction

It has become much clearer, as a result of numerous historical, sociological, interpretive, and conceptual studies completed during the last quarter century, that changes in the curriculum of both public schools and universities are often tied to broader social, political, and economic shifts (Apple, 1979; Apple & Weis, 1983; Beyer & Apple, 1988; Franklin, 1986; Kliebard, 1986). From the decline of "faculty psychology" and mental discipline almost a century ago, to the problems associated with the Great Depression and the world wars, to the development of a cold war ideology that became more strident with the launching of *Sputnik*, to current concerns with an increasingly multicultural population, individuals and groups have sought to alter educational institutions and their curricula in an attempt to respond to what they have taken to be crises in the social order. In contemporary U.S. society, the development of the "new math," the push to return to "the basics" and to articulate a "new basics," the movement to foster "choice" and promote closer alliances between businesses and schools—all reflect this tendency for the curriculum to become an instrument for avoiding perceived social perils or for strengthening particular social initiatives. It is not an overstatement to say that we cannot understand the construction and reconstruction of public school and college curricula if we do not understand how they are intimately tied to these larger social currents and crosscurrents. The "crisis reports" of the 1980s, the meetings of the National Governors Association, and now the attempt to establish national standards for the evaluation of schooling through the National Education Goals Panel are only the most recent examples of a longstanding pattern of reevaluating and reforming the school curriculum so as to alleviate some current or future shortcoming—whether real or imagined.

The curriculum field as an area of inquiry with a formal status within higher education has also undergone periodic and substantive revisions over the course of its history, in response to similar institutional pressures and social forces. Beginning more or less in the middle of the second decade of this century, the field of curriculum studies has been affected both by debates involving those working within the field as well as in allied disciplines and by the changing social landscape within which it functions. Scholarly debates and social shifts themselves cannot be neatly separated, as one often responds to or serves to orient the other. One of the realities that makes curriculum studies so exciting, as well as at times so exasperating, is the relatively fluid, permeable boundaries that separate it from other academic pursuits and from ongoing social, political, cultural, and economic phenomena.

Scholarly and public debate increasingly focused on both public school and college curricula during the 1980s. Consistent with general political and cultural shifts, the mainstream discussion of educational problems during this decade tended to promote the perspective of the political right wing, or the "new right" (Shor, 1986). For example, Allan Bloom (1987) and E. D. Hirsch (1988) argued that the legacy of the 1960s left schools with a watered-down curriculum, one unable to guide or advance the education of public school and college students. *A Nation at Risk* (National Commission on Excellence in Education, 1983), the influential report of the Reagan administration's Department of Education, cited schools as contributing to a myriad of economic, social, and military shortcomings. Studies by Diane Ravitch (1983), Chester Finn (1984), and Lynne Cheney (1988) maintained that the public school curriculum no longer emphasized valuable content. Controversy over the curriculum at Stanford and Harvard, for example, underscored the conflict between a more conservative view that sees "the Western tradition" as fundamental and of transcendent intellectual importance, and a more critical orientation that claims such a position denigrates and devalues less powerful cultures, thus maintaining patterns of cultural and social domination (P. Keller, 1982). During this decade the press corps offered reports of then Secretary of Education William Bennett's flights around the country. In those reports he continually bemoaned the sorry state of public educational institutions and maintained, like Bloom, Hirsch, Ravitch, Finn, Cheney, and others, that a more conservative approach to curriculum content portends not only a return to past mores but a more vigorous, strengthened, and promising future (Bennett, 1989). In short, during the 1980s, and into the 1990s, the political right has articulated a critique of current public school and college curricula and a vision for their transformation. It has been an articulation that relies on critiques of previous, purportedly liberal and progressive, educational practices while offering conservative alternatives. These conservative formulations are not new— despite occasional allegations to the contrary. They echo arguments and claims made throughout this century and earlier (Apple, 1985; Franklin, 1986; Kliebard, 1986).

More recent discussions have focused on the determination of some scholars within higher educator to foster what has been termed "political correctness" within the curriculum of the academy. There has developed an antagonism between (1) those who argue that race, social class, and gender are important aspects of all claims to knowledge and thus must be taken into account in discussions of the "body of knowledge" that can and should be central to teaching and research—especially in the humanities and social sciences, but in the natural sciences as well; and (2) those who see such a position as allowing politics to intrude on scholarly endeavors and "the pursuit of truth" through objective research. Among those who argue for the latter perspective is a relatively new group, the National Association of Scholars, established to resist what it sees as a growing tide of vocal critics of the traditional humanities view (Mooney, 1990).

Similarly, the Madison Center for Educational Affairs, founded by William Bennett and Allan Bloom, with Chester Finn as its president, has been created to "promote traditional values in the humanities" (Mooney, 1991, p. A16). A meeting at the Madison Center during the week of January 20, 1991, reflected something of the state of affairs in higher education:

> The conference reflected the polarization of the academy in recent years into opposing camps that often talk about—but seldom with—each other. . . . [Those advocating the centrality of race, gender, and class] have been labeled "politically correct" by critics who, like many of the participants in last week's conference, advocate the study of Western culture and an "objective" approach to scholarship. (Mooney, 1991, p. A15)

As in other decades, the rise of interest in cultural and social issues as a part of research, curricular, and teaching activities in colleges and universities has resulted in a conservative reaction that seeks to return to a "golden age" of reason, rationality, and objectivity that may be, in important respects, mythical and sentimental. Spokespersons for this reaction seek to discredit the growing chorus of voices urging greater sensitivity to nondominant groups in both research and teaching activities.

Such conflicts document an important, often overlooked point: It is simply a mistake to assume that the educational community ever speaks with one, uncontested voice. Even during the 1980s, when much of mainstream educational discourse was dominated by the forces of the new right, important alternative traditions and voices could be heard and in fact gained in strength and even academic respectability (one of the reasons for the creation of the Madison Center and similar efforts). In the same way, it is inaccurate to assume that cohesive, viable alternatives did not exist during earlier periods of school and curriculum reform. Therefore, while it is important to document dominant themes and movements in educational theory and practice, it is equally important that we keep in mind that those working to reform education—even members of powerful groups with institutional backing—do not constitute a monolithic force. In researching the movements of the 1980s, for example, the influence of the political right needs to be contrasted with those studies and visions that reflect a more progressive orientation. It is within such an orientation that we place our own work, while we seek to extend its grasp.

We must admit at the outset that, as in some earlier eras, more progressive responses to the educational and political trends of the 1980s and early 1990s have sometimes been lacking in clarity and incisiveness. Moreover, these responses have at times been excessively abstract, with insufficient attention paid to the current realities of education as well as to alternative visions with which to articulate revised educational practices. In what may be a mirroring of the larger political arena, leftist educational responses to the new right were not always able to formulate a curricular or broader educational agenda to counteract the conservative momentum of the last decade. Certainly there were many progressive analyses running counter to the conservative educational proposals that were dominant. Taken together, however, these progressive movements tended to speak as a cacophony of voices rather than as a coherent, albeit distinct, set of perspectives (see Beyer & Apple, 1988; Giroux & McLaren, 1989; Liston, 1988; Pinar, 1988; Ross, Cornett, & McCutcheon, 1992; Schubert, 1986; Sears & Marshall, 1990). The progressive tradition in educational scholarship, and perhaps especially in curriculum studies, is internally splintered and divided. For educational, intellectual, and political reasons, the articulation of a coherent progressive vision and practice is essential if we are to have substantive input into helping redirect educational experience.

Numerous and very distinct progressive voices have been heard within the curriculum field within the last 15 to 20 years. Differences are not only among people writing across these various traditions, but within them as well. And, of course, such differences are very real, reflecting the different frames of reference, styles, and social, material, and historical locations of the authors who provide them, as well as the traditions and communities in which they are embedded. It would be a mistake to presume that such divergent voices can easily reach some unanimity about what are the most important issues facing us currently and what are the most efficacious responses to them. Indeed we concur in general with the view that a search for consensus that disregards diversity and conflict is one of the important failings of the mainstream educational field and of the "new right." And yet we also recognize that, while the celebration of difference is important, it carries with it significant dangers. Since curriculum studies as a field, as well as the nature and direction of public school and university curricula, are thoroughly (though by no means exclusively) political matters, we are convinced that the differences that often divide progressive voices make improbable substantive change—change that almost by definition will require *collective* action. If the differences that are represented by the range of progressive thought and action within the curriculum field continue to be divisive, our ability to enact any sort of transformative educational vision will be diminished. We believe that what is needed now is a coherent yet inclusive synthesis of a progressive tradition that challenges both the curricular status quo and the recent attempts at a conservative restoration, a synthesis that points to possible common goals, concerns, and commitments. Moreover, we believe the curriculum field provides perhaps the most promising domain in which to situate and further the larger educational debate that continues to develop regarding the proper means and ends of education. As we argue throughout this volume, and as we will in fact demonstrate, curriculum studies provide both the parameters within which the current debates in education can be clearly seen, and an important avenue for the redirection of educational practice.

CURRICULUM: THE FIELD AND ITS CENTRAL ISSUES

The reasons for highlighting the field of curriculum studies within current educational debates have already been alluded to and can be elaborated here. First, the curriculum is the centerpiece of educational activity. It includes the formal, overt knowledge that is central to the activities of teaching, as well as more tacit, subliminal messages—transmitted through the process of acting and interacting within a particular kind of institution— that foster the inculcation of particular values, attitudes, and dispositions. In both its manifest and latent versions, the curriculum represents the essence of what education is for. It is often the focus of what teachers and professors see as their central preoccupation, what parents expect their offspring to master, and what community members and politicians focus on when, for example, debates take place regarding what students may or may not read, see, and listen to.

Second, struggles over the shape of the curriculum are often protracted and heated precisely because they relate directly to competing visions of "the good life," and, therefore, what sort of future we may have. James B. Macdonald (1975) made the following comments about the nature of curriculum theory and development, which illuminate this facet of the curriculum:

> I suspect that in many ways all curriculum design and development is political in nature; that is, it is an attempt to facilitate someone else's idea of the good life by creating social processes and structuring an environment for learning.

Curriculum design is thus a form of "utopianism," a form of political and social philosophizing and theorizing. If we recognize this, it may help us sort out our own thinking and perhaps increase our ability to communicate with one another. (p. 293)

The centrality of the curriculum as a political and cultural force in contemporary social life can, in fact, be clearly seen in the debates between those advocating "political correctness" and those who seek to restore the conservative values of the traditional humanities.

Third, the curriculum field is intimately tied not only to other fields of educational inquiry (philosophy of education, policy studies, history of education, educational psychology, etc.) but to other disciplines normally considered separate from educational studies. The work of curriculum scholars frequently is concerned with issues in epistemology, political and moral philosophy, sociology of knowledge, and the physical and biological sciences. Whatever the boundaries that normally separate academic disciplines, they must, in the case of curriculum studies, be at least semipermeable. Those engaged in curriculum scholarship occupy a relatively open-ended, integrative domain that serves to differentiate it from other, more insulated areas within the university. This, together with the curriculum field's intimate connection to educational practice and to the larger social and cultural contexts in which it is embedded, serves to differentiate curriculum studies from other important domains within education.

Thus our decision to make the curriculum field the center of our analysis of the social and political positions reflected in current educational debates is hardly arbitrary. Yet even our points about the connectedness of curriculum issues and ideas with other educational domains, and with disciplines usually located outside the study of educational phenomena, have been, and to some extent still are, contentious within the field called curriculum studies. For the place of the curriculum field within both other scholarly domains and the larger social universe has been a central issue that has, in fact, actually helped to define the field. Rather than thinking about curriculum studies as defined by a set of characteristics or parameters about which there is substantial consensus, we would suggest that it is more fruitful and more responsive to the historical and contemporary dimensions of the field to think of it as constituted by a set of questions to which a variety of responses have been and continue to be made. It is just this feature of curriculum studies that makes it perhaps the best arena with which to analyze recent educational debates and proposals for practice.

These defining questions of curriculum studies highlight specific, context-dependent issues and more global concerns regarding curriculum matters. They harbor epistemological, ethical, and cultural frames of reference and issues. The central frameworks and questions we find most compelling include the following:

1. *What knowledge and forms of experience are most worthwhile?*

This is perhaps the central question of the field and one that has historically guided much curriculum development. Important issues here include, on the one hand, an array of complex epistemological questions and assumptions regarding, for instance, the nature of knowledge, knowing, and justification. On the other hand, ethical issues that always surround judgments of worth must be taken up, necessitating some axiological framework within which alternative ways of constructing and valuing knowledge can be considered and evaluated.

2. *What is the relationship between the knowledge embodied in the formal curricula and those who are involved in enacting it?*

It has often been assumed that "knowledge" can be thought of, at least analogically, as an entity or thing, or a set of propositions that can be stated and verified independently of those who are to acquire this knowledge. Yet there is a considerable body of both theoretical and empirical evidence that the histories and immediate cultural constructs of the people engaged with any curriculum unavoidably shape the experiences that result and, consequently, that knowledge is always *constructed*, rather than *discovered*. This emphasis on the interpersonal construction of knowledge undermines assumptions about the nature of knowledge as an entity that can be objectively transmitted through a disinterested curriculum form. The view that an individual's biography, capacities, life experiences, and psychological tendencies serve to interpret and give differential meaning to forms of knowledge (even those thought "most worthy") complicates what are already quite complex curricular issues. Such interpersonally diverse realities are of central importance in regard to both issues in curriculum studies and to thinking through what it means to teach and to become an educated woman or man.

3. *What types of educational and social relationships are required or desirable in order to facilitate curricular experiences?*

The enactment of any curriculum will affect the sort of human and social relationships that are possible or encouraged in the classroom. Thus, when generating a curriculum, we confront a number of normative options: To what extent should interactions among students be based on individual activities, to what extent on shared experience; in the case of the latter, should they be focused on competitive or cooperative activities? In addition, what ought the relationship be between teacher and student in formal institutions of education? Depending on our responses to the previous questions about the nature and worth of knowledge, the role of individual and social differences, and so on, we may well conceptualize pedagogical possibilities quite differently. Thinking about knowledge as an objective entity, for instance, leads to a quite different set of social relations between teacher and student than if we see knowledge as emergent within an ongoing set of actions and modes of discourse, just as priorities regarding social relations affect participants' conception of knowledge and its value.

4. *How do larger social, political, and institutional contexts affect the experiences students have with the curriculum?*

In addition to considering individual variations that mediate curricular exchanges, how do the complex and interacting realities of race, social class, ethnicity, gender, sexual orientation, cultural identity, and the like affect people's understandings and their curricular experiences? Conversely, how should such realities affect what is included or excluded in the curriculum? Different social and cultural groups have alternative forms of language, values, priorities, and structural locations within the wider society. These often significantly affect how people understand and make sense of the knowledge and values made accessible in any formal curriculum. The extent to which the cultural histories of students are taken into account in the design and implementation of the curriculum thus raises important ethical questions regarding how we treat students and how their futures are affected by the responsiveness of the curriculum.

5. *What are the implicit (and explicit) conceptions of democracy within the curriculum?*

Within modern democratic societies, education and a system of public schooling have come to be viewed as central means for ensuring the vitality and cohesiveness of a democratic way of life. The curriculum, constituted as either a set of proposals or as whatever practices currently exist in a school or university, is directly linked to the possibilities for democratic participation. The conception of knowledge contained within the curriculum, the relationships among students, the curriculum, and the teacher, and the role of the curriculum in examining persistent social issues are all elements that point to an implicit, if not explicit, conception of the connection between education and democracy. Moreover, there are a number of conceptions of democracy itself, some of which are, in fact, incompatible. This further complicates our ability to understand and critique forms of education and their contribution to a democratic way of life. Indeed part of the problem here is that "democracy" can become a kind of slogan, used to garner support for whatever practices we favor, without a sustained analysis of the concept itself and the kinds of curricular practices that can contribute to its enactment and attainment.

6. *What are the implicit (and explicit) visions of students' social, political, and economic futures, and how does the curriculum prepare students for these futures?*

Whatever else we may think education consists of or is good for, it is certainly related to students' futures, and so it cannot be divorced from a consideration of what kind of world we envisage and help create with students. The range of possibilities in this regard may not be openly debated and discussed, for teachers often assume that the social status quo is the world for which they are preparing their students. Yet it is clear that this is not the only choice. As a normative enterprise, education must be concerned not only with the particular forms of knowledge, values, dispositions, and habits of heart and mind that are being transmitted, but with the social world that such individuals might create and inhabit as a result. For example, in some curriculum designs there is an attempt to sort and select what knowledge goes to what students, while in other curricula there is an attempt to treat students more equitably. Assumptions about students' possible futures play a key role in determining the type, quality, and distribution of knowledge. These assumptions in turn will affect what kinds of futures are possible and students' ability to participate in those futures.

The questions raised here have decidedly philosophical and normative emphases. Unfortunately, large segments of the curriculum field have frequently, especially in their more mainstream reiterations, paid insufficient attention to such issues as they have sought ameliorative responses to immediate problems or "crises." This has led to a kind of narrowness, even brittleness, that has not served the field well. We want to argue that an abiding concern with philosophical and normative questions provides an important route to effective and valuable curriculum deliberation, especially as we seek to alter educational practices. In this particular work we will argue that these questions provide the best means to examine and analyze current educational debates.

Any set of questions such as the one just elaborated must itself become part of the ongoing debate about what constitutes education and an appropriate curriculum; we make no pretense to completeness or veridicality, just as we recognize that the provision of any framework must be incomplete and somewhat tentative. Yet these questions do provide a starting point around which our own positions, assumptions, and interpretations may be clarified. Partly as a result of such clarification, and in facilitating a critique of our positions, we join and extend those debates that are so central to education and to our collective and individual futures.

AN OUTLINE

In this work we essentially contrast recent conservative and progressive educational proposals so as to justify and legitimate a more durable and sustaining reform movement. Our concern is to assess in a fair but pointed manner the relative merits of recent proposals and to offer a route for a more thoroughgoing progressive orientation.

Curriculum in Conflict consists of seven chapters, addressing some crucial controversies in the curriculum of the public schools and universities. In Chapter 1, "The Historical Legacy," we present an overview of the field of curriculum studies. We examine the central epistemological assumptions and the overriding values that have governed past curriculum debates. This chapter serves as both a prelude and an introduction to our examination of the central issues that arise when one examines the conservative arguments that have recently gained momentum and the more progressive challenges to existing educational practices. We look at the historical background to the current situation, focusing on conservative and progressive traditions that have offered analyses of and recommendations for educational reform. In Chapter 2, "The New Right: Individualism, Free Markets, and Character," we examine the educational agenda of the new right and the philosophical and normative assumptions that undergird it. In particular, we examine the work of William Bennett, Chester Finn, and Diane Ravitch, focusing on both the general outlines of their educational agenda and their views of moral and multicultural education. We also explore classical liberal conceptions of the individual, market economies, moral deliberation, and the state that inform and guide the new right's educational proclamations. In Chapter 3, "Modern Liberalism and the Welfare State," we outline more progressive educational agendas, particularly those related to revised understandings of democracy and social justice, and their relationship to an altered form of (modern) liberal consciousness. We include an analysis of various movements and ideas designed to soften the effects of unrestrained capitalism, particularly those undergirding the formation of the modern welfare state. In Chapter 4, "Dominating Dynamics: Radical Critiques of Class, Gender, and Race," we focus on educational critiques motivated by neo-Marxist, feminist, and racial/ethnic scholarship. We highlight both the shared and the distinctive features of these radical frameworks. We maintain that central to the radical analysis is an examination of structures of domination in schools and the society at large. In Chapter 5, "Postmodernism," we examine one of the more recent developments in social and educational theory—postmodern analyses of school and society. We highlight the central tenets of postmodern analyses and underscore what are for us particularly difficult paradoxes. We maintain that postmodern critiques are guided by a suspicion of the "metanarratives" of both liberal and radical thought, a criticism of any sort of epistemological realism, and a concern for the other. In Chapter 6, "Our Social and Democratic Vision: Toward a New Progressivism," we incorporate the concerns that have led to an embrace of new right proposals on the part of many, while suggesting alternative ways to conceptualize the nature of freedom, character, and community. Going beyond the ideas of modern liberalism, we also explore alternative ways to think about work in the United States, particularly ways in which it may be made more meaningful and democratically organized. These alternatives have important implications for educational policy and practice, which we explore in Chapter 7, "One Progressive Agenda." In this final chapter we suggest strategies for the progressive renewal of schools and universities, focusing again on curriculum debates and issues.

Any response to the social and educational difficulties that continue to face Americans will entail concerted, conjoint action across differences. Yet this need for communal action cannot be allowed to hide the different voices that make up any progressive orientation. As a result, we do not end on a note of synthetic resolution to all the issues and concerns raised by the critical scholarship with which we are affiliated. We do offer in this volume a way to build a cultural solidarity within the progressive community of scholars, researchers, and teachers that we hope may lead to effective action.

CHAPTER 1

The Historical Legacy

You must be efficient, you must be able to hold your own in the world of politics, the world of business, able to keep your own head above water, to make your work satisfactory, to make it pay. If you do not, you cannot do good to others. You must be efficient. You must never forget for a moment that, so far from being a base theory, [scientific management] is a vital doctrine, a doctrine vital to good in this country.

—Theodore Roosevelt, 1913 (cited in Callahan, 1962, p. 46)

In the group of great industrial nations, there has come forward in recent years one that has taken place in the very front rank among industrial competitors. That nation is Germany. . . . I am firmly convinced that the explanation of [Germany's] progress can be encompassed in a single word—schoolmaster. He is the great corner-stone of Germany's remarkable commercial and industrial success. From the economic point of view, the school system of Germany stands unparalleled.

—Frank A. Vanderlip, Vice President, National City Bank of New York, 1905 (cited in Callahan, 1962, p. 12)

In this chapter we analyze the dominant values and interests that have historically guided curriculum discourse and practice and look at how they are related to broader social movements. In the process, we uncover both the educational and social assumptions on which such discourse and practice have been based. These assumptions, as we will see in later chapters, can still be seen within more contemporary debates about the means and ends of education for students in the United States. The ideas examined below not only lay the historical groundwork for understanding the educational and curricular debates of the 1980s and 1990s but also continue to provide support for many of those advocating contemporary educational changes. Indeed by simply substituting "Japan" for "Germany" in the above quote from Mr. Vanderlip, we would arrive at a significant understanding of the perceived crisis in education that, in the view of many current commentators, has faced us for the last dozen or so years.

1

EARLY EDUCATIONAL PATTERNS

The emergence of a separate, discrete curriculum field took place nearly 100 years ago, in the early decades of the twentieth century. Decisions regarding what are the most important ideas and values to transmit to younger generations, how best to organize activities and to provide experiences that promote understanding or, to use more recent terminology, that will enhance student learning, have of course been taken up since people gave conscious thought to teaching. Yet such decisions until recently took place without the benefit of a substantial or focused institutional framework.

Even before the beginning of the common school movement in the second quarter of the nineteenth century, the teacher had been the central figure of the informal schools that existed at that time. This reality was to continue throughout most of the ensuing century. The preparation provided early common school teachers was rather limited, to say the least, with teachers often only marginally older and with barely more years of schooling than their charges. Prospective teachers' formal preparation was often quite rudimentary; it was aimed at replicating existing patterns of instruction and methods of socialization, and fitting into the social mores and expectations of the communities that hired them (see Beyer, Feinberg, Pagano, & Whitson, 1989; Mattingly, 1975). The eminent curriculum historian Herbert M. Kliebard (1982) has summarized the period preceding the development of the curriculum field:

> At the heart of America's educational system in the 19th century was the teacher. Ill-trained, harassed, underpaid, and often immature, it was the teacher who was expected to embody the standard virtues and community values and, at the same time, to mete out stern discipline to the unruly and dull-witted. (p. 16)

The curriculum of the rural, one-room schoolhouse had few, if any, commercially produced textbooks or other standardized curriculum materials. Usually organized only loosely and subject to direct, local oversight, the curriculum of the early public schools was characteristically composed of whatever materials and books lay easily at hand or could be purchased at low cost; the Protestant Bible was apparently a central element of many early schools. Still, there were important social and ideological messages that were to be communicated through the teachings that were incorporated into these schools. As David Tyack (1974) comments regarding the early curriculum in use within schools, "often these books wedded the dream of worldly success to an absolute morality; cultivation meant proper diction and polite accomplishments" (pp. 19–20). The primary goal of the common school was to commence or extend the processes of cultivation and socialization. The focus was on what we now refer to as a "hidden curriculum" (Jackson, 1968) that would provide refinement through the social and moral parameters imposed on student conduct (Vallance, 1977). By incorporating a hidden curriculum emphasizing respect for authority, hard work, diligence, promptness, and individual success, working-class and immigrant children could be prepared for the factory work that was becoming increasingly common, especially in the East. Preparation for the demands of factory capitalism was especially important since cottage industries and older craft-oriented patterns of work and apprenticeships were replaced by larger and more impersonal work patterns in the burgeoning factories of the time (Violas, 1978; Nasaw, 1979). Parents with the requisite wealth and connections, of course, could continue to send their children to the more prestigious private schools, which offered access to much different social and economic opportunities.

The dominant pedagogical orientation to teaching during this time was based on faculty psychology and some version of "mental discipline," by which the mind-as-muscle could be strengthened. The specific content or knowledge conveyed through the teacher-dominated lesson mattered less than its contribution to the orderly development of the student's mind (Kliebard, 1986). Recitation was frequently the basis for the pattern of interaction between student and teacher, which might combine the assumptions of faculty psychology with the values and character traits central to the hidden curriculum.

The curriculum of early institutions of higher education was much less elaborate than the one in place in today's colleges and universities and, in fact, reflected a uniformity and predictability that is noteworthy. Muelder (1984) notes that this nineteenth-century curriculum

> was so uniform for all students and so common to colleges that it could be printed on one page of the first catalogue [of Knox College], which was published in the summer of 1842. The courses were strong on classical languages and literature, mathematics, and philosophy or religion. There was some science but no modern literature, no modern languages, and no modern history. (p. 7)

Such a curriculum also promised a sort of cultivation for those able to pursue higher education and a route to the high-status professions. Its lineage could be traced in some respects to the classical university of the Middle Ages, with its emphasis on the seven liberal arts—grammar, rhetoric, logic, geometry, arithmetic, astronomy, and music. The appeal was to a "community of scholars" engaged in the dissemination of sanctioned forms of knowledge and appropriate moral precepts, especially in private, sectarian colleges and universities.

Yet with the progression of the nineteenth century and its quite revolutionary effects on business, technology, communication, the family, and social life generally, it became increasingly clear to many that the older, more removed curriculum of the university, the commitment to faculty psychology, and the recitation method that typified the schools were not adequately preparing students for the changed future that was shortly to be upon them. It was within a significantly changing social landscape—characterized by dramatic innovations in science, technology, and communication; changing patterns of employment and production; progressive and sometimes muckraking cultural and journalistic forms; and the ascendancy of values associated with the industrialist and commercial success generally—that education was to be transformed.

THE CONTEXTS OF MODERN
CURRICULUM CONCERNS

The emergence of the curriculum field as a centerpiece in educational policy and practice cannot be understood or appreciated outside the context of the changes that took place just before and after the turn of the century. These changes catapulted the curriculum into a national issue, as they made clear the inadequacy of current educational practices and institutions for the rapidly industrializing, and increasingly urban, American society. Simultaneously, the curriculum became increasingly enmeshed with the social, political, and ideological currents of the day.

Within higher education, one response to the changing social situation was to support greater efforts at research and an increase in specialized fields. This in turn led to a more fragmented system of higher education in the United States, with the formation of a number of subdisciplines that came to constitute departments within the complex, modern university, thus altering forever that uniform curriculum that had dominated so much of college life in the United States, and elsewhere, throughout the nineteenth and earlier centuries.

The issues surrounding the enactment of the proper course of study in the public schools—especially given the increased emphasis placed on school attendance, the development of the comprehensive high school, and the role of schooling in promising both social stability and mobility—became matters of serious concern for students and their parents. Even more prophetically, the shape of the curriculum became a matter of keen concern for those presumably concerned with the well-being of society generally (who, of course, operated with definite visions of the social good).

A Growing Faith in Science and Progress

Hand in hand with the unfolding of the Industrial Revolution went a faith in the ability of scientific procedures and calculations to predict and place objective controls on a variety of procedures and activities. The invention of new technologies, such as those associated with mass production, were made possible at least in part by scientific discoveries and the applied sciences. Such scientific and technical breakthroughs promised to make goods both more reliable and more widely available. Furthermore, such technologies were widely seen as enabling advances in the social welfare. In this sense social progress became linked in the minds of many, as well as in the culture at large, to the value of science and the scientific enterprise in ways that extended far beyond the laboratories and experiments of natural scientists. Among other things, the development of departments and schools of science within higher education, the creation of new laboratories, and the appearance of new technologies and inventions during this era reflect this concern with the scientific method and its social virtues. At the level of college and university curricula, this interest in science helped alter the curriculum, away from the older tradition of a community of scholars pursuing the timeless verities, toward a more research-oriented, future-focused set of activities that would help usher in the new prosperity (Beyer, 1988b).

The advent of scientific discoveries and scientifically grounded procedures helped in no small way to generate both a new epistemology and the basis for managed social change. By properly designing and regulating procedures in the laboratory, on the shop floor, and in schools, we could arrive at certain results that would be replicable and also spur social progress. The growth in scientific activities and a faith in the methods of scientific investigation thus would lead to the remediation of a host of social, political, and economic problems. By integrating the scientist's commitment to predictability, certainty, and objectivity within a number of social institutions, we might help ensure public approval for our undertakings and the promise of a better life for all.

If an area is to become scientific, its practices must be seen as based in the natural sciences. Methodologically, this means that it must be committed to systematic, quantitatively recorded and analyzed, objective observations that can lead to the formulation and testing of hypotheses. Within education, it is probably within the development of educational psychology as a discrete field that this commitment to scientific aspirations can be most clearly seen, especially as it was committed to various forms of behaviorism. The positivist-inspired world view of these early educational scientists was one in which interactions were mechanically ordered around stimuli and responses. Absent were such metaphysical and unscientific entities as mind, intentionality, and introspection. At its most schematic, this view of the world reduces events and actions to the impersonal and controllable appearance of physical and chemical processes. Such a view has obvious affinities with materialist theories of mind (for example, see Armstrong, 1968). Behaviorists postulate an arena that is consistent with the preeminence of the scientific method, and one that is said to contain a good deal of social as well as educational utility. As Edward L. Thorndike put this view:

> We should regard nothing as outside the scope of science, and every regularity or law that science can discover in the consequence of events is a step towards the only freedom that is of use to men and an aid to the good life. If values do not reside in the orderly world of nature, but depend on chance or caprice, it would be vain to try to increase them. The world needs, not only the vision and valuation of great sages, and the practical psychology of men of affairs, but also scientific methods to test the worth of the prophets' dreams. (cited in Marvin, 1937, pp. 196–197)

In his 1897 doctoral dissertation, Thorndike sought to develop systematic procedures for reinforcing approved behaviors and diminishing undesirable ones in animals. Through such a system, we might make inferences regarding the control of human behavior, including the control of learning (Franklin, 1986). For Thorndike (1935), both ideas and emotions could be controlled and rationalized:

> We now know that the fundamental forces which can change desires and emotions, directing them into desirable channels, are the same as change ideas and actions. A human being learns to react to the situations of life by such and such wants, interests, and attitudes, as he learns to react to them by such and such precepts, ideas, and movements. In both cases, the task of education is to cause the desired connection to occur and to attach the confirming reaction to it. (p. 217)

Expressing something of the world view of the educational scientist, Thorndike believed that by connecting rewards to actions or traits deemed desirable and punishments to ones declared contemptible, instructional systems could be developed that would be scientifically verifiable and generate certain and efficacious results. Such systems would be not only more reliable, but also more precise and predictable, than the theory of mental discipline and the methodology of the recitation that they would replace.

They could also make the job of teaching more scientific, with more predictable individual and social outcomes.

Other areas of education, especially administration and curriculum, were to be strongly affected by the growing trust in science as well. To understand these effects at their deepest levels, however, we must see the tools of the scientist in the context of other, closely related social and economic realities.

The Age of Efficiency

Well before the changes wrought by the Industrial Revolution, American notables such as Benjamin Franklin and Thomas Jefferson reflected a belief in progress, perfectibility, and practical industriousness as a kind of individual and social bedrock. The values of progress and practicality have been implicated in the need to reform social institutions as well as individual psyches. Along with this, the typically American character has embodied a kind of pragmatic inclination that sometimes reveals itself as a form of anti-intellectualism. The tendency to separate reflection from action, scholarship from daily life, may be a reflection of these typically American tendencies and traits. Tocqueville noted some of these with a mixture of admiration and alarm during his visits to the United States in the 1830s:

> The man of action . . . has occasion perpetually to rely on ideas that he has not had leisure to search to the bottom; for he is much more frequently aided by the seasonableness of an idea than by its strict accuracy . . . a rapid glance at particular incidents, the daily study of the fleeting passions of the multitude, the accidents of the moment, and the art of turning them to account decide all its affairs. (cited in Borrowman, 1956, p. 32)

This progressive pragmatism and its appearance in the late nineteenth century alongside the expansion of industry may be seen as providing the parameters of two interrelated social currents: the glorification of the business leader and the uncovering of graft and corruption through the muckraking press. Although the muckrakers of this era were critical of many aspects of industrial expansion, their criticisms tended to be couched within yet another American tradition, that of individualism. Thus greed and corruption were interpreted as failings of individual people and their faulty characters, rather than as structural weaknesses requiring changes in economic or social institutions. Such an ameliorative response to social failings may reveal yet another facet of the American character.

The techniques of capitalist production introduced in rudimentary form in nineteenth-century America were refined and accelerated, and even transformed with the advent of the new technologies, as the century progressed. Wealth and power were increasingly centralized in those who headed the new corporations. Commenting on the growing influence of big business and its leaders, Callahan (1962) notes:

> In wealthy America, the tremendous industrial and material growth under the capitalistic system was clearly visible. Visible, too, with their vast fortunes, were the great industrial and financial leaders—men such as Andrew Carnegie, John D. Rockefeller, J. P. Morgan, Edward H. Harriman, and the rest. By 1900 these men had been accorded top status by most of their countrymen, and quite naturally their values and beliefs were widely admired and accepted. Indeed, the acceptance of the business philosophy was so general that it has to be considered one of the basic characteristics of American society in this period. (p. 2)

The glorification of business leaders and values was supported by a number of factors. The hidden curriculum of the early common schools, already discussed, may be seen as one contributor, in its emphasis on a strict morality, thrift, and success tied to hard work. Horatio Algier and other rags-to-riches stories no doubt also fueled enthusiasm for individual hard work and a belief in the possibility of individual success, as epitomized in the Carnegies and Morgans. Similarly, tales from one of the first widely available standardized curriculum texts, the McGuffey Readers, provided further support for the admiration of a business philosophy. From these readers students learned "not only the idea that success was a result of honesty and hard work but the idea that success was *material* success . . . [the models for whom were] usually bankers or merchants" (Callahan, 1962, p. 2). Underwritten by longstanding preferences for pragmatic action, progressivism, and industriousness, the developing system of corporate capitalism provided for the American public an image of the good life that was supported by stories of self-made men and powerful captains of industry that were compelling indeed.

Andrew Carnegie himself extolled the virtues of the "practical life" as he criticized the remoteness of higher education. Distinguishing between real and artificial educational activities, Carnegie told the American public that students who have attended college

> have in no sense received instruction. On the contrary, what they have obtained has served to imbue them with false ideas and to give them a distaste for practical life. *In my own experience I can say that I have known few young men intended for business who were not injured by a collegiate education.* Had they gone into active work during the years spent at college they would have been better educated men in every sense of that term. The fire and energy have been stamped out

of them, and how to so manage as to live a life of idleness and not a life of usefulness has become the chief question with them. (Carnegie, 1902, pp. 79–81; emphasis added)

The "philanthropic" educational actions of many industrial giants were, it must be noted, even less benign than Carnegie's ideas regarding higher education. For example, shortly after the end of the Civil War, northern industrialists including J. P. Morgan, John D. Rockefeller, Sr., and Robert C. Ogden helped create and finance the General Education Board. This Board sought to "educate" former slaves so that they would be "kept in their places" within the social and economic structures of the South, continuing patterns of racial and economic exploitation (Anderson, 1988). Thus the educational institutions developed during this time contain a number of racial, as well as class and gender, characteristics regarding which corporation heads were hardly innocent bystanders.

One of the overarching commitments of both industrial leaders and the general public at the time was to a more utilitarian or functional education. College and school curricula that were not directly tied to social life, especially to the aims and values of industry and commerce, would be seen as increasingly irrelevant. On the other hand, schooling that could contribute to economic growth, then as now, was seen as virtually a panacea for the social and economic difficulties facing America (competition from foreign countries, especially Germany; inflation; increasing numbers of immigrants and resulting unemployment; "soldiering" on the shop floor and mismanagement of the workplace; etc.).

The certain, replicable knowledge available through the modern procedures of science discussed in the previous section, and the technological innovations that in part resulted from it, did not go unnoticed by the industrial and financial giants. Such new forms of knowledge and technology would simultaneously promote industrial growth and social progress. As larger, more complex corporations replaced more and more locally owned and run entrepreneurial ventures, a premium was placed on enhancing productivity among workers and increasing the efficiency of the machinery and the operations of production and distribution. Such efficiencies would maximize profit margins for the company and simultaneously serve the common good by providing more jobs and making available more time-saving goods.

However, the proliferation of working people's unions and other organizations with different and potentially dangerous political and social values might portend the disruption of efficient manufacturing practices and social stability generally. This possibility necessitated, from the managers' point of view, greater control of the labor process not only to maximize profits but to control the workers themselves. The possibility of making business more scientific and efficient—standardizing the processes of production, quantifying both results and means of evaluation, and centralizing decision making—might promote smoother internal operations and a more compliant workforce (Braverman, 1974; Edwards, 1979; Lasch, 1984; Noble, 1977, 1984). One of the most important methods by which the process of productive labor could be controlled and made more efficient was through the employment of efficiency experts. The work of Frederick Winslow Taylor and his associates was especially influential in this regard.

Taylor was chiefly concerned with engineering and the development of scientific research projects that would make manufacturing practices more precise and replicable, and hence more cost-effective. Little was known about the man or his methods by the general public until his approach to industrial efficiency was discussed in a hearing before the Interstate Commerce Commission (ICC) in November 1910. The ICC hearing involved a request from some railroads in the Northeast for an increase in freight rates. Though Taylor did not himself appear at this hearing, several witnesses referred to his ideas, and the term "scientific management" was coined by a group assembled by Louis Brandeis, the attorney for the trade association who led the opposition to the rate increase request (Callahan, 1962). Though new to the American public at the time of the ICC hearing, Taylorism was to take the country by storm, as part of a virtual frenzy of efficiency-mindedness whose applicability was not limited to industrial and business operations. His ideas were to be extended by a group of his disciples, for example, Harrison Emerson (1913), who spoke with even greater fervor and zeal, not to mention moral conviction, than did Taylor. Moreover, Taylor's influence was to extend well beyond the United States, as exemplified by the fact that his *Principles of Scientific Management* was to be translated into 10 foreign languages (Callahan, 1962, p. 23). Taylor himself would come to regard his system of scientific management as containing ideas that could be "applied with equal force to all social activities: to the management of our homes; the management of our farms; the management of the business of our tradesmen, large and small; of our churches; our philanthropic institutions, our universities, and our governmental departments" (F. W. Taylor, 1911, p. 8). Taylorism was to exert a pivotal influence on the formation of the curriculum field.

The father of scientific management, Taylor strove to make work as rationalized as possible, thereby ensuring maximal productivity from workers:

> The principal object of management should be to secure the maximum prosperity for the employer, coupled with the maximum prosperity for each employee . . . maximum prosperity for each employee means not only higher

wages than are usually received by men of his class, but, of more importance still, it also means the development of each man to his state of maximum efficiency. (F. W. Taylor, 1911, p. 9)

Reflecting the influence of scientific rationality, the key to guaranteeing worker efficiency lay in making the operations of the workplace more regular and systematic, less subject to individual interpretation and initiative. Centralization of the decision-making process went hand in hand with this search for efficiency through the control of work and workers. Managers were thus to assume "the burden of gathering together all the traditional knowledge which in the past has been possessed by the workmen and then of classifying, tabulating, and reducing this knowledge to rules, laws, and formulae which are immensely helpful to the workmen in doing their daily work" (F. W. Taylor, 1911, p. 36). Reflecting a compartmentalization of work that came to be seen as commonsensical, the manager was to conceptualize the work to be done on the shop floor, identify the skills that were required in order for the end result to be obtained, and regularize and make more systematic the actual movements that were required for that end result to be efficiently generated. The worker's job was thus "to do what he was told to do by management. . . . In [Taylor's] system the judgment of the individual workman was replaced by the laws, rules, principles, etc., of the science of the job which was developed by management" (Callahan, 1962, pp. 27–28). Workers became quite literally appendages to the machine, means to an end over which they had no independent control, and engaged in mostly isolated, individual actions requiring little thought, thus both ensuring productivity and preventing worker solidarity. The clearest example of this system is the assembly line, where each worker completes one specific, simplified, and monotonous task. In this fashion resistance to the hierarchical nature of productive activities might be made at least more difficult to organize.

By discovering the scientific principles in accord with which work is to be organized, segmented, and carried out, the process of production is made efficient, just as the required knowledge is centralized within the corporate hierarchy. The incorporation of what Frederick Winslow Taylor (1911) called "motion and time studies" became a crucial method by which this efficiency could be ensured. These studies involved the scientific analysis of the productive process; its division into minute, segmented tasks; and the organization of work brigades so that each person was responsible for only one narrow and specialized activity. The work process would then be standardized along the scientific lines discovered by the efficiency expert. Just as important, the worker was to be paid not an hourly wage or even a piece-rate schedule. Rather, workers would be paid on the basis of a "bonus plan." The basic idea was to pay workers at a higher rate than previously for doing the work at a faster pace and ensuring them that this pay rate would be permanent if that pace was maintained, and to punish (with lower pay rates coupled with the fear of possibly being fired) those workers who were unable to maintain the pace. "Perhaps the most prominent single element in modern scientific management," Taylor wrote, "is the task idea. . . . This task specifies not only what is to be done but how it is to be done and the exact time allowed for doing it" (F. W. Taylor, 1911, p. 39).

The growth of industry was, thus, importantly promoted by the growing fascination with scientific standards and methodologies that would guarantee the efficient organization of work, the wider distribution of goods, and at least in part the values of social control through the hierarchical organization of the workplace. The shop thus became a bureaucracy in which science, the increased specialization and division of labor, technical control, and efficiency were crucial influences. The worker became the cog in a much larger and somewhat mysterious machine, given the segmentation of work and the simplification of individual tasks that became the watchword for industrial efficiency (Haber, 1964). Yet scientific management and efficiency were also, wrote Taylor, beneficial for the workers, who became "not only more thrifty but better men in every way; that they live rather better, begin to save money, become more sober, and work more steadily" (F. W. Taylor, 1911, p. 74). Thus scientific management was a boon not only to the corporate capitalist and manager but also to the individual worker. The Age of Efficiency was, in this way, truly named for a central value in the new industrial democracy.

Ideology and Cultural Difference

In addition to reflecting a fascination with scientific rationality, the control of labor through rationalized and hierarchical procedures, and the pursuit of social control as a part of productive work, the development of the curriculum field took place as concerns grew about the increasing numbers of immigrants. These new arrivals posed a special threat to those who were already settled in this country—especially to those with social and economic power. The threat to a sense of community, as this idea was filtered through a number of ideologies and class-based attitudes, was seen as potentially undermining the established order. This threat needed somehow to be defused.

Already buffeted by changing social and familial patterns produced by industrialization and urbanization, both social stability and progress were challenged by increasing numbers of immigrants—especially those who spoke unfamiliar languages, held different values and priorities, and had different customs. Theoretically at least, unmanaged immigrants might upset the dynamics of power that the centralization of wealth and influence had shored up. Thus a central question became how to "Americanize" these immigrants so that social stability, traditional community values, and patterns of control and power could be maintained.

The notion of community is especially salient in this context, as schools became one of the chief instruments by which it would be maintained. Apple (1979) discussed the events that transpired:

> The cities were increasingly being populated by immigrants from eastern and southern Europe and Blacks from the rural South. These diverse people were seen as a threat to a homogeneous American culture, a culture centered in the small town and rooted in beliefs and attitudes of the middle class. The "community" that the English and Protestant forbearers of this class had "carved from a wilderness" seemed to be crumbling before an expanding urban and industrial society. (p. 71)

Reflecting a nostalgia for rural and small-town life that seems endemic to many writers in American politics and letters, many saw a rededication to consensus and a set of agreed-upon values as the essence of small-town life. Such a way of life might be reinvigorated even within the growing urban centers of the United States. Thus many in higher education and in politics took the view that "order and progress were dependent on the degree to which beliefs and behavior were common and shared . . . they argued for the maintenance of a unitary culture rooted in the values, beliefs, and behavior of the middle class" (Apple, 1979, p. 72).

Such a maintenance orientation was hardly benign from the point of view of those to be acted upon. Indeed it was often attached to blatantly racist and ethnocentric positions and practices. Within this orientation immigrants were not only different from "us," but inferior. This meant that people could devise plans for their "purification" that might be couched in a "helping" or progressive language, regardless of their possibly draconian consequences. A report by the New York State Assembly warned that "like the vast Atlantic, we must decompose and cleanse the impurities which rush into our midst, or like the inland lake, we shall receive their poison into our whole national system" (cited in Kaestle, 1973, p. 141). Included in the cause of purification were a number of attempts at social engineering linked to the eugenics movement (Selden, 1988).

We see here a response to the potential for social breakdown that not only has antecedents in American history but that, in its search for a common culture and social homogeneity, is strikingly similar to many of the most widely touted contemporary calls for changes in the curricula of the public schools and colleges. In danger of being lost, according to these protagonists, is a way of life or world view in which homogeneity, face-to-face interaction, and a unified system of beliefs and values prevail. A primary means by which to retain this way of life is, and was, seen to involve changes in the public school and college curriculum.

The process of Americanizing immigrants was also to be assisted, in the early decades of the century, by a movement that was aided by educational scientists like Thorndike, Termin, Goddard, and their followers. This movement—"mental measurement," or intelligence testing—could be used to distinguish among students on the basis of allegedly natural ability or native/genetic mental endowment. With the creation of IQ and other standardized tests during and after World War I, a presumably objective and scientific means had been found to differentiate students and curricula (Karier, 1975). In the process, issues that had revolved around social class, race, gender, and ethnicity were altered so that they were pictured instead as related to ability or intelligence—the objectivity of the tests themselves being accepted by many as given, created as they were by men of science. Yet when such men of science identified those with greater intelligence, they referred to lawyers, scientists, and businesspeople—all, like themselves, members of the middle and upper classes. The "masses," especially African Americans and southern Europeans, were accordingly considered unintelligent or lacking in native ability. Thus, as Apple (1979) concludes:

> What was originally seen by American intellectuals as a cultural problem of ethnic and class differences was redefined in the seemingly neutral language of science as a problem of differences in intelligence, as a problem in differing "abilities" to contribute to the maximization and control of "expert" moral and technical knowledge. . . . Social control, hence, became covered by the language of science. . . . By controlling and differentiating school curricula, so could people and classes be controlled and differentiated as well. (pp. 76–77)

By employing the tools of allegedly scientific objectivity, neutrality, and certainty to the construction of test instruments, and then using the results to differentiate curricula for students whose schoolwork would thus guarantee their "proper" futures, social control, economic harmony, and cultural cohesion could be promoted. In the process, the Americanization of the foreign-born, as well as the values of science, technology, and bureaucratic oversight, might be integrated and promoted.

The key to resolving the problem of immigration also provided the solution to the problem of how to maintain the allegiance of the lower classes: the development of a cultural cohesion within which commonalities could be assumed even as new differences became instantiated. The institutionalization of standardized testing and other forms of scientific measurement were to prove useful to this process. Earlier, cultural differences between "settled" and "new" immigrants—in terms of social customs, moral values, religions, political ideologies, and more general ways of life, for example—might have been seen to involve normative questions regarding whose values or beliefs or customs are preferable and therefore ought to be permitted or mandated, in schools and other institutions. This way of thinking about culture, however, might well allow for diversities that could prove to be destabilizing for the status quo. These diversities might, given the social and intellectual currents of the early twentieth century, be transformed into different kinds of questions—for example, as related to the level of intellectual development of those who hold them.

If scientific and objective instruments are able to make distinctions among people that reflect their natural predilections and abilities, we might transform normative questions into scientific or technical ones. Suppose there are, as the National Association of Manufacturers had reported earlier, in 1912, naturally occurring distinctions between those who are "hand-minded," "head-minded," and "the great mass in between these" (cited in Nasaw, 1979). Now suppose that there are natural differences in intelligence and temperament that we can measure through scientific test instruments, the results of which we can use to promulgate a differentiated curriculum that respects those natural differences. What we are developing, following these suppositions, is a system of education that is meritocratic even as it maintains the social status quo. And by allowing the working-class and immigrant populations to pass through such a meritocratic system, we will be simultaneously protecting their interests and furthering the expansion of corporate capitalism.

But something in addition to the notion of an educational, and hence social, meritocracy is required. Recall that for many intellectuals and educators there was a pronounced fear of losing a sense of community as American society became more urbanized and industrialized. The resuscitation of the norms of community might well be consistent with the expansion of capital, the acculturation of immigrants, and the socialization of the working class. The problem of what to do with potentially dysfunctional immigrants was clear to people like Finney (1922), who, like other early curriculum writers, longed for a return to community:

> The immigrant working class had to hold the same firm commitments to their work which [Finney] attributed to people from his own class. It was this commitment, he believed, that would reduce their potential revolutionary threat by making them happy performing the "humbler" economic functions that he saw as the future lot of the mass of the American population in an industrialized society. (cited in Apple, 1979, p. 73)

Capitalist production requires for its maintenance and expansion the development of specific classes and, more recently, class segments. While it is easy to justify this in the eyes of those at the top of the hierarchy created by this need for a stratified labor force, it is less clear how allegiance might be obtained from those at the lower rungs of the capitalist system. One answer, of course—and one that continues to have a significant measure of validity—is to perpetuate a "reserve army" of potential employees. The unemployed, underemployed, and others in the potential labor pool make radical interventions by workers less likely, especially when such intervention carries with it the risk of unemployment, lack of health care, decreased opportunities for their children, and the like. Yet in the long run a more cultural response to the problem of maintaining the allegiance of the working classes involves again the aura of community. If we are told that the capitalist enterprise involves a kind of harmonious relationship among all of those involved, within which a kind of community needs to be perpetuated, immigrants and workers may come to see their role in this enterprise as a communal one requiring cooperation. Then, too, given the notion of meritocracy, such workers and citizens may see that role as both necessary and valuable.

THE BIRTH OF CURRICULUM STUDIES

What came to be the modern American curriculum field is in large measure a conglomeration of responses to the social, economic, and cultural conditions discussed above. As articulated by academics in the university and the newly emerging class of professional administrators in the schools, debates about the shape and structure of the curriculum became infused with a number of central concerns. While not all people shared these concerns, of course, and while different responses were made to them, they do represent something of the mainstream of early curriculum studies and so represent an important segment of the intelligentsia who had the influence to effect educational policy and curriculum thinking. Foremost among these concerns were the following:

1. How students who were "different" (racially, ethnically, socially, culturally, linguistically) could be acculturated so as to promote social and economic stability. Like a well-oiled piece of machinery, the social order needed the proper lubricant to protect its component parts from the damages of friction so that it could perform effectively. Political and business leaders, aware of the labor strife and political upheavals in many foreign countries, and worried about the increasing economic power of Germany,

sought a way to ensure tranquillity among an increasingly diverse population. One response to this concern was to standardize the formal curriculum, thereby promoting cultural homogeneity. Another was to provide, through a value-laden hidden curriculum, experiences that would generate the "correct" values, attitudes, and beliefs—especially in troublesome poor and immigrant children who needed to be Americanized.

2. How educational institutions generally could be scientifically organized and run so as to promote efficiency, standardization, and predictable results. The desire to eliminate waste within the context of education was to provide a set of principles for the use of the school "plant," for the attainment of prespecified and particularistic educational ends, and for the eventual production of a stratified work force to meet changing industrial needs and political prerogatives. Through the adoption of systems management strategies, technical measures of accountability, and quality control procedures in schools that had their origins in Taylorism as applied to industry and the control of labor, students would be prepared intellectually and culturally to fill the economic, social, and political positions that awaited them. Moreover, this new course of study, and the educational activities it helped enact, would be responding to the socially felt need to modernize. By ridding itself of such outdated ideas as mental discipline and the traditional liberal arts curriculum favored by the humanists (Kliebard, 1986), the school curriculum could be more practical and functional.

3. How the expansion of political power and local forms of democratic involvement—especially as propagated by those affiliated with labor unions and other workers' associations, as well as a variety of nonmainstream political groups—could be contained so as to protect the interests of the status quo. This was accomplished partly through the break-up of local or "ward" control in the urban areas and the creation of centralized governmental institutions. Exposés in the popular press by muckraking journalists also identified political corruption and abuse. Publications such as *The Saturday Evening Post* and, the most noted of the muckraking publications, *McClure's*, pointed to the evils of business and educational practices. These writers did not, however, "attack the business system; indeed . . . their solution to many of the problems was the application of modern business methods" (Callahan, 1962, p. 5). Within the schools, a curriculum that was socially relevant and properly sanitized would be helpful in eradicating dangerous political ideas as it readied future workers for their roles in life. A Taylorized educational system would help undercut dangerous political ideologies.

4. How the provision of a differentiated curriculum for students could be established while still maintaining the appearance of meritocracy. Wealthy families, as before, might send their children to private, elite schools

that provided access to high-status professions. But how could the public schools stratify their teaching and curricular practices without arousing working-class opposition? This is, of course, a problem endemic to a society with essentially contradictory social and ideological forces at work: some favoring inequality and stratification, some fostering equal protection and rights (Beyer, 1988a). By basing curriculum decisions in part on scientific findings from IQ and other tests, and by implementing activities that embodied the norms of scientific methods, educators were seen as providing experiences that almost magically seemed to respond to both the individual predilections of students and the needs of society. A functional curriculum must, of course, serve social and individual needs, and if these needs could be combined and then accommodated by scientifically regulated procedures that reflected students' capacities, such a curriculum would be both efficacious and just.

The curriculum field, and, frequently, curricular practices in the schools and universities became directly implicated in responses to these concerns. Curriculum studies and practices became, in fact, a center for the myriad social and political dynamics that were unfolding, housed as they were in cultural institutions—which schools and universities are, virtually by definition. Summarizing the immediate context of the founding of the curriculum field, Kliebard (1975b) writes:

> The tenor of the times was a mélange of post–World War I nationalism, a drive for "Americanization" of immigrants, a faith in the methods of science, and a concern for the uplift of the masses. To a large extent the curriculum field seems to have been shaped by this atmosphere and a reaction against what was believed to be a kind of education that was static, irrelevant to modern life, and nonfunctional. The reformers proposed a school program that was perpetually innovative, directly related to the ongoing world of affairs, and supremely utilitarian in orientation. (p. 40)

Recall that the increase in industrialization in the United States was accompanied by the search to find new ways to control workers and the processes of production. Through the efforts of people like Taylor, work became segmented, rationalized, and framed within hierarchical modes of interaction. These ideas became guiding features of the emerging curriculum field, and of curricular practices in schools, as metaphors were articulated and developed that served to orient curriculum work. "Scientific management" was not only the watchword for industrial productivity but also the framework for curricular decision making. The infiltration of scientific management principles into the early curriculum field, as well as into the school more broadly and into the practices of teaching, is nowhere more clear than in the declaration of Ellwood Cubberley (1916) that

> every manufacturing establishment that turns out a standard product . . . maintains a force of efficiency experts to study methods of procedure and to test the output of its works. . . . Our schools are, in a sense, factories in which the raw products (children) are to be shaped and fashioned into products to meet the various demands of life. The specifications for manufacturing come from the demands of twentieth-century civilization, and it is the business of the school to build its pupils according to the specifications laid down. This demands good tools, specialized machinery, continuous measurement of production to see if it is according to specifications, the elimination of waste in manufacture, and a large variety in the output. (p. 338)

For men like Franklin Bobbitt (1918), W. W. Charters (1927), David Snedden (1921), and Ross Finney (1929)—virtually "the founding fathers" of the curriculum field—the school was to be modeled after the factory. Within such an institution, educational efficiency, standardization, and predictability could be seen. Following the general outlines of Cubberley's comments, Bobbitt (1912) expressed his fourth principle of scientific management:

> Work up the raw material into the finished product for which it is best adopted. Applied to education this means: Educate the individual according to his capabilities. This requires that the materials of the curriculum be sufficiently various to meet the needs of every class of individuals in the community; and the course of training and study be sufficiently flexible that the individual can be given just the things he needs. (p. 269)

In keeping with the general precepts of scientific management, Bobbitt further indicated the kind of quality control mechanisms that should be implemented within schools (Kliebard, 1975a, p. 57). Just as other industries require precise calculations to make sure their products are within acceptable limits, Bobbitt (1913) recommended that, based on standard scores reported elsewhere:

> The third-grade teacher should bring her pupils up to an average of 26 correct [arithmetic] combinations per minute. The fourth grade teacher has the task, during the year that the same pupils are under her care, of increasing their addition speed from an average of 26 combinations per minute to an average of 34 combinations per minute. If she does not bring them up to the standard 34, she has failed to perform her duty in proportion to the deficit; and there is no responsibility upon her for carrying them beyond the standard. (pp. 21–22)

While we may speculate about the actual impact such quality control ideas had on teachers in the third and fourth grades, scientific management did have some affect on those working in mathematics education in universities (Stanic, 1988). At the very least, some justifications for mathematics education had to be couched in terms that would be persuasive within the groundswell of support for making the curriculum more functional and efficient. One mathematics educator, David Reeve, was a primary proponent of a "unified" view of mathematics—that is, of eliminating the barriers between mathematics and other fields and between the various subareas within mathematics. He saw some social efficiency ideas as providing support for that view of the field. Reeve's embrace of scientific management ideas, however, created additional problems for the support of mathematics within the school curriculum:

> Uncritically accepting the language of social efficiency gave support to a movement that threatened the traditional place of mathematics in the school curriculum. Reeve's use of the social efficiency metaphor meant that the social efficiency educators could, in a sense, define the situation. The school curriculum was viewed through the lens of social efficiency, and using such a lens restricted the possible outcomes for Reeve's general mathematics program. Instead of the rigorous college preparatory course of study he originally wanted, general mathematics became almost a remedial course for students deemed incapable of handling the traditional coursework. (Stanic, 1988, p. 220)

We see here that the immersion of educational ideas within movements that become prominent at a given time, so as to elevate the status of those ideas and thus gain popular support, is quite problematic. For the net effect of this process is to reshape and perhaps transform those ideas in ways that may contradict reformers' original impulses. This is as dangerous a pattern for curriculum reform in the late twentieth century as it was 75 years ago.

The setting up of definite standards based on scientific analysis and measurement was not alone sufficient to ensure an adequate curriculum, of course. Equally important was the ability to forecast students' future places in the social order. Just as business relies for much of its success on predetermining the nature, number, and quality of products to be manufactured, the curriculum must also predetermine its end points. "There is a growing realization within the educational profession," Bobbitt declared, "that we must particularize the objectives of education. We, too, must institutionalize foresight, and, so far as the conditions of our work will permit, develop a technique of predetermination of the particularized results to be aimed at" (1920, p. 738). The emphasis on predictability was thus closely allied for these early curriculum theorists to predestination. The particular outcomes of the curriculum would be identified with specific abilities and objectives, prespecified in quite minute detail. For instance, Charters (1924) reports in another context that a study of homemakers revealed 4,500 activities they completed, which might then be systematized and sequenced in building a curriculum for future domestic work. These could then provide the necessary guidance for efficient and quality controlled curriculum practice. In general, the efficient ordering of the work of curriculum making required the elimination of waste through precise articulation of the ends to be accomplished and the means that would accomplish them; such precise and regularized ordering of materials and activities became as vital for the "curriculum manager" as time and motion studies were for the industrial manager. Predestination through curriculum also meant educating each student so that he or she would be temperamentally and intellectually suited to the probable economic and social position that awaited him or her. This, of course, entailed curriculum differentiation or tracking, so that only the "appropriate" forms of knowledge and habits would be acquired by each group of students. Summarizing these tendencies of the early curriculum field, Kliebard (1975a) notes, in terms reminiscent of Cubberley's orientation to schooling:

> This extrapolation of the principles of scientific management to the area of curriculum made the child the object on which the bureaucratic machinery of the school operates. He became the raw material from which the school-factory must fashion a product drawn to the specifications of social convention. What was at first simply a direct application of general management principles to the management of schools became the central metaphor on which modern curriculum theory rests. (p. 56)

By attuning education to the values of efficiency, productivity, and scientific management, individual students schooled in differential curricula would acquire not just the forms of knowledge, but also the habits, values, and social outlook necessary to fit into a particular occupational and social niche. "The schoolchild became something to be molded and manipulated on his way to filling his predetermined social role" (Kliebard, 1975a, p. 62). The school, thus conceived, functioned as an effective conservative force, maintaining social and economic stability and furthering the interests of corporate America, among at least a partially socialized body of employees for whom Taylorism had already been a part of their social experience through schooling. Coming to regard the scientific management of one's work in schools—with the class, gender, and racial configurations and hierarchical structure that accompanied that work—as natural or commonsensical could promote a way of life and culture that would be functionally useful within an increasingly industrialized and Taylorized capitalist economy.

Beyond the specific ends served by this approach to curriculum, a culture of schooling was also being promoted by the founders of the curriculum field. The school, rather than being a site for intellectual inquiry, the exploration of curiosity, or creative activity, is portrayed as a mechanism in which students passively work to accomplish prespecified ends—ends that often bear little or no relationship to their own interests and histories but that are presumably geared to their probable futures. The "factory model" of curriculum development that emerges from the early years of the field emphasizes a technical or means–end rationality tied to an emphasis on efficiency and predictability: To accomplish the ends of education, we must know beforehand the specific objectives at which we aim, and we must eliminate as fully as possible those activities that are wasteful in terms of reaching those objectives. To be eliminated, therefore, are the student's wonders, beliefs, understandings, and musings, which are hardly scientific and are plainly irrelevant. Thus, for "social efficiency" educators (Kliebard, 1986), the enactment of the curriculum is accompanied by a real sense of impersonality that, together with the search for efficiency, neutrality, and objectivity, became the hallmarks of the modern bureaucracy.

Equally bureaucratic is the culture of teaching for those employed within efficiency-minded schools. This culture was promoted by a system of bells announcing the beginning and ending of classes; the development of the "egg-crate" school design, with separate compartments for different subject matters and classes; and the creation of a new class of educational administrators, analogous to middle-level managers in corporations, who would "oversee production," resulting in the proliferation of what Ella Flagg Young (1901) had earlier called "the dull routine" of teachers' lives. This is not to suggest that teaching before the advent of the curriculum field was immune from dull, repetitive, and routinized tasks, or that the oversight provided in earlier schools was always more enlightened than those forms that emerged in the early twentieth century. Indeed, it is clear from the early accounts of some teachers that local control of schools could be as arbitrary, insidious, and sexist as more bureaucratic systems management procedures (see, for example, Kaufman, 1984). Yet it seems fair to say that the nature of teaching did undergo a significant alteration with the implementation of the ideas and values of the early curriculum theorists, and that a culture of teaching was created which, in important ways, continues to shape school practice (Beyer, 1989). The teacher became cast as a manager of personnel (students) and materials (texts, other curriculum materials) and as an overseer of a process of production (the achievement of minute and prespecified objectives) that in some ways was as disconnected from her own interests and values as it was from students'. She became a task master who oversees typically impersonal procedures so that predicted outcomes can be facilitated. Moreover, the teacher increasingly had available to her a battery of "objective" information and data (IQ and other test scores, previous school attendance patterns and examination marks, behavioral notations, etc.) that could assist in the process of tracking students into their "appropriate" subjects and classes, with ability grouping and curriculum differentiation aiding this process.

THE CURRICULUM FIELD IN MATURITY

Several caveats need to be made about the historical development of the curriculum field outlined here and the effect this would have on its continuation. First, it would be a mistake to assume that the scientific management fetish surrounding the birth of the field predated and obliterated alternative approach and foundations. Using Kliebard's (1986) classification of the field, it is important to see that the school of thought that was central to much nineteenth-century educational theory, humanism, not only embodied older and equally passionate commitments but also was defended during the ascendancy of scientific management and survives to this day. Similarly, the articulation of proposals from the developmentalists and social meliorists/reconstructionists, as well as the various combinations of values and ideas from all the curriculum interest groups, have frequently ended up as strange bedfellows and "untidy compromises" at one time and location or another (Kliebard, 1982). We cannot assume that any one school of thought has ever so dominated the curriculum field as to obscure other ways of theorizing about and enacting curriculum. Even during the heyday of scientific management, there were spokespeople for alternatives, notably Dewey, Kilpatrick, and other progressives, as well as alternative schools and universities that were created and thrived (Teitelbaum, 1988).

Second, we have less evidence than we might like about the actual impact the ideas that were instrumental to the formation of the curriculum field had on classroom practice. It would be, at best, speculative to suggest that teaching underwent wholesale changes that were directly attributable to scientific management and other ideas that were so prevalent at the time (for the complexities involved here, see, for example, Beyer, 1982; Franklin, 1982). The linkages among educational and specifically curriculum theory, educational policy, and classroom practice are complex, rarely if ever reflecting a cause-and-effect relationship. What we have documented here are the ideas of curriculum theorists and reformers, not the actual practices of teachers and professors.

Yet there are some good historical and contemporary reasons to think that school practices have in fact been significantly affected by social effi-

ciency thinking. For example, Cuban (1984) has documented the relative
constancy of conservative teaching practices over time, and Sirotnik (1983)
has documented the continuing power of a hidden curriculum promoting
apathy, respect for authority, linear thinking, and so on, in different contemporary school settings. Both these patterns have also been the subject
of critique for decades and even, in some respects, centuries. Some set of
forces must, therefore, be implicated in what is at one level a picture of
constancy over time and across geographic regions that is remarkable. We
believe the constellation of assumptions, intellectual trends, social forces,
and ideologies discussed in this chapter accounts more fully for this constancy than any other available explanation.

Then, too, as employees of the state and subject to local and more global political influences, teachers are hardly immune from whatever contemporary intellectual and social currents become central concerns of the day.
Whether this involves the question of what to do with poor and immigrant
children at the turn of this century, or the problems associated with the
homeless, the scourge of AIDS, and computer literacy of later decades, educational institutions have hardly been immune from a variety of public
pressures. In part this reflects something we have already commented on
and will refer to often in this book: the fact that schools and universities
are cultural institutions whose aims, values, and internal processes are linked
in complicated and sometimes contradictory ways to the social fabric with
which they are interwoven. It would be strange indeed if there were not
some tangible effects of the social efficiency movement in curriculum on
the practices of teachers.

Last, there are significant continuities between the ideas that led to the
development of the curriculum field and more recent educational proposals
and events. These, too, ought to make the history of curriculum studies an
abiding interest for those concerned with the future of American education.

Perhaps the individual who has had as much effect on more recent
curriculum theory and policy as anyone is Ralph Tyler. He is best known
perhaps for his role as director of evaluation for the Eight-Year Study (Aiken,
1942; E. R. Smith & Tyler, 1942) and for his synthesis of the "commonsense"
of the curriculum field in what was the virtual Bible of the field for generations, *Basic Principles of Curriculum and Instruction* (Tyler, 1949). In the latter work Tyler lays out what became known as "the Tyler rationale"—a
4-step approach to curriculum development—which became the common
sense of curriculum planning. It is not so much that Tyler's book (essentially his syllabus for a course at the University of Chicago) represents a novel
or imaginative rendering of curriculum deliberation as that it codifies what
mainstream thinkers, since the founding fathers, had advocated.

The Tyler rationale entails four steps. First is the development of objectives—a crucial first step since all other aspects of curriculum planning depend on the precise articulation of achievable ends. The second step involves the creation of learning experiences that will lead to the attainment of those objectives, with the third step involving the ordering of those activities in an effective way. In the final step the curriculum designer/ teacher evaluates how successfully students have accomplished the objectives identified in step 1 (Tyler, 1949, p. 1).

In addition to this rationale for curriculum design, Tyler says that curriculum content may be drawn from three sources: studies of students, studies of contemporary life, and subject-matter specialists. By filtering them through what he calls philosophical and psychological "screens," these content areas can be incorporated into the curriculum design rationale for which Tyler is known, with a curriculum for the schools being the final product.

Barry Franklin, in an essay that deals with lesser-known works by Tyler, notes similarities between Tyler's approach to curriculum and those of earlier advocates of scientific curriculum making. Having grown up in small-town Nebraska and graduated from Doane College in that state, Tyler, like earlier theorists, had an attachment to small-town, middle-class life that was to affect his social understanding of the purposes of curriculum: "Products of the nation's rural, small towns, Anglo-American in heritage, and Protestant in religion, these intellectuals saw the small town they knew from their youth with its like-mindedness and face-to-face relationships as *the virtual embodiment of democracy*" (Franklin, 1988, p. 279; emphasis added). Fearing for the loss of small-town life, men like Bobbitt and Charters sought a way to incorporate the homogeneity of middle-class, Protestant, small-town life into the growing urban centers of the country. And, as suggested above, they were "so impressed with the seeming ability of scientific management principles to harmonize the interaction between management and labor, that they saw the corporation with its hierarchical work relationships as a model for twentieth century American society" (Franklin, 1988, p. 280).

Tyler's social ideas, however, were less closely tied to scientific management and corporate capitalism than were those of the earlier generation of theorists. Indeed in a talk given before the Conference of Administrative Officers of Public and Private Schools in 1942, Tyler noted that "the social distance between employer and employee has widened," therefore adding to the dissolution of the face-to-face relationships that he believed typified more agrarian life. He further noted that "the worker feels himself a cog, and a replaceable cog, in an immense economic system" (cited in Franklin, 1988, p. 281). Tyler's response to this situation was to urge more cooperative activities within schools and to have students deal with social realities; he suggested, for instance, that social studies classes "should be expanded to include an examination of the problems of the social and personal effects of technology," while home economics "should study the nature of family life in the urban environment" (cited in Franklin, 1988, p. 282).

Tyler broke with earlier theorists as well in regard to the value of making the curriculum more functionally related to the prerogatives of corporate capitalism. Separating education from a strict social efficiency orientation, Franklin (1988, p. 285) cites another speech by Tyler in which he declared, "'The school is not a business institution; it is not seeking to make a profit or to distribute material goods.' Rather, it was an institution dedicated to the education of youth." As such it might serve to promote "human welfare." In this sense Tyler seems to have believed that using schools to help achieve the narrow purposes of social efficiency was unjustified; equally unjustified would be curricula that sought to help construct an alternative social order, as advocated by the social meliorists/reconstructionists. Yet Tyler did have a social vision related to his own past and to what he saw as the requirements for democracy, and this vision became a part of the framework for his proposals for more cooperation among students and more direct inclusion of urban problems into the school curriculum.

The Tyler rationale, the linear/rational mode of thinking that it embodies, and its widespread acceptance of the "common sense" of the field, may owe a good deal to the ideas and values that were embraced by Tyler's predecessors. Beyond the admittedly important differences that Tyler had with Bobbitt, Charters, and Snedden over the place of scientific management and the attainment of social and economic ends through the curriculum, his orientation to curriculum design shares some important underlying epistemological assumptions with the earlier generation. Both that generation and Tyler saw knowledge as an entity that can be transmitted from one person to another and as something that is made accessible through the proper development, ordering, and sequencing of learning experiences. The rational/calculative character of the Tyler rationale reflects a mode of thinking and deliberation that was begun decades earlier and, of course, reflects as well a typically Western mode of thought with much deeper philosophical and historical roots.

Kliebard (1977) notes a number of problems with the Tyler rationale: the overlapping nature of the sources from which objectives are to be developed, the derivation and defensibility of the values that are incorporated into the philosophical screen through which objectives are to be filtered, and the lack of substantive detail included within the process as a whole. Because of such shortcomings, one wonders whether the long-standing insistence by curriculum theorists that the first step in making a curriculum be the specification of objectives has any merit whatsoever. It is even questionable whether stating objectives at all, when they represent external goals allegedly reached through the manipulation of learning experiences, is a fruitful way to conceive of the process of curriculum planning. (Kliebard, 1977, p. 65)

Some of the ideas associated with John Dewey may form part of the basis for Kliebard's criticisms here—for instance, that the means and ends of education are mutually constitutive, that subject-matter knowledge and student interest are aspects of the same process, that the conditions of growth are the conditions of education, and that the social and the psychological must somehow be integrated (Dewey, 1916, 1902/1956a). As we detail in Chapter 3, these ideas challenge many of the assumptions on which the curriculum field from Bobbitt to Tyler rests.

Those social and educational assumptions continue to have an effect on educational thinking. For example, the "back-to-basics" movement, especially strong in the early 1970s, was at least partly an attempt to make the curriculum more systematic and functional, dominated by a "skill-and-drill" orientation that was a response to what many saw as the overconcern with "relevance" and "open education" (which we might say embodied elements of developmentalist and social meliorist thinking [Kliebard, 1986]) in the 1960s. More recently, the development of the "new basics" (National Commission on Excellence in Education, 1983) sought to forge a curriculum that would respond to the economic, cultural, and military shortcomings identified by the Reagan administration's committee. It thus sought a utilitarian curriculum for the schools to bring them into line with perceived needs and to avoid a host of alleged social perils (Beyer, 1985). The ideas of central concern in Chapter 2 dealing with the attempts of the new right to reconfigure the school and college curriculum are tied to yet another attempt to make the curriculum reflect the needs not of industrial or corporate capitalism but of what has been called post-industrial society. Such an attempt in many ways reinstantiates the curriculum movement at the turn of the twentieth century. The ideas of Bobbitt, Charters, Snedden, Finney, and Tyler are thus very much alive and well in contemporary society.

Kliebard ends his 1977 essay (originally published in 1970) by claiming:

[For his] moderation and his wisdom as well as his impact, Ralph Tyler deserves to be enshrined in whatever hall of fame the field of curriculum may wish to establish. But the field of curriculum, in its turn, must recognize the Tyler rationale for what it is: Ralph Tyler's version of how a curriculum should be developed—not *the* universal model of curriculum development. Goodlad once

claimed that "Tyler put the capstone on one epoch of curriculum inquiry."
The new epoch is long overdue. (p. 65, emphasis in original)

We would note in passing that the closest we may have so far come to
developing a "curriculum hall of fame" is the creation of a "Distinguished
Contributions to Curriculum Award" through Division B ("Curriculum
Studies") of the American Educational Research Association (AERA). It is
worth noting that this award was inaugurated in 1981 and that Ralph Tyler
was a recipient that first year. It is also interesting to note that this award
was subsequently sanctioned by the AERA as a professional organization (as
opposed to only the membership of Division B) in 1991 and that the recipient of the award that year was Herbert M. Kliebard.

Many have struggled before and since the publication of Tyler's *Basic
Principles of Curriculum and Instruction*, not to mention Bobbitt's *The Curriculum*, to formulate alternative ideas, values, and educational theories that
could help usher in a "new epoch" in the field; perhaps no one has been
more influential in contemporary times than Kliebard himself in this regard.
In any case, we see this book as part of that same struggle, as we build on
the work of others in the effort to help construct a new curriculum approach.

CHAPTER 2

The New Right:
Individualism, Free Markets,
and Character

[Our common culture] is our civic glue. [It] serves as a kind of immunological system, destroying the values and attitudes promulgated by an adversary culture that can infect our body politic. Should our common culture begin to break down, should its fundamental premises fail to be transmitted to succeeding generations, then we will have reason to worry. One vital instrument for the transmission of the common culture is our educational system, and we need to ensure that our schools meet that responsibility.
—*William Bennett (1992, p. 195)*

In their recent writings William Bennett (1992), Chester Finn (1991), Diane Ravitch (1990), and Edward Wynne (Wynne & Ryan, 1993) have repeatedly underscored one theme: The United States is perilously close to a state of cultural, economic, moral, and educational disintegration. They argue, and fear, that the "center will not hold." These analysts maintain that today the United States lacks common values and standards, that our country's economic edge has dissipated, and that our schools' curricula present neither the facts nor a commitment to the disinterested search for truth. Our country and our public schools, they reason, require an enhanced focus on the educational three Cs: content, character, and choice. It falls to our nation's teachers to enhance students' intellectual and moral faculties through a curriculum that teaches cultural, moral, and scientific truths.

The analysis from the new right is persuasive for many individuals. When Chester Finn (1990, 1991) denounces the effects of rigid educational bureaucracies and worries about the flabbiness of our national will, many readers are likely to nod their heads in assent. When William Bennett (1992) maintains that the body politic is infected and weakening under the strain of cultural antibodies, and that in order to become healthy we must do battle, the medical and martial metaphors can be persuasive. These messages mesh well with a corresponding focus on market mechanisms, individual strivings, and moral duty. The apologists for the new right speak frequently of *the* moral "tradition," a concern for "traditional" values, and the need to instill in students a sense of moral propriety. They exhort students and citizens to improve their station in life through hard work and moral responsibility. Their analyses tug at individuals' memories and beliefs in evocative and persuasive ways.

Exhortations from the new right touch sensitive nerves because the stakes are so high. Armed with a sense of moral duty and feeling somewhat besieged, it becomes easy to believe that something drastic must be done. William Bennett (1992) puts it bluntly: "We are in the midst of a struggle over whose values will prevail in America" (p. 11). And for this struggle members of the new right have undertaken an all-out "battle" to win the "war." It is unabashedly an ideological battle, and one that liberal and radical educational scholars have tended to ignore. In what follows we present the educational critique and prescriptions of the new right, as well as the central assumptions that guide and mold this educational platform. Central to this task is an elaboration of the political, social, ethical, and economic ideas and theories that undergird that platform.

ELEMENTS OF A PERCEIVED CRISIS
AND A PREFERRED SOLUTION

> All Americans . . . would benefit from an education system that produced informed citizens. (The streets would probably be safer also.) Education isn't just a service we obtain for our daughters and sons and grandchildren. It is a public good, after defense perhaps our most important form of common provision and, in a sense, itself a defense against the ills that plague us at home. (Finn, 1991, p. xvi)

Public schools, members of the new right claim, can serve as an antidote to the domestic ills that plague our country. Claiming that the body politic is ill, they pursue the medical metaphor and maintain that once the illness is diagnosed, the prognosis can be formulated. The diagnosis includes an etiological assessment: Our ills are both societal and educational in origin.

The societal ills that hamper our national progress are not seen as structural or systemic in nature but rather are construed as weaknesses that lie within individuals, weaknesses that are multiplying and portend a social crisis. Chester Finn (1990, 1991) and William Bennett (1988, 1992) portray us as a nation of individuals who have lost our determination and nerve. Our pathology is a behavioral one—and it is most evident among the poor. America's poor, in brief, no longer exhibit self-discipline or commitment. For William Bennett (1992), the central problem is a loss of character:

> It's hard to estimate what self-discipline and the ability to commit to a task could bring about if every child in America had them. At least they would eliminate much remedial education, much of our drop-out problem and much social pathology among the poor. But one cannot simply wave a wand and create virtue and social character in people. (p. 199)

Utilizing Charles Murray's arguments, Bennett (1992) focuses on the behavior of the poor:

> For black women with a high school education, 91.5% live above the poverty line. But for a black woman to attain this, she has to avoid becoming pregnant before marriage. "A poor woman who wishes to get out of poverty ought not to have a baby out of wedlock," reads the Murray report. "This is not a moral statement but an empirical one."
>
> But of course it is a moral one as well. This is just one obvious example of the intimate link between educational attainment and success on the one hand and values on the other. Behavior affects attainment, and nothing—race, class or family background—more powerfully affects behavior than one's beliefs and convictions. (p. 197)

Infuse character, commitment, self-discipline, and proper virtues in the populace, and our societal (i.e., aggregate individual and behavioral) ills will be healed.

For members of the new right, schools are central, albeit problematic, sites for this behavioral enhancement. They concede that the task before the American public is not simple. Over the years the public schools have become part of the problem. Today schools have grown to be "tyrannical" bureaucratic machines that ignore their consumers (i.e., students) and end up serving the "educrats" (bureaucratic educational administrators) who run them. For Chester Finn (1991), the "internal dynamics and rivalries of the education system have pushed the public interest aside" (p. 180). And, as Bennett (1992) maintains:

> [Instead of confronting the problems and] . . . beginning the hard task of improving education, the education establishment—that wide array of professional organizations putatively representing teachers, administrators and other educators—by and large offers a steady stream of defenses, denials, ultimatums, and repeated calls for more money. Many of these education bureaucrats, or "educrats," have abdicated their responsibility; they should abdicate their authority as well. The few who occasionally break rank and point to the problems in the system are usually quickly brought back into line or punished. Too

often this education establishment itself is the single greatest obstacle to education reform. (pp. 43–44)

The problems have to be confronted squarely, and while effort needs to be directed at transforming the educational establishment, the site for educational enhancement is the classroom and the person responsible for this enhancement is the teacher. It is the teachers' task to bring an emphasis on content and character into the classroom and thus forestall the social crisis.

Content

Schools exist, say new right advocates, to improve students' cognitive and moral capabilities. To accomplish this, teachers need to return to the foundational features of the curriculum. There are a number of common strands to this agenda. Prominent among them is the proposition that shared background knowledge is an indispensable educational ingredient and one of the most important elements in our shared cultural identity. The emphasis on "common knowledge" operates on both a societal and a textual level. On the societal level, in order to participate in a country's shared legacy its citizens need to understand the prominent features of that legacy. Common knowledge serves both as a kind of societal glue and as a set of background tools for political participation. At its most basic textual level, the claim of the new right is that in order to read, in order to comprehend any meaningful text, one must understand the references and allusions to our fund of common cultural knowledge. Students need to have some passing acquaintance with the basic elements of knowledge that most Americans already know. Without an immersion in these elements, which provide a shared cultural literacy, students cannot share in the common legacy that is uniquely and truly American. As E. D. Hirsch (1983) writes:

> Without appropriate, tacitly shared background knowledge, people cannot understand newspapers. A certain extent of shared, canonical knowledge is inherently necessary to a literate democracy.
>
> For this canonical information I have proposed the term "cultural literacy." It is the translinguistic knowledge on which linguistic literacy depends. You cannot have the one without the other. . . . School materials contain unfamiliar materials that promote the "acculturation" that is a universal part of growing up in any tribe or nation. Acculturation into a national literate culture might be defined as learning what the "common reader" of a newspaper in a literate culture would be expected to know. (pp. 165–166)

Hirsch maintains that these building-block bits of knowledge are often best learned in a rote fashion. Most new right proponents agree. What is clearly stated in their educational proposals is that content-specific foundations are needed. Hirsch (1987/88) argues:

> Only recently have we come to understand that "Jack and Jill" and "George Washington" belong to an alphabet that must be learned by heart, and which is no less essential to higher-order literacy skills than the alphabet itself. . . . The methods by which children learn these higher-order ABC's can be exciting and fun, or they can be deadening and painful. . . . But learning the higher-order ABC's, like learning the alphabet itself, does require learning by heart and piling up information. (1987/88, p. 67)

Chester Finn reinforces this assessment when he focuses his analysis on the college level. After citing statistical indicators that our current college students are ignorant about the facts, he states that, "surely college ought to transport one's intellect well beyond factual knowledge and cultural literacy. But it's hard to add a second story to a house that lacks a solid foundation" (Finn, 1991, p. 17).

Similarly, William Bennett (1992) maintains that we must "give greater attention to a sound curriculum emphasizing English, history, geography, math and science" (p. 51). This is exactly what he attempts to do. In the introduction to *James Madison High School: A Curriculum for American Students*, Bennett (1987), then U.S. secretary of education, writes:

> We want our students—whatever their plans for the future—to take from high school a shared body of knowledge and skills, a common language of ideas, a common moral and intellectual discipline. We want them to know math and science, history and literature. We want them to know how to think for themselves, to respond to important questions, to solve problems, to pursue an argument, to defend a point of view, to understand its opposite, and to weigh alternatives. We want them to develop, through example and experience, those habits of mind and traits of character properly prized by our society. And we want them to be prepared for entry into the community of responsible adults. (p. 4)

In the educational world such aspirations are common and frequently stated. In Bennett's (1987) outline of high school social studies (history, geography, and civics), he prescribes the following scope and sequence: Western Civilization (ninth grade); American History (tenth grade); Principles of American Democracy (eleventh grade, first semester); and American Democracy and the World (eleventh grade, second semester). In each section Bennett declares that certain topics and eras ought to be covered and that written assignments ought to be required. The central claim is that "too many of our students are unfamiliar with the basic facts of their national history and government," and so the "James Madison High School history curriculum is designed to provide a solid grounding in the European and American past" (Bennett, 1987, pp. 20–21). In spite of a proclaimed emphasis on cognitive abilities and moral sensitivities, it is the "facts" that have to be "covered."

This example illustrates one of the basic orientations and general directions of the curriculum reform efforts associated with the new right. Their emphasis is on a return to basic, elemental, and foundational knowledge. Despite stated desires to enhance students' "habits of mind" and general cognitive processes, the facts are to be laid down as the prerequisite "building blocks." The concern seems to be with a rather thin approach to knowledge. The new right does not depict knowledge as powerful or rich lenses through which to view our natural and social worlds or as a human inheritance with great disciplinary or interdisciplinary depth. For the new right, knowledge is much thinner and apparently not very substantial. Furthermore, how character and cognition are to be enhanced in this process is not clear. In addition, who will choose the content that informs students' character and cognition remains a pertinent but largely ignored question. What is clear is that such questions are directly related to the broader social vision of the new right, as discussed below. For now, it is enough to notice that the new right's educational vision tends to be guided more by political imperative than by educational reflection. The driving force behind their analysis is a set of convictions about the requirements for a good society that is not matched by an attention to educational contexts and practices. Students tend to be seen as carriers of social functions and politically inscribed meanings rather than as active, independent, creative people whose interests and backgrounds need to be considered within the context of curriculum and teaching. As a result, the educational positions of the new right lack a substantial consideration of how we might bring the student and the curriculum together in a manner that is educationally defensible, an omission that undermines both their political purpose and any corresponding set of actual educational practices. These deficiencies in the new right agenda will become even more evident in the next two sections.

Culture and the Curriculum

Given the emphasis on shared knowledge and shared understanding, the arena of multicultural curriculum becomes a pressing one for the new right. Proponents of multicultural curricula purportedly highlight differences, not similarities—a perspective that threatens to undermine the cultural cohesion that is central to the new right perspective. The most articulate spokesperson of the new right in this debate is Diane Ravitch, the former assistant secretary of education under George Bush and a historian by training. In an article entitled "Multiculturalism: E Pluribus Plures," Ravitch (1990) maintains that there are two sides to the multicultural debate: the pluralists, who desire a cohesive approach, and the particularists, whose ideas point to a divisive and antagonistic future. For pluralists the goal is to "understand that part of our national history in which different groups competed, fought, suffered, but ultimately learned to live together in relative peace and even achieved a sense of common nationhood" (p. 340). Pluralists want to "demonstrate that neither race nor gender is an obstacle to high achievement. They teach all children that everyone can achieve self-fulfillment, honor, and dignity in society if they aim high and work hard" (p. 340). The pluralistic orientation, Ravitch maintains, already exists within our public schools, and its presence represents an accomplishment that has not come easily. Pluralists have painstakingly achieved a recognition of the "diversity of voices" (p. 339) that have contributed to our common culture. In their support for the "new history," they recognize that history "is—indeed, must be—a warts-and-all history; it demands an unflinching examination of racism and discrimination in our history" (p. 340).

Particularists, on the contrary, "insist that no common culture is possible or desirable" (p. 340). According to Ravitch, the particularist perspective represents a deterministic, separatist orientation that tries to raise children's self-esteem and academic achievement through a curriculum that focuses on minority students' cultural legacy. Their history is an ideologically laden one: "The brand of history that they [particularists] espouse is one in which everyone is either a descendant of victims or oppressors. . . . [It has] its intellectual roots in the ideology of ethnic separation and in the black nationalist movement" (pp. 341–342). Particularists threaten our social fabric by letting loose "unfettered group rivalry" (p. 340), and they undermine the canons and standards of scholarly inquiry.

In her analysis, Ravitch (1990) acknowledges that our schools do not educate well the minority populations they serve. She writes:

> Many of the children in these districts [where the majority of students are African American and Hispanic] perform poorly in academic classes and leave school without graduating. They would fare better in school if they had well-educated and well-paid teachers, small classes, good materials, encouragement at home and school, summer academic programs, protection from the drugs and crime that ravage their neighborhoods, and higher expectations of satisfying careers upon graduation. These are expensive and time-consuming remedies that must also engage the larger society beyond the school. (p. 349)

While this passage might lead others to consider what education and schooling mean to poor black and Hispanic students, Ravitch does not pursue the topic further. Instead she ends her analysis with a recurrent warning from the new right. The real problem is the particularist approach to multicultural education, an approach that

> will detract attention from the real needs of schools and the real interests of children, while simultaneously arousing distorted race pride in children of all races, increasing racial antagonisms and producing fresh recruits for white and black racist groups. (1990, p. 349)

Building on the need for the kind of social cohesion that provides for social harmony, the new right sees multicultural education as both inimical to the history and spirit of America and as leading to cultural and racial separation. It reflects the politicization of education and an abandonment of a search for truth.

Character and Moral Education

In William Bennett's (1992) most recent critique of liberal privilege and his documentation of the decline of America, the former secretary of education asserts that in the late 1960s and 1970s:

> We saw a sustained attack on traditional American values and the place where those values had long had a comfortable and congenial home—the school. Many of the [liberal] elite correctly understood that civilization's major task is the upbringing of children; if they could alter the ways we raised children by changing the way we teach them, they could then alter American society to suit their view of the world. Academics provided much of the intellectual heavy artillery—citing how endemically corrupt and sick America is. Once the traditional teachings were discredited and then removed, the vacuum was filled by faddish nonsense, and the kids lost. (pp. 51–52)

Bennett and other new right defenders want to restore traditional values to their "rightful" place in the American school.

In a discussion of schools and traditional values, two questions seem particularly pressing: (1) Why should schools teach traditional values? and (2) What is entailed in teaching those values? The new right does not respond to these questions with a singular voice, but many of these commentators share common beliefs about values, education, and schooling. William Bennett (1988) and Edward Wynne (1987) view our present social order as disordered and morally decaying, and they call for character education as an integral response to this disorder. They claim that our moral and social crisis is caused, in part, by a personalistic, me-oriented ethos—one in which students are unable to delay gratification or work together in a meaningful fashion. Purportedly today's students lack character, and past forms of moral education have been too process-oriented. Given this situation, the new right calls for an education that emphasizes traditional values and character indoctrination. Only in this context, they maintain, can characterless students be initiated into a larger, more traditional moral order—a moral community.

Edward Wynne maintains that character education must focus on indoctrinating students into the "great" tradition. Both he and William Bennett consistently stress that students must learn "our" traditional values. Wynne (1985/86) states that, "on the whole, school is and must be inherently indoctrinative" (p. 9). Teachers should indoctrinate students into the "great tradition" that emphasizes "good habits of conduct as contrasted with moral concepts or moral rationales" (p. 6). William Bennett (1992) claims:

> There are values that all American citizens share and that we should want all American students to know and to make their own: honesty, fairness, self-discipline, fidelity to task, friends, and family, personal responsibility, love of country and belief in the principles of liberty, equality and the freedom to practice one's own faith. (p. 58)

For many teachers the question that immediately arises is: How should these values be taught? According to Bennett (1992), that question "deserves a candid response, one that isn't given often enough"; the core of that response is to be found in "exposing our children to good character and inviting its imitation," through which we will, "transmit to them a moral foundation" (p. 58). Teachers should model good character, and students should be exposed to stories and tales that extol and underscore the virtues that inform the good life.

Both Wynne and Bennett are careful to note that their approach to character formation does not negate the importance of moral reasoning. But they are practical men who understand the importance of the common dictum—first things first. Wynne (1985/86) writes:

> The [great] tradition was not hostile to the intellectual analysis of moral problems. Adults recognize that life occasionally generates moral dilemmas. In the Jewish religious tradition, learned men were expected to analyze and debate Talmudic moral issues. . . . [But] instruction in exegetical analysis commenced only after the selected neophyte had undergone long periods of testing, memorized large portions of semididactic classics, and displayed appropriate deference to exegetical experts. (p. 7)

And Bennett (1992) proclaims:

> We need not get into issues like nuclear war, abortion, creationism or eutha-
> nasia. This may come as a disappointment to some people but the fact is that
> the formation of character in young people is educationally a task different
> from and prior to, the discussion of the great, difficult controversies of the
> day. First things first. We should teach values the same way we teach other
> things: one step at a time. (p. 60)

As noted earlier, many in the new right want schools to teach both
cognitive and moral lessons. Wynne (1987) believes it is important to integrate moral and cognitive lessons, and he discusses the process by which
an inner-city elementary school staff attempted to alter the deviant behavior of young female students. In this school, girls who were considered discipline problems were encouraged to take part in the school's "charm class"—
a class that stressed proper dress, makeup, poise, good grooming, posture,
and etiquette. Wynne (1987) states that, "such activities need to be a part
of the academic program because academics are an important part of the
business of any effective school. If collective activities are segregated from
academics, a critical message is being given: Academics are the really
important thing for ambitious students" (p. 110). The "charm class" represents one way in which the new right supports inculcating traditional values
"in" students, and how these purportedly "traditional" values represent elements of larger collective norms.

Character education proposals of the new right focus clearly and
unerringly on the individual. Amidst social disorder and moral decay, its
proponents maintain that students need to be initiated into larger moral
communities. They assume that in spite of the dominance of the social disorder and the moral decay they decry, worthwhile and valuable moral communities exist into which students ought to be initiated. This somewhat
puzzling assumption fits well with their focus on individual responsibility.
For it is only through a focus on the individual that their moral order can
be sustained. And, finally, a third element has gained widespread support
from the new right: a commitment to providing new educational alternatives for students and their parents.

School Choice

One of the most popular of the proposals that continues to be promoted
by members of the new right is the idea of school choice. Though there are
several versions of this approach to school reform and restructuring, they
have at least one thing in common that is directly related to their general

orientation. Schools have become overgrown and lethargic bureaucracies, in part—as we shall explore in the next chapter—because of the growth of the welfare state. As a result, elementary and secondary educational institutions are unresponsive to both parents and national needs; they must be taken out of the hands of government, reestablished on the principles of the free market, and organized to maximize the right of parents to choose which schools their children will attend. This will expand personal freedoms of parents, increase educational quality, and better serve our national interests.

One of the first proposals for school choice was apparently authored by Milton Friedman (1955). In this essay Friedman says that he will assume as his starting points "a society that takes freedom of the individual, or more realistically the family, as its ultimate objective" and a social system that relies on "voluntary exchange among individuals" (pp. 123–124)—ideas that lie close to the center of the new right's social vision. While federal and state monies have underwritten much of the cost of public schooling, there are alternatives to such state intervention that maximize student and parental choice. Schools could be financed, Friedman (1955) says, "by giving parents vouchers redeemable for a specified maximum sum per child per year if spent on 'approved' educational services. Parents would then be free to spend this sum and any additional sum on purchasing educational services from an 'approved' institution of their own choice" (p. 127).

Central features of many voucher plans include allowing private and parochial schools to be funded with public monies and giving parents greater choice in determining which schools their children will attend. What this represents is the importation of a market mechanism into "public schooling." Through the process of consumer selection and producer competition, it is believed, the best schools and the brightest students will surface and thrive, and the bureaucratic obstacles that currently bedevil schools will diminish.

Friedman draws a distinction between general education, aimed at educating students for citizenship, and vocational education, the aim of which is to enhance the professional pursuits of students. His educational proposals vary between these two aims, though for both he provides an outline for a market-oriented system that provides a grounding for the current efforts to enact school choice. Reflecting the perspectives of contemporary spokespeople for the new right, Friedman acknowledges the need for a social cohesiveness beyond that provided in collections of self-interested actors. He says that "a stable and democratic society is impossible without widespread acceptance of some common set of values and without a minimum degree of literacy and knowledge on the part of citizens. Education contributes to both" (Friedman, 1955, pp. 124–125). This social cohesion must be maintained even within a market-oriented set of educational choices. This creates significant educational problems for new right advocates of school choice and, as we shall see, raises serious questions about their embrace of moral relativism.

THE NEW RIGHT'S "CALL TO ARMS"

The educational "call to arms" of the contemporary new right was sounded by one of the earliest of the reform proposals to emerge in the contemporary educational crisis—the publication of the Reagan administration's *A Nation at Risk* (National Commission on Excellence in Education, 1983). Claiming that "the educational foundations of our society are presently being eroded by a rising tide of mediocrity that threatens our very future as a Nation and a people" (p. 5), it is evident that the new right also blames purported educational shortcomings for many social, economic, cultural, and military failings. This report also contains a number of recommendations for restructuring schools so as to assist in social renewal. A key aim is the rekindling of a competitive spirit that would enable the United States to be more globally competitive through a restructured curriculum founded on the New Basics as well as higher standards for academic performance and student conduct (National Commission on Excellence in Education, 1983, pp. 23–36). As noted earlier, William Bennett's (1988) three Cs (choice, content, and character), along with a concern for strengthening the connections between schools and corporate capitalism, constitute central elements of the new right's educational platform.

The new right's belief that schools must more effectively serve the interests of corporate capitalism is already being realized in concrete practices in our public schools. For example:

• Worklink was created and put into practice in Florida, with assistance from the Educational Testing Service (Rothman, 1992). This program responds to the "skills gap" that allegedly exists between high school graduates and the demands of the workplace by providing computerized means for schools to respond to skill deficits that businesses identify in their workers.

• Chris Whittle, the man who brought Channel One into our schools, has attempted to create a new, for-profit high school plan, dubbed the Edison Project, which included Chester Finn as a founding member. It was initially assisted by such corporate giants as Time Warner and Phillips Electronics (Walsh, 1992b).

• A number of high schools are already providing "competency guarantees" that offer to retrain, at no cost to employers, those graduates who exhibit inadequate job performance.

- Adopt-A-School programs are beginning the process of worker socialization early on in high school and junior high school students' careers, under the rubric of making the world of work understandable and less intimidating. Some have even suggested vocational education programs as early as kindergarten.
- A Corporate Academy for at-risk students has been initiated through the auspices of Burger King, so that schooling can better serve those students and respond more effectively to the prerogatives of corporate America (Walsh, 1992a).
- Various programs have been created for non–college bound high school students, in part to better prepare them for the world of work. These often go under the name of "tech-prep" programs, with the curriculum geared toward more "usable" knowledge.
- Private companies have contracted with some schools and school districts to take over the administration of their schools.[1]
- Harlem High School in Rockford, Illinois, is paying students enrolled in an apprenticeship program "cash incentives for success": $1,300 for As and $1,150 for Bs ("Rockford School Offers," 1992). In cases such as this, the notion that education is part of a market system ceases to be a metaphor.

The new right, in sum, advocates a combination of educational emphases and directions in response to the crisis they perceive. Identifying this crisis in individualistic terms, they point to the need to instill social cohesion through attention to a thin, discipline-based content focus for all and to character education, especially for the poor. Curriculum content focused on the common heritage of Americans, and on discipline-specific subject matter, will serve to enforce the necessary cultural cohesion. This, combined with an emphasis on hard work, diligence, and personal responsibility, will help avert the social crisis. In this nationally promulgated vision, public schooling would be more responsive, and more open and flexible, if it were taken out of the control of the government bureaucracy, if parents were directly provided a more comprehensive set of options (perhaps through a system of vouchers), and if ties between classrooms and boardrooms were strengthened.

Beyond the perceived social and educational crises identified and responded to by members of the new right, we need to understand the undergirding assumptions and orientations that shape their analyses. For educational proposals are unavoidably embedded in larger intellectual traditions and social realities, not created *sui generis*. The reforms analyzed here embody such larger domains even as they help construct (or reconstruct) them. The calls for school and curriculum reform from the new right contain strands of political and moral discourse and action that are themselves embedded in a distinctive world view. Educators must understand that world view if we are to assess the social, political, and ethical import of the educational changes this group advocates.

CLASSICAL LIBERAL THEORY AND SOCIETY

> Nothing could more strikingly demonstrate the positive value of self-interested action than that its denial destroys civilization and enslaves men. In "capitalism" we have a freedom of moral choice, and no one is *forced* to be a scoundrel. But this is precisely what we are forced to be in a collectivist social and economic system . . . [because] the satanic rationale of the system presses us into the service of the state machine and forces us to act against our consciences. (Ropke, 1960, p.121; emphasis in original)

The heritage of the new right can be traced in significant part to the tradition widely referred to as "classical liberalism." This school of thought, emerging in the seventeenth and eighteenth centuries, contains philosophical, social, religious, moral, political, and economic dimensions, constituting a world view that has significant repercussions for day-to-day life. While it is not possible to discuss each of these dimensions in depth, it should be noted that classical liberalism generally challenged the status quo of an aristocratic, tradition-bound world within which those who governed were seen as in some sense anointed, with leadership determined by the inheritance of a certain status and genealogy. Classical liberalism was also connected to intellectual and epistemological shifts. Instead of religious doctrines or philosophical speculations, classical liberals highlighted empiricist science and human rationality more generally as the arbiters of truth and the engines of social progress. Physical processes and calculations, rather than received religious doctrines or metaphysical speculations, became the basis for claims to transcendent knowledge. The importance of the individual—autonomous, self-determining, and free—also became a fundamental part of classical liberal beliefs. Regarding political theory, classical liberals asserted the importance of constitutional guarantees protecting the individual rights of free persons. Together classical liberal perspectives challenged many longstanding assumptions and traditions. One commentator has said, summarizing these perspectives:

> [Classical] liberalism, as even its major critics admit, was novel, revolutionary and profoundly unsettling. . . . Dissatisfied with the rigidity and iniquity of ancient privilege and arbitrary authority, seventeenth- and eighteenth-century liberals sought, above all else, to free men from the constraints of arbitrary power. All social relations, including political relations, these early liberals

argued, ought to be based upon the mutual and free consent of equally sovereign individuals. (Koerner, 1985, p. 3)

The mutual and free consent of independent agents is precisely what a market economy was designed to support. This freedom of personal agency, in both economic and political spheres, is what animates much of the new right's world view.

The Priority of Free Markets

In their introduction to *Free to Choose*, Milton and Rose Friedman (1980) unequivocally assert their position on the economic and political vitality of the United States and its historic promise: "The story of the United States is the story of an economic miracle and a political miracle that was made possible by the translation into practice of two sets of ideas—both, by a curious coincidence, formulated in documents published in the same year, 1776" (p. 1). The documents to which the Friedmans refer are Adam Smith's *The Wealth of Nations* (here cited as A. Smith, 1776/1910a, 1776/1910b) and the Declaration of Independence.

In the new right's world view, "economic freedom" is guaranteed through the alleged social, political, and moral advantages of a capitalist social order, especially as compared with other systems. Capitalism creates open markets that provide two kinds of opportunities: for producers, the chance of creating efficient, profitable organizations and processes for the manufacture and distribution of goods, which in turn generate more and better processes of production; and for consumers, the chance to procure goods and services that will improve their quality of life.

The pursuit of individual interests originates, according to Adam Smith, in "the desire of bettering our condition, a desire which, though generally calm and dispassionate, comes with us from the womb, and never leaves us till we go into the grave. . . . An augmentation of fortune is the means by which the greater part of men propose and wish to better their condition" (1776/1910a, p. 305). Since complete satisfaction with our life situation is not a human possibility, seeking a better condition through an increase in capital is as natural as the processes of birth and death themselves. An explosion in the availability of consumer goods made available under capitalism offers virtually limitless opportunities for pursuing the good life—or at least an incrementally better one.

An operating market system allows unencumbered choices and expands the total productive capacity and wealth of the society. This is aided by one of its defining features—the division of labor. This is, of course, not a new proposal for organizing social life. Yet early capitalist industry created a rigorously reinforced, highly segmented division of work that—assisted by the invention of modern machinery and the hierarchical management of production—reinforced specialization and promoted efficiency. As a result, a greater variety in production and more widely available goods are made possible. Small wonder, then, that Adam Smith pronounced, "it is the great multiplication of the productions of all the different arts, in consequence of the division of labor, which occasions, in a well-governed society, that universal opulence which extends itself to the lowest ranks of the people" (1776/1910a, p. 10). This view is echoed in more modern times by the observation that, with the advent of capitalism and the opportunities it generates, "the ordinary man has been able to attain levels of living never dreamed of before" (Friedman & Friedman, 1980, p. 146).

The mechanisms internal to the operation of a free market also promote social stability. These mechanisms are to be supported, as we shall see, by procedural rules maintained by a limited state, as well as by cultural values and symbols incorporated into educational processes such as those espoused by Hirsch (1988), Bennett (1992), and Wynne and Ryan (1993). Through such market mechanisms as prices, the division of labor, and the relations of supply and demand, goods are voluntarily exchanged that serve the interests of both producers and consumers, thereby helping maintain order through a decentralized economic system.

The market system takes advantage of what many new right advocates believe is another natural human characteristic—our competitive drive. This is manifested in our relations with other people, our acquisition of products, and our general determination to become materially better off. One of the protections built into a market economy is the competition among businesses to produce better products or to generate goods of equal quality at lower prices. Competition ensures that more efficient firms will drive out less efficient ones, resulting in more and cheaper goods than is the case under more centralized economic systems, which restrict competition. Personal competition among workers will also enhance productivity and increase the wages of those who are more deserving.

As a form of economic organization, in sum, capitalism is held to provide several advantages over previous and contemporary alternatives:

1. The lack of centralized control, giving people the opportunity to pursue interests as they define them
2. The opportunity to further the natural drive to better our life
3. The chance to procure an unprecedented array of goods and services made available through market mechanisms, which include the free rein of competition, the forces of supply and demand, a system of pricing, and the division of labor

4. An unprecedented increase in the total wealth of a society that will improve the quality of life for the masses
5. The operation of an orderly system of exchange produced through individual initiative
6. The exercise of personal liberty rather than coerced choice, in terms of both consumption and production activities

Free Markets and Human Capital

Skilled, disciplined workers are a central requirement of a market economy, as is the development of technology and systems of management to oversee production. In simple terms, a company's profitability amounts to the difference between the sale of goods and the costs of production. In a system designed to foster competition, increasing productivity and efficiency are central if a firm is to survive and flourish. The resources available to increase productivity can be divided into two general types—physical capital and human capital. Physical capital—machinery, tools, plants—was central to the success of the Industrial Revolution. The efficient use of machinery also had clear implications for work patterns and the need for new forms of human capital:

> The decision-making process was two steps removed from the worker. The machine dictated to the employer who arranged work patterns and conditions according to its requirements. Punctuality was important—workers had to be on time to feed the machinery. Accuracy was crucial—the machine had to be tended properly. Order was necessary—the machine dictated how work must be performed. Diligence was essential—an hour wasted by the worker was an idle hour for the machinery and a profitless one for the employer. Perseverance was required—expensive machinery had to be run from dawn to dusk to pay off its costs with profits. (Nasaw, 1979, p. 36)

The efficient operation of machinery is not possible unless workers are adequately socialized and trained and unless managers implement the appropriate methods of supervision. The educational implications of this are rather straightforward: What the schools must emphasize, in the case of future workers, are those dispositions, mannerisms, and personality traits consistent with efficient, predictable, and productive work habits. This meant that the emphasis in the early common schools was not on the knowledge conveyed through the formal curriculum but on the moral guidance provided through a hidden curriculum (Jackson, 1968; for a historical account of the hidden curriculum, see Vallance, 1977). Especially for working-class students, "the common schools were to be the institutions in which the poor would receive the character training necessary for success";

students "who learned the virtues of hard work, frugality, and temperance in the common schools would never forget them" (Nasaw, 1979, p. 37). The human capital requirements of early U.S. society would be served by promoting a hidden curriculum that was consistent with the values of Adam Smith, Benjamin Franklin, and John Calvin and that was central to capitalist production.

INDIVIDUALISM AND LIBERTY

The classical liberal tradition outlined above has many correlates in the contemporary new right. One of the primary of these is the view that human beings are fundamentally social isolates—separate, self-formed, and self-determining. Our thoughts, feelings, and values are, hence, individually formed and validated. More than a narrowly economic matter, the primacy of the individual constitutes an ontological position that is a central part of the classical liberal legacy, continued in the new right's social and educational agenda. Within this ontology, people are

> pictured abstractly as given, with given interests, wants, purposes, needs, etc., while society and the state are pictured as sets of actual or possible social arrangements which respond more or less adequately to those individuals' requirements. . . . The relevant features of individuals determining the ends which social arrangements are held (actually or ideally) to fulfill . . . are assumed as given, independently of a social context. (Lukes, 1973, p. 73)

The primary unit of analysis is the individual, who must create and organize social conditions that best meet the needs and interests that he or she has antecedently identified.

Proposals from the new right to introduce a more stringent character education, as we have seen, focus exclusively on individual defects and routes for their amelioration. Amidst what they see as social disorder and moral decay, they maintain that if individual students are adequately initiated into moral traditions of a certain sort, our social ills will be combated. They claim that worthwhile moral values exist that can be recaptured through a focus on the moral "enhancement" of individuals. Such a position fits with the legacy of classical liberal theory and its ontological individualism. It is also tied to an orientation that embraces competition as a means of individual betterment. Any sustained attention to larger contextual features would, in this view, undermine individual responsibility and misdirect educational efforts.

In their much-discussed work on the collapse of communal bonds and the rise of "radical individualism," Robert Bellah and his colleagues (1985) document the personal and social costs of the tendency to regard people as socially and morally self-sufficient. As the authors of *Habits of the Heart* put it:

> The American understanding of the autonomy of the self places the burden of one's own deepest self-definitions on one's own individual choice . . . the notion that one discovers one's deepest beliefs in, and through, tradition and community is not very congenial to Americans. Most of us imagine an autonomous self existing independently, entirely outside any tradition and community, and then perhaps choosing one. (p. 65)

As we will see when we discuss the moral underpinnings of the new right, this emphasis on the autonomy of the self has resulted in forms of moral relativism. An ontological individualism has important social, political, and moral consequences.

The individualistic tenor of classical liberal views on which proponents of the new right draw is underscored by the presumption that human beings possess natural drives and inclinations upon which a capitalist economy builds. Taken together, this constellation of drives constitutes a partial picture of human nature that is traceable to the tradition of natural law and rights. The emphasis on natural processes and drives in *The Wealth of Nations* is not inconsequential for social or educational policy, nor is it accidental. For, in addition to writing perhaps the most famous early treatise on political economy, Adam Smith was himself vitally concerned with the doctrines of natural liberty. He was chair of Moral Philosophy at Glasgow in 1752 and published his *Theory of Moral Sentiments* in 1759 which, like most works of that era, reflected a belief in natural theology; our natural affirmations lie first with ourselves, then with our families, and then (in a weaker sense) with the nation or state. In the Introduction to *The Wealth of Nations* it is said that one of its "fundamental ideas" is natural liberty (Seligman, 1910). In that work, Smith (A. Smith, 1776/1910a) says:

> All systems, either of preference or restraint . . . being thus completely taken away, *the obvious and simple system of natural liberty establishes itself of its own accord.* Every man, as soon as he does not violate the laws of justice, is left perfectly free to pursue his own interests in his own way, and to bring both his industry and his capital into competition with those of any other man or order of men. (pp. xi–xii; emphasis added)

Rid of artificial systems, organizations, and social confines, human beings' natural rights and obligations may emerge, forming an important basis for day to day actions. As a matter of natural right, we are essentially individuals, disconnected from others and responsible ultimately to our own selves and the choices we make within our own frameworks and situations.[2]

This tradition depicts human beings as naturally endowed with certain rights that must be protected and maintained. This way of thinking provides a basis for making political decisions that cannot, as such, be challenged; "nature" provides a bedrock for the enunciation of rights that are transcendent and must be respected. We might refer to this as "political naturalism." Others have suggested that nature provides a basis for making claims to knowledge—what we might call an "epistemological naturalism." This latter position is related to many of the views outlined by Allan Bloom in *The Closing of the American Mind* (1987).

Horrified by the lack of civility among new students in the "great universities," Bloom longs for a return to a university constituted by scholars committed to the study of the verities and the eternal questions, to "man" in general and the intellectual canon as its own end—in short, to that image of scholarly inquiry and teaching as the disinterested pursuit of knowledge.

The social movements that helped give voice to alternative curricular initiatives, such as feminism and multiculturalism, are rejected by Bloom because, among other things, they violate his epistemological naturalism. The fundamental problem with feminism, on this account, is that in trying to overthrow "natural" laws and processes, feminists attempt what is both impossible and socially dangerous. Thus feminism "ends, as do many modern movements that seek abstract justice, in forgetting nature and using force to refashion human beings to secure that justice" (Bloom, 1987, p. 100). If women would just respond to their natural inclination to have and raise children ["children have always been, and still are, more the mother's anyway" (Bloom, 1987, p. 105)] and men were allowed to develop their own natural instincts toward protectiveness and aggressiveness ["to make them 'care' [is a] project [that] must inevitably fail" (Bloom, 1987, p. 129)], we would not only be respecting nature but serving the interests of social, intellectual, and emotional harmony.

Claims concerning natural rights and epistemology, respectively, have implications for political doctrines and educational policies. Rooted in the ontological individualism that is central to classical liberal ideas, these claims reinforce the emphasis on lone individuals who are removed from any important social context. Yet the classical liberals also argue that individual endeavors and perspectives will, by themselves, help procure the social good.

Personal Liberty and the Social Good

A reliance on self-interest as the route to the social good stems partly from Adam Smith's view that "every individual endeavors to employ his capital as near home as he can" if such investments bring returns roughly equal to or greater than other possibilities (1776/1910a, p. 398); further, these domestic investments are made by people, "so to direct that industry that its produce may be of the greatest possible value" (1776/1910a, pp. 399–400). In maximizing our own monetary interests, we assist the accumulation of capital by the industry in which we invest, increasing in turn the total wealth of a nation. Self-interest and the social good are in reality co-extensive:

> As every individual . . . endeavours as much as he can both to employ his capital in the support of domestic industry, and so to direct that industry that its produce may be of the greatest value; every individual necessarily labours to render the annual revenue of the society as great as he can. He generally, indeed, neither intends to promote the public interest, nor knows how much he is promoting it. By preferring the support of domestic to that of foreign industry, he intends only his own security; and by directing that industry in such a manner as its produce may be of the greatest value, he intends only his own gain, and he is in this, as in many other cases, led by an invisible hand to promote an end which was no part of his intention. . . . By pursuing his own interest he frequently promotes that of the society more effectually than when he really intends to promote it. (Smith, 1776/1910a, p. 400)

From Adam Smith's "invisible hand" in the eighteenth century to Ronald Reagan's "trickle down economics" in the twentieth, many have held that regulatory activities imposed by government agencies are unnecessary and destructive. Whereas regulating activities erode personal liberties, capitalism provides impersonal mechanisms whereby we help procure the social good without having to consciously do so—indeed, without having to consider it.

The kind of personal liberty available under capitalism is also related to a particular conception of equality. Recall that for writers like Milton Friedman, the other seminal document that appeared in 1776 (in addition to *The Wealth of Nations*) was the Declaration of Independence. There Jefferson proclaimed that we possess certain "inalienable rights," including the right to life, liberty, and the pursuit of happiness. And among the self-evident truths he celebrated is that "all men are created equal." This on the face of it presents significant problems for the classical liberal view, since social inequalities are generated through the division of labor and the variability of income associated with market conditions; Adam Smith (1776/1910b) himself noted that, "for one very rich man there must be at least five hundred poor, and the affluence of the few supposes the indigence of the many" (p. 199). The individual liberties provided by a classical liberal economic orientation promote gross inequalities. How are such liberties related to Smith's "invisible hand," and how can they be reconciled with the right to pursue happiness and the presumption of equality so cherished by classical liberal political perspectives as well as by the founders of our own country?

Members of the new right outline a conception of liberty, distinct from various forms of equality, that is said to be in keeping with the views of the founding fathers and consistent with a market economy. They argue that neither equality as identity nor equality of result is consistent with individual liberty. Instead, a selective interpretation of equality of opportunity is the only safeguard of liberty and the only kind of "inalienable right" we possess. Liberty, as we have seen, is associated with rights that have a natural origin. In this view, each person "is entitled to serve his own purposes and not to be treated simply as an instrument to promote someone else's purposes. 'Liberty' is part of the definition of equality, not in conflict with it" (Friedman & Friedman, 1980, p. 129). We are, in other words, largely entitled to be left alone, to put the actions allowed by our liberties in the service of whatever aims we prefer as long as they do not curtail the liberties of others. The equality protected by this tradition does not presume people to have the same mental or physical abilities or attributes—a view that would violate the "naturalness" of human difference. There are differences in aptitude, personal and vocational aspirations, ability, and temperament that make people inescapably different. The opportunities provided by personal liberty are the very social goods that enable us to pursue our particular interests, tempered by our unique capacities. Such liberty permits each person to succeed (or fail) to whatever degree her or his abilities allow, with natural differences in ability guaranteeing different levels of success.

In the United States, the political and educational implications of this view were clear as early as the writings of Thomas Jefferson, who presumed a "natural aristocracy" based on virtue and talents (Lee, 1961, p. 162). While Jefferson believed that the diffusion of knowledge through the masses would provide the way to enlightenment and progress, his educational agenda plainly contains a filtering process for the masses that acknowledges this natural aristocracy. Friedman and Friedman (1980), noting Jefferson's belief in a natural aristocracy, conclude that while he "had no doubt that some men were superior to others, that there was an elite," this fact "did not give them the right to rule others" (p. 129). Even though electoral equality was assumed, economic equality was not—indeed, the latter is "unnatural."

Within the economic sphere, the liberty that allows a natural aristocracy to rise to prominence is both inevitable and in the interest of all, as it maximizes personal well-being and the social good. Natural differences generate natural aristocracies, necessitating economic liberty conceived as treating people as their own ends and generating social inequalities that are themselves natural and productive of the social good.

According to the new right, the danger in the welfare state advanced by contemporary liberals is that equality understood as unfettered freedom to pursue individual interests (with its limiting condition being those pursuits that curtail the liberties of others) will be extinguished by a view of equality at odds with the natural elite recognized by Jefferson and facilitated through the market. In this regard, Friedman and Friedman (1980) cite Alexis de Tocqueville, who, during his visit to the United States in the nineteenth century, cautioned against a certain form of egalitarianism he saw manifested in this country. Americans, according to Tocqueville, often exhibit

> a manly and lawful passion for equality which incites men to wish all to be powerful and honored. This passion tends to elevate the humble to the rank of the great; but there exists also in the human heart a depraved taste for equality, which impels the weak to attempt to lower the powerful to their own level, and reduces men to prefer equality in slavery to inequality with freedom. (Friedman and Friedman, 1980, pp. 130–131; Tocqueville, 1838/1900, vol. 1, p. 53)[3]

A different interpretation of equality, as equality of outcome that aims at the "leveling down" Tocqueville feared, would destroy liberty, undermine economic growth, and necessitate a more intrusive type of centralized government. Just as "personal equality" in the sense of identical attributes and abilities is an impossibility, so, too, is equality of opportunity interpreted in a strict sense. For, according to Friedman and Friedman (1980):

> One child is born blind, another with sight. One child has parents deeply concerned about his welfare who provide a background of culture and understanding; another has dissolute, improvident parents. One child is born in the United States, another in India, or China, or Russia. They clearly do not have identical opportunities open to them at birth, and there is no way that their opportunities can be made identical. (pp. 131–132)

The problem with both personal equality and equality of opportunity interpreted as promoting a "level playing field" is that they fly in the face of what we know about people's natural mental and physical endowments. Just as important, efforts to guarantee such equal opportunities undermine that exercise of liberty which enables the more talented to obtain positions of authority that their talents justify and that improve all of our lives. Natural differences that serve the social interest can, together with cultural affirmations and symbols, provide a kind of social cement that holds society together without abridging personal freedoms.

Jefferson's plan for an educational system has not been adopted in twentieth-century America. Undoubtedly it has been rejected, among other reasons, because of its gender specificity and its denial of opportunities to so many children. It is equally clear that most Americans would not say their political leaders constitute a "natural aristocracy" we have had the good sense to put in positions of power. Yet many have not given up the idea that a natural aristocracy makes educational distinctions unavoidable and contributes to the general welfare.

At the college level, consider Allan Bloom's (1987) advocacy of meritocratic arrangements. The reason for Bloom's disdain of an inclusive curriculum is that an emphasis on merit is being replaced by a politicization of the curriculum. Political struggles of this sort must be superseded by the natural business of the university—the discovery of truth by those who are most meritorious, which for Bloom has its basis in the thought of Plato. The contemporary university may espouse a political commitment to equality through its sanctioning of women's studies and multiculturalism. But its abiding concern must be with the elite who are capable of genuine thought and reflection.

There seem to be, then, four objections to equality and a comprehensive equality of opportunity that are central to the new right:

1. Any notion of strict personal equality simply flies in the face of natural facts about human difference.
2. Even if an equalization of opportunities could be envisioned, the system of governmental intercession required would be so intrusive that its enactment would violate the principles of liberty that must be protected if we are to enjoy the natural rights to which we are entitled.
3. The basic principle of a society founded on liberty is not equality (of condition, result, or strictly defined opportunity) but meritocracy.
4. The appearance of a free market economy serves the general interest, thus making a commitment to social equality unnecessary.

Like the invisible hand in promoting the general social good, capitalism has promoted the particular interests of the poor and working classes. For members of the new right, capitalism makes available not only unprecedented personal freedoms but the most compelling forms of social justice.

MORAL JUDGMENT

Any set of social ideas or policies carries with it preferences about what is a desirable way of life, just as any vision of what constitutes a good life necessarily establishes priorities that serve as a guide for choices to be made and actions to be undertaken. The preferences and priorities of the new right serve to create a normative framework that must be analyzed and made a part of an analysis of their social and educational proposals.

It is not surprising that many new right advocates have attempted to provide a basis for moral judgment consistent with their larger world view, as a way of providing social direction. Moreover, as outlined in the first portion of this chapter, the new right recognizes a need for social cohesion that provides social stability. This emphasis on social cohesion becomes a part of their normative framework as well.

To deal with the moral dimensions of the new right's agenda, we examine here three kinds of frameworks, which we refer to as (1) moral judgments and matters of taste, (2) morality as middle-ground humanism, and (3) moral choices and social pluralism. Each of these embodies a kind a moral relativism, though with different emphases and implications. This is followed by a discussion of utilitarianism, the system of ethics most compatible with classical liberalism.

Moral Judgments and Matters of Taste

Some members of the new right embrace a straightforward relativism that is directly linked to their individualistic ontology. For example, Friedman (1982) suggests that there is no extra-individual moral qualifier to be exercised with respect to the actions permitted by our freedoms. Our moral duty extends to protecting those freedoms, but it has no jurisdiction over the actions we undertake as a result, short of the injunction not to interfere with the liberties of others. In fact, "a major aim . . . is to leave the ethical problem for the individual to wrestle with" (Friedman, 1982, p. 12). The values on which we act are those that we, as isolated, self-contained individuals, embrace and find persuasive. When considering alternative courses of action, therefore, we will choose on the basis of whatever we find most pleasing or comfortable, or in accord with whatever is consistent with our idiosyncratic "tastes."

The implications of this position are clear in Friedman's discussion of racial discrimination. This practice harms African Americans, to use Friedman's example, just as tariffs harm foreign trade. For Friedman, racial discrimination is like "import discrimination" in terms of the status of both offenses. For, the author says, "the man who exercises [racial] discrimination pays a price for doing so. He is, as it were, 'buying' what he regards as a 'product.' *It is hard to see that discrimination can have any meaning other than a 'taste' of others that one does not share.*" In a related and equally telling passage, Friedman asks, "is there any difference *in principle* between the taste that leads a householder to prefer an attractive servant to an ugly one and the taste that leads another to prefer a Negro to a white or a white to a Negro,

except that *we sympathize and agree with the one taste and may not with the other?*"
(Friedman, 1982, p. 110, emphasis added). Racism, preference in music,
and choice in hiring servants are all matters of taste, inhering in individuals who apply their own individual preferences.

Choices and positions that are regarded as matters of taste reflecting only
a personal preference cannot justify coercive restraint. A thoroughgoing
relativist framework for decision making effectively denies a moral status to
activities such as racist hiring practices, nullifying what we ordinarily regard
as a moral point of view (Baier, 1958) and embracing a form of emotivism
(MacIntyre, 1984). As a result, the moral categories of "right and wrong" are
supplanted with the personal ones of "like and dislike," which carry no moral
force (see also Bellah, Madsen, Sullivan, Swidler, & Tipton, 1985).

When confronted with the imperatives of individual freedom and social
justice, what we get is not extended analysis, but a simple statement implor-
ing us to action of some kind: When equality and freedom come into conflict, "one must choose. One cannot be both an egalitarian . . . and a [clas-
sical] liberal" (Friedman, 1982, p. 195). A possible basis for choosing is
conspicuously absent. Regarding moral judgments as matters of taste,
bounded by individual preference, effectively ends the possibility of meaningful discussion across individual preferences.

Morality as Middle-Ground Humanism

Other new right advocates have taken positions on moral issues that are in
some ways at odds with the emotivist, economistic platform of Friedman.
Instead of seeing individual liberties and market exchanges as embodying
the summit of human life, some writers have argued that an obsession with
material objects overlooks more important values and ideas. These values
must be attended to, even by economists. Ropke (1960) observes:

> Nobody would dream of denying that the aspect of society with which the
> economist deals belongs to the world of means, as opposed to ends, and that
> its motives and purposes therefore belong to a level which is bound to be low,
> if only because it is basic and at the foundation of the whole structure. . . . To
> take a drastic example, what interests economics is not the noble beauty of a
> medieval cathedral and the religious idea it embodies, but the worldly and
> matter-of-fact question of what place these monuments of religion and beauty
> occupied in the overall economy of their age. . . . We are fully aware that what
> concerns us as economists is, as it were, the prosaic and bare reverse side of
> the decor. (p. 106)

The extent to which these views contrast with those of a Milton Friedman
is clear when Ropke (1960) says that we must beware of the economist, "who,

watching people cheerfully disporting themselves in their suburban allotments, thinks he has said everything there is to say when he observes that this is not a rational way of producing vegetables"; such an economistic attitude fails to grasp that such gardening activities "may be an eminently rational way of producing happiness, which alone matters in the last resort" (p. 92).

Instead of a kind of economism, Ropke (1960) would opt for a new brand of humanism, one in which "the market and the spirit are reconciled in common service to the highest values" (p. 116). Key to this reconciliation is a moral schema, neither angelic nor base, within which operate the values of the middle class—that "bourgeois spirit" necessary for capitalist production. This value system can be identified as one in which "there is nothing shameful in the self-reliance and self-assertion of the individual taking care of himself and his family . . . [which has led us to] assign their due place to the corresponding virtues of diligence, alertness, thrift, sense of duty, reliability, punctuality, and reasonableness" (Ropke, 1960, p. 119).

To counteract "the curse of commercialization," we need to recognize and value a *nobilitas naturalis*, or an elite group of people potentially representing all walks of life, with the moral values and priorities that will protect the social good by helping tame the excesses that are possible under capitalism. This would amount to a kind of moral aristocracy to counteract the worst aspects of Jefferson's "natural aristocracy."

Moral Choices and Social Pluralism

Michael Novak (1982) claims that something more substantial than the physical trappings of capitalism accompanied the creation of a market economy:

> Apart from some new spirit, it is almost impossible to define capitalism. Its economic features do not define it. Neither industry nor factories, neither commerce nor profits, neither private property nor incentives, neither the division of labor nor international trade, appeared first in modern times. Yet something new is universally held to have appeared . . . and that something new is pluralism. (p. 49)

Novak anticipates here the criticisms offered by postmodern writers in rejecting the tendency to postulate a cosmic unity or commonality. While such presumptions have taken hold of both religious and secular institutions, they are neither necessary nor productive of the common good.

An important moral contribution of democratic capitalism, Novak (1982) tells us, is that it realizes that the unity presupposed in modern societies is fictitious, socially unnecessary, and generative of much evil in the world. Conflicts between members of rival religious and ethnic groups, each of which believes its way of life offers not only a better alternative but the correct one, provide examples of how a commitment to unity and universality are often socially undesirable. Democratic capitalism does not begin with the premise that it embodies moral precepts that necessitate any such unity with which people must comply. Instead, it has "left the circle of freedom bare" (Novak, 1982, p. 51).

Recognizing that sin is a part of our human character, a basic question for democratic capitalists like Novak (1982) is what kind of system will be most likely to work for good rather than evil. In his words:

> Democratic capitalism does not promise to eliminate sin. It certainly does not promise equality of results (an outcome which, in any case, would run counter both to nature and to justice). It does not even promise that all those who have wealth or who acquire wealth will do so according to moral merit. Its sense of meritocracy is not a judgment upon individuals but is based upon the system *qua* system. It holds that a system which permits individual families over time to rise and to fall in wealth in accord with their own actions and circumstances will, *on the whole*, better reward familial performance than any other form of society. The judgment of individual cases may be left to God. (p. 85; emphasis in original)

Like Ropke (1960), Novak claims a pragmatic realism in democratic capitalism, which, as a system, recognizes that we are not saints and adjusts for this by propounding a political, economic, and moral system that minimizes social sinfulness.

What may we conclude about the three positions on moral judgment analyzed here? It appears that, while there are notable differences among them, there are some important commonalities as well.

If Friedman consistently held to an emotivist view of moral judgment, there would be no apparent way to substantiate the value of the liberties he thinks capitalism provides. The new right may argue, as a working principle, that "the circle of freedom [is left] bare" (Novak, 1982, p. 51) within capitalism. But they cannot leave bare the "normative circle" of external justifications for capitalism if they want to show its normative superiority in comparison with other social and economic possibilities. And that is indeed what they want to show. If the superiority of capitalism is more than a subjective preference, on what basis can other normative issues be limited to such a preference?

Utilitarianism

We have noted at several points in this chapter that classical liberals and members of the new right are committed to ontological individualism. This individualistic point of reference is a key component of their world view, as seen in the position that the social good is revealed in and through the actions of independent, self-motivated individuals; that more encompassing orientations to the nature of justice are either unnecessary or implausible; and that overcoming social problems is a matter of individual striving and character uplift. It should not be surprising, therefore, that utilitarianism has been embraced within the new right's world view.

Simply put, utilitarians believe that human beings act so as to maximize their desires or satisfactions or utilities, and to minimize pain and suffering. As rational, calculative beings, we seek to obtain the greatest possible utility from whatever sources are available through our experiences. As self-interested beings, we may seek out those experiences that will maximize our utilities or create situations in which they may be enhanced. This, of course, means that the individual interests people have will sometimes conflict with the interests of other individuals. Thus there is in utilitarianism, as in other types of moral theory, a perspective on human nature, a sense of who we are as people and how we make decisions.

There is a social element to utilitarianism as well. For any social group, like any individual, will try to maximize its utility (or, more properly, the individuals who make up that body will try to maximize their own utilities through the actions sponsored by that social group). This means that government must be made accountable to the governed and must be able to be reined in when necessary, so as to protect the interests and utilities of the individuals it serves. Thus, as Held (1987) argues:

> Bentham, Mill and the Utilitarians generally provided one of the clearest justifications for the [classical] liberal democratic state, which ensures the conditions necessary for individuals to pursue their interests without risk of arbitrary political interference, to participate freely in economic transactions, to exchange labor and goods on the market and to appropriate resources privately. . . . The state was to have the role of umpire or referee while individuals pursued in civil society, according to the rules of economic competition and free exchange, their own interests. . . . A key proposition was that the collective good could be properly realized in many domains of life only if individuals interacted in competitive exchanges, pursuing their utility with minimal state interference. (p. 67)

The moral perspectives discussed here, especially utilitarianism, share the view that personal liberties constitute the primary good. Yet from Milton Friedman (1955) through William Bennett (1992), members of the new right have recognized that there must be some type of civic glue that binds us together as a society and as a force for producing and purchasing material goods. This civic glue requires a minimal social cohesiveness that organizes

human interactions and generates social order. Moreover, the spokespeople
for the new right have charged that the central threads of our societal fabric are unraveling, requiring a fundamental change in the operation of our
educational institutions. In addition, and consistent with their ontological
individualism and embrace of utilitarianism, the new right has suggested a
limited role for the state—especially in protecting our personal liberties and
value preferences.

THE ROLE OF THE STATE

Members of the new right focus on the establishment of constitutional
guarantees, legal ordinances, formal contracts, and other documents that
provide procedurally fair rules for social engagement. Consistent with
Novak's (1982) emphasis on the centrality of process within a democratic
pluralism, the ultimate ends of life must remain at the discretion of individuals, not codified into laws that preempt human choice in such matters. Thus within the new right there is an emphasis on "negative freedom"
in political life (Berlin, 1969). What must not be stipulated are the positive
values or aims to which we give allegiance or the substantive actions in which
we are to engage. This leads to a view of the state in which its actions are
justifiable only when they are "undertaken within a set of rules which were
derived in a neutral way, and . . . directed towards policies which are, as far
as possible, neutral between different conceptions of the good life" (Plant,
1991, p. 77). The meaning of justice is thus restricted to procedural matters and the promulgation of rules guaranteeing procedural fairness, as well
as to the rights (to a fair trial, equal treatment under law, freedom of speech
and of the press) that go with fair procedures.

The state must remain silent on the proper distribution of goods, since
intervention in such matters presupposes a social design derived from moral
principles that transcend individuals. Distributive justice, in short, has no place
within the state advocated by the new right. For example, we may deplore
the appearance of poverty within capitalism, yet it does not result from the
intention of any individual who engages in (voluntary) market exchanges.
Poverty thus constitutes a natural calamity with (amoral) consequences for
the general populace not unlike those associated with other natural disasters
such as tornadoes or floods: We may feel sympathy for the victims, but we
are not obligated, as a matter of justice, to provide for them through the
agencies of the state. As proclaimed by Ludwig von Mises (1956):

> Men, cooperating under the system of the division of labor, have created all
> the wealth which the daydreamers [i.e., detractors of capitalism] consider as a

> free gift of nature. With regard to the "distribution" of this wealth . . . [w]hat matters is not the allocation of portions out of a fund presented to man by nature. The problem is rather to further those social institutions which enable people to continue and to enlarge the production of all those things which they need. (pp. 81–82)

For members of the new right, all that need be done regarding the distribution of wealth is to ensure continued economic expansion and thus the increased production of goods that contribute to that wealth.

In this connection, it is hardly surprising that George Will (1995) commented recently that "a society that values individualism, enterprise and a market economy is neither surprised nor scandalized when the unequal distribution of marketable skills produces large disparities in the distribution of wealth. . . . There is a presumption in favor of respecting the market's version of distributive justice" (p. A12). Whatever the actual distribution of wealth in the United States, it is de facto just, rewarding those with the requisite skills and attributes, providing an incentive for others to acquire them to the extent their abilities allow. What is required for the operation of a polity is not an independent theory of distributive justice but the further expansion of capitalist techniques, machinery, and forms of organization that have generated the tremendous wealth we enjoy. Friedrich A. von Hayek (1976), a former colleague of Milton Friedman's at the University of Chicago, reflects this view, claiming that the disparate benefits that result from the autonomous, morally neutral capitalist system could be viewed as unjust

> if [they] were the result of a deliberate allocation to particular people. But this is not the case. Those shares are the outcome of a process the effect of which on particular people was neither intended nor foreseen. . . . To demand justice from such a process is clearly absurd, and to single out some people in such a society as entitled to a particular share evidently unjust. (p. 65)

Governmental incursions lead inevitably to bureaucratic control that is economically inefficient, constrains individual choice, and assumes a transcendental moral unity. Governmental constraints that infringe on individual liberties are, following John Stuart Mill, only justified in those cases where a failure to enact them would result in the curtailment of the freedoms of others. In perhaps his most frequently cited precept, Mill (1859/ 1956) says:

> The sole end for which mankind are warranted, individually or collectively, in interfering with the liberty of action of any of their number is self-protection. That the only purpose for which power can be rightfully exercised over any member of a civilized community, against his will, is to prevent harm to others.

> His own good, either physical or moral, is not a sufficient warrant. . . . The
> only part of the conduct of anyone for which he is amenable to society is that
> which concerns others. (p. 13)

Government powers must, accordingly, be stringently limited, enacted only
when their absence leads to even greater evils. The market, in addition,
"provides an offset to whatever concentration of political power may arise.
The combination of economic and political *power* in the same hands is a
sure recipe for tyranny" (Friedman & Friedman, 1980, p. 3; underlining
added, italics in original).

The proper role for government is discussed by Friedman (1982) in
Capitalism and Freedom. In the first chapter, "The Relation Between Economic Freedom and Political Freedom," Friedman tells us early on the thesis of the chapter: that "there is an intimate connection between economics and politics" and that "only certain combinations of political and
economic arrangements are possible" (p. 8). The intimacy characterizing
the connection between economics and politics is one of virtual opposition,
grounded as it is in the classical liberal view of liberty and in utilitarian ethics:

> A citizen of the United States who under the laws of various states is not
> free to follow the occupation of his own choosing unless he can get a license
> for it, is . . . being deprived of an essential part of his freedom. So is the man
> who would like to exchange some of his goods with, say, a Swiss for a watch
> but is prevented from doing so by a quota. . . . So also is the farmer who
> cannot grow the amount of wheat he wants. And so on. Clearly, economic
> freedom, in and of itself, is an extremely important part of total freedom.
> (Friedman, 1982, p. 9)

As we have seen, intrinsically worthwhile individual freedoms are the
mainstay of a market economy. But this is not their only virtue. For economic freedoms are also important as means to the end of political freedom, and this instrumental value gets us back to the connection between
economics and politics. For "economic arrangements are important because
of their effect on the concentration or dispersion of power. . . . Competitive
capitalism . . . promotes political freedom because it separates economic
power from political power and in this way enables the one to offset the
other" (Friedman, 1982, p. 9). The operations of a competitive capitalist
economy serve to decentralize power and individualize decision making,
while the tendency within politics is toward the centralization of power and
decision making.

The exercise of our personal liberties, given the fact that most of us do
not qualify for sainthood, requires procedural rules that form the basis for

interactions. Because some people will naturally be stronger (physically and/or mentally) than others, and hence more likely to force or manipulate the less strong in ways that violate the latter's freedom, some third party must exercise oversight. Within political theory, reference is often made to the views of Thomas Hobbes. In the *Leviathan*, for example, it is argued that the absence of any state will result in "that condition which is called war, and such a war as is of every man against every man" (Hobbes, 1651/1958, pp. 104–106). In enforcing a truce in "the war of all against all," civil authorities maintain an order that permits us to act on the freedoms offered in the private sphere. As Locke proclaimed:

> Men being . . . by Nature, all free, equal and independent, no one can be put out of this Estate, and subjected to the Political Power of another, without his own *Consent*. The only way whereby any one devests himself of his Natural Liberty, and *puts on the bonds of Civil Society* is by agreeing with other Men to joyn and unite into a Community, for their comfortable, safe, and peaceable living one amongst another, in a secure Enjoyment of their Properties, and a greater Security against any that are not of it. (1690/1960, pp. 374–375; emphasis in original)

Social order is a necessary condition for the exercise of our individual freedoms, and the state that guarantees it is sanctioned to the extent that those freedoms are preserved.

There is, as suggested already, an evident tension between two fundamental aspects of the new right's orientation. On the one hand, there is an ontological individualism that sees people as independent, self-forming, and endowed with natural rights, against which the state is seen as virtually a necessary evil, to be curbed so as to allow for the free expression of individual choice. The rights we enjoy have, as well, an individual origin and could be enhanced through the addition of choice plans for schools. Social problems tend to be seen as having individual causes and directions for their remediation—for example, in the need for character education in schools and the recommendation to create a New Basics to make the United States more globally competitive. On the other hand, the new right acknowledges the need for social cohesion and bemoans its loss in contemporary U.S. society and its educational institutions. There is a revealing conflict here between individual realities and problems and the need for specific forms of social/communal constraints and directions. This conflict is unresolved within the orientation of the new right. It is taken up in modern liberal and radical perspectives, as outlined in succeeding chapters, as well as addressed overtly when we discuss our own social orientations in Chapter 6.

CONCLUSION: THE NEW RIGHT
AND SOCIAL/EDUCATIONAL PRACTICE

The center of human existence for the new right is in critical respects the sphere of economic exchange. We are restricted only by our level of individual merit; capitalism offers us the opportunity of pursuing whatever occupation we find meaningful. Free from outside constraint, we may enjoy those labors that provide intrinsic satisfaction and/or that generate the level of material wealth necessary to procure ends we have individually chosen. Thus do we enact the explicit promise of our Declaration of Independence that we can pursue (if not necessarily attain) our individually defined sense of happiness.

The market mechanisms entailed in these processes of production and consumption (pricing, competition, the division of labor, and so on) underscore our individual liberties and collectively ensure the social good. This, combined with the unfettered operation of a natural aristocracy that is similarly productive of a common good, spontaneously allows our actions to further the material interests of all and frees us to choose in our private lives whatever conceptions of the good life we find compelling. The freedoms to produce, consume, reflect, and act as we see fit will be accompanied by procedurally fair, socially neutral rules that maintain social order. Such rules may be established to enforce the contractual market obligations voluntarily entered into, to protect the individual rights of other people, to guarantee forms of national sovereignty and domestic tranquility that are required for the exercise of liberty, and to provide for certain elements of the infrastructure required to maintain commerce. The freedoms we enjoy within economic interactions and institutions, together with those we are granted because of the disinterestedness of governmental procedures aimed at equality under the law but not equality of condition, promise the fullest opportunity possible to define and lead our life as we see fit. The basic virtue of such a system is, by intention, personal liberty or lack of external control.

Since any social system requires a minimal amount of cohesiveness, it is important that certain values be adopted, as a matter of practical necessity, even though there can be no unanimity regarding the ultimate ends or meaning of human life. These values are justified because of their natural origin, or because of their utility for economic growth and capital accumulation, or because of their traditional importance to the West in general and the United States in particular. Educational activities have a special place within the moral-cultural domain (Novak, 1982) that will supply this cohesiveness. The new right has posited an educational orientation dedicated to reviving character traits that have all but been abandoned by public schools and colleges alike, emphasizing skills and forms of knowledge that will make the United States once again a competitive force in the increasingly global economic realm, and restoring the canons of dispassionate scholarly inquiry. Within public schools, an emphasis on "the facts," cultural literacy, and moral character, increased constraints on student behavior, and more rigorous academic standards will serve our national needs and the traditional values of education. Regarding college education, Lynne Cheney (1992) has put forward a common new right sentiment about the dangers of censorship allegedly promoted by liberal and radical scholars and teachers. Cheney says that "the aim of education, as many on our campuses now see it, is no longer truth, but political transformation—of students and society" (p. 7); leftist scholars, she asserts, have abandoned the traditional goal of teaching—the "disinterested" pursuit of knowledge, which aimed to "discover the truth." Against such scholars, she says that "to abandon truth and objectivity as goals and put political expediency in their place is to move perilously close to the world of George Orwell's 1984, the world where two and two make five—if it's politically useful" (Cheney, 1992, p. 20). Like other new right proponents, Cheney suggests that professors stop trying to manipulate their students by rejecting the negativism and divisiveness of much teaching and scholarship, substituting instead the "common truths" of America (Burd, 1992).

Democracy within the orientation of the new right takes on a particular meaning. The role of government officials is largely to protect the private, individual prerogatives of people and to guarantee those inalienable rights specified in our country's founding documents. The work of politicians is limited to generating neutral, fair procedural rules that leave questions of distributive justice to a disinterested market economy. A representative government composed, ideally, of those "natural aristocrats" we elect to protect our individual interests is best suited to such a society.

Members of the new right insist upon a strict separation between the individualistic, protected domain of private individuals and larger social goods or governmental actions. Indeed, much effort has gone into protecting the former and demarcating the proper role of a rather minimalist state (Nozick, 1974). Yet as we have seen, the new right also acknowledges that social cohesion of the sort that can be encouraged through education is a primary social requirement, one related to the very need for a state to rescue us from a turbulent and dangerous state of nature. There is in this a central tension between individualism and communitarianism that is not resolved. Part of the distinctiveness of the modern liberal tradition is that it offers a different perspective on human and social life in an attempt to resolve this tension. This perspective is related to a distinctive world view, a different orientation to social justice, a broadened understanding of democracy, and a particular educational agenda. It is that tradition to which we now turn.

NOTES

1. Education Alternatives, Inc., in Bloomington, Minnesota, has been especially prominent in this regard (see Celis, 1993).

2. Friedman does say that "the ultimate operative unit in our society is the family, not the individual"; yet he follows this by saying that "the acceptance of the family as the unit rests in considerable part on expediency rather than principle" (1982, p. 33). Therefore, in terms of what might be considered the central ethical values associated with the view of the new right—freedom, autonomy, responsibility, and so on—it appears that Friedman holds consistently to the view that the individual is the primary unit of analysis.

3. The term "incites" in the first line of this quotation from Friedman and Friedman (1980) appears as "excites" in Tocqueville (1838/1900).

CHAPTER 3

Modern Liberalism
and the Welfare State

Those involved in creating the interventionist state . . . rejected the negative concept of freedom espoused by classical liberals, calling it the freedom to starve, to fail, to be out of work, to risk one's life in factory or mine, or to live in dangerous housing. They replaced it with a positive concept, seeking to create minimum standards of human well-being as an essential prerequisite to the true exercise and enjoyment of liberty. This was best accomplished, they believed, by greatly expanding the role of government.
—Coleman (1989, pp. 54–66)

Both supporters and critics of classical liberalism have noted the ability of capitalism to generate goods and services that in certain ways have undeniably enriched human life. The mass production and widespread distribution of automobiles, household appliances, food, newspapers, magazines, books, single-family homes, and so on, made practicable by a market economy, have increased the standard of living of citizens in capitalist societies, often in dramatic ways. Their material productivity seems uncontestable.

Yet the development of a free market economy in the United States was accompanied by social, cultural, and political effects that, accelerating in the latter stages of the nineteenth century, became an increasing cause for concern and, ultimately, for governmental action. A new generation of muckraking journalists and novelists took as their subject the tendency for wealth to become centralized in the hands of a relative few while conditions in the factories and new corporate structures robbed work of its dignity and meaning; for poverty to become a way of life for many, especially in times of economic recession and depression; for economic power to become joined with political influence; and for technological breakthroughs and bureaucratic modes of operation to increasingly isolate and dehumanize people (for example, see McClure, 1914; Sinclair, 1906; H. S. Wilson, 1970). In response to these tendencies, a progressive tradition developed that sought to counter the excesses of capitalist development. One outcome of this development was the creation of alternative social, ethical, and political theories that were to vie for precedence with classical liberalism. Spokespersons for the welfare state argued that governmental policies and interventions of various kinds were needed to provide a basic level of care, a guarantee of a certain minimum welfare, for all citizens. As one commentator has put it, an Age of Reform took place in the late nineteenth and early twentieth centuries that was "the start of an evolutionary process in which the American people fashioned their government into an instrument for the humanization of capitalism" (Greenberg, 1985, p. 74).

It is not possible to assign a specific date to the birth of the welfare state. The ideas on which it was founded in the United States and other industrialized nations had a significant portion of their roots in older traditions (see Held, 1987). Nor is it the case that the welfare state, once it was institutionalized in the United States, became a permanent fixture consistently supported by broad-based consent. Indeed, the debate over what are the most enlightened political, social, and economic theories and practices—like the debate over what are the most enlightened educational theories and practices—is not the sort of dispute that has clear, long-term winners and losers. Instead, the attempt to win political and educational influence is a continuing struggle, with policies and practices gaining acceptance over some period of time, to be replaced by alternative policies and practices at another. The reemergence of central elements of classical liberalism in the new right in the 1970s and 1980s, and apparently intensifying with the American elections of November, 1994, testifies to the contested nature of political discourse and public policy in the United States.

Yet the appearance of welfare state principles and programs did signal a crucial shift in American life—a shift that affected educational policy and the role of schools in American society. The echoes of arguments and perspectives that helped form the modern welfare state can be heard in the current climate of educational criticism and reform. This chapter analyzes modern liberal forms of consciousness, ethical principles, political commitments, and social policies that helped create the welfare state, as well as their connection to the domain of education. As we shall see, the broad ideas of welfare state advocates provide a clear contrast with those of classical liberals, at a fundamental level: Is the good life better promoted by a planned, centrally modified economy and a social policy committed to extra-individualistic fairness and social justice, enforced by regulatory state agencies; or by a free market, laissez-faire economy accompanied by a minimalist state, which highlights individual liberties and a utilitarian ethic?

A CRITIQUE OF CLASSICAL LIBERAL THEORY AND SOCIETY

Challenges to Classical Liberal Doctrines

In discussing the shift to modern liberalism, John Dewey notes three "enduring values" for which classical liberalism stood. These values are "liberty, the development of the inherent capacities of individuals made possible through liberty, and the central role of free intelligence in inquiry, discussion and expression." Even as these values endured, however, their prior affiliations with classical liberalism "colored every one of these ideals in ways that rendered them either impotent or perverse when the new problem of social organization rose" (Dewey, 1935, p. 32). One of Dewey's central undertakings in this regard is to dislodge liberty, the development of human capacities, and intelligence from the misguided trappings of classical liberalism. Among the most important of the failings of the older tradition was that its proponents lacked a sensitivity to the historically conditioned nature of their ideas and values. This lack of historical sensitivity caused classical liberals to mistakenly regard their ideas as immutable, timeless truths. This is the case, for example, when Adam Smith says:

> All systems, either of preference or restraint . . . being thus completely taken away, the *obvious and simple system of natural liberty* establishes itself of its own accord. Every man, as soon as he does not violate *the laws of justice*, is left perfectly free to pursue his own interests in his own way, and to bring both his industry and his capital into competition with those of any other man or order of men. (1776/1910a, pp. xi–xii; emphasis added)

The problem with such ideas is that they are assumed to be descriptions of a "natural" reality, one that is transcendent. Instead, modern liberals contend, we need to see such ideas for what they are: human-generated assertions about what sort of social arrangements are most advantageous and thus open to challenge and replacement.

There is a second problem with the lack of historical consciousness among classical liberals, Dewey says, that is equally lamentable. As we saw in Chapter 2, writers in the older liberal tradition sought to challenge the accepted social and religious hierarchies, challenging the status quo of an aristocratic, tradition-bound world. Many highlighted empiricist science and a particular form of human rationality for both its epistemological and social benefits, challenging the preeminence of theology and classical philosophy. The new intellectual framework adopted by classical liberals, with its social, economic, and political ramifications, sought to create new processes and, in a sense, new people. Yet when that framework was widely adopted and embedded into social practices, it became, according to Dewey, "the vested interest, and [classical liberal] doctrines, especially in the form of *laissez faire* liberalism, now provided the intellectual justification of the *status quo*." Dewey continues: "The tragedy is that although these [classical] liberals were the sworn foes of political absolutism, they were themselves absolutist in the social creed they formulated" (1935, pp. 33–34). Classical liberals believed that social change could take place only through the development of an unfettered economic system in which individual liberties and economic productivity would flourish. Other sources of significant social change seemed all but unthinkable within this framework.

Another central element in the classical liberal tradition was that individually guided economic pursuits would generate unintended social advantages. As more efficient, productive industries are able to outperform their competitors, they make more goods available at lower prices, ensuring their wider availability for consumers, whose individual lives will thereby be improved. Moreover, while individual consumers intend only to procure goods that will benefit them, within the dynamics of laissez-faire capitalism they are led by Adam Smith's "invisible hand" to promote the social good (1776/1910a, p. 400). This leaves questions of distributive and substantive justice to one side, so that larger moral questions related to the social good need not be formally addressed. Indeed, such questions are to be resolved by free, socially unencumbered individuals, since moral precepts are not to be prespecified by a community or state, since this would have the effect of limiting personal liberties. As Novak (1982) puts it, a market-oriented society leaves "the circle of freedom bare" (p. 51), or morally contentless.

What the classical perspective overlooks, say modern liberals, is the tendency for business enterprises to take advantage of employees, the environment, and the social welfare generally as they pursue their own narrow economic interests. As Dewey put the conceptual point: "In many cases personal profit can be better served by maintaining artificial scarcity and by . . . [the] systematic sabotage of production" (1935, p. 35). This tendency was in fact in evidence in the United States as businesses formed virtual monopolies within and across industries to the detriment of social life and the welfare of individual workers. The patterns of artificial scarcity, sabotage, and exploitation manifested in the era of corporate capitalism were part of the impetus behind modern liberalism. Such economic realities may have benefited the new industrialists, but they did so, the new liberals claimed, at the expense of workers and the quality of social life.

Economic Realities and the Social Good

Social classes and social inequality have flourished since the founding of the United States. Indeed, even before this nation became independent, people of color—both those who had lived here for centuries before the arrival of Europeans and those brought here by force from Africa—were enslaved and brutalized in the process of ensuring the survival and development of the U.S. economic and social systems. The nature of those systems has, of course, undergone significant changes since the eighteenth century. We moved from relatively small, cottage industries and a guild system located within the community, to large-scale factories requiring new forms of specialization, divisions of labor, and capital—not to mention expanded markets. We explore here the ways in which altered forms of capitalist production affected patterns of inequality, how these compared with the views of the classical liberals, and why the effects of an unbridled capitalist economy led to calls for the development of the welfare state.

We may understand something of the early social dynamics of industrialization by looking at the value of capital over the course of the latter nineteenth and early twentieth centuries. If we understand "active capital" to include "the machines, buildings, tools, railroads, trains, vessels, live stock, etc., which assist in the creation of new wealth" (King, 1915, p. 42), we can note some interesting trends. Between 1850 and 1910: (1) The value of active capital in the United States went from $2.8 million to $48 million—an increase of more than 17-fold; (2) this growth, even when adjusted via a price index, was continuous; and (3) increases in the value and quantity of consumer goods produced during that time period were of similar scope (King, 1915, pp. 46–48).

These data begin to reveal something of the magnitude of economic growth and industrialization in the United States during this period. How did this pattern of growth affect the distribution of capital and goods, and the relative income or wealth of the citizenry?

Several trends can be noted regarding the value of probated male estates by looking at data for 1859–1861 and 1889–1891 (King, 1915, p. 68, table IX).[1] In particular:

1. The total value of estates increased by 3.7-fold.
2. People in the poorest three categories went from 90% to 86% of the total population, while the average value of their estates went from 19.6% to 13% of the total.
3. People in the wealthiest three categories went from less than 1% to 2.6% of the total population listed, while the average value of their estates went from 17% to over 27% of the total.
4. In terms of relative wealth, a man in the poorest aggregate had an estate average that went from 10% to 7% of the total, a 30% decrease; while a man in the wealthiest aggregate had an estate average that went from 11% to 18% of the total, a 61% increase.
5. In absolute numbers, the poorest aggregate went from 14,000 to 30,000, while the wealthiest aggregate went from 15 to 93.
6. There were marginally more wealthy people as time went on, but the number of poor people increased dramatically over time—both in absolute numbers and in terms of their percentage of the total population.

Looking at U.S. family income figures for 1910, we see a similarly unequal distribution (King, 1915, table XLIII, pp. 224–226). For that year, a total of 50 income ranges, from $0 to $50,000,000, are reported. The bottom three groups (totaling more than 2 million people, or 7% of the total) averaged $350 in annual income, while the highest three groups (totaling 56, or .0002% of the total) averaged $6.3 million. Group number 25 (totaling 77,000) had an average income of $3,078. The largest single group (numbering 3.6 million, or 13% of the total population) had an annual income of $665. In sum, for 1910, there was a total reported family income of $30.5 trillion. Slightly more than 51% of the families had an annual income of less than $800, representing 28% of all income received that year; the wealthiest 56 families had an average annual income of over $6 million (King, 1915, table XLIV, pp. 228–229). These figures document staggering disparities between the very rich and the very poor in 1910, even as the total national value of active capital had increased 17-fold in the previous 60 years. Such realities raise serious doubts about the ability of an invisible hand to promote the social good.

The centralization of capital before and after the turn of the last century provides another indication of disparity and functioned as an additional impetus for the creation of the welfare state. Among other factors, the Civil War provided a catalyst for the creation of new systems of mass production, which became commonplace as they revolutionized factories, especially in the period following World War I. Of prime importance in this regard was the development of products utilizing interchangeable parts; the establishment of conveyor belts, assembly lines, and systems of standardization; the isolation and control of labor to both make the processes of production more efficient and control the work force; and the increasing monopolization of capital.[2]

Writing in 1931, Harry W. Laidler says that the earlier image of the "rugged individual" was no longer appropriate to American economic and social life. While the previous system of production in which one person or a small group was responsible for all stages of production flourished for a time,

> its doom was sealed when steam and electricity supplanted hand power as the source of industrial energy; when the machine made possible a growing expansion of production and when new methods of communication and transportation extended the market from the village or city to the state, the nation, and even to the outside world. These changes necessitated the pooling of constantly larger quantities of capital and gave rise successively to the partnership and the corporation. (pp. 3–4)

The movement from small proprietorships to large corporations intensified the disparities in the distribution of wealth already noted, while often promoting social relations in the factory that were increasingly intensified, standardized, and dehumanized.[3] The trend toward larger economic enterprises, toward more tightly controlled and managed relations within growing hierarchical structures, and toward the concentration of economic production and wealth is clear during this era.

For example, Brody (1980) discusses the personal, organizational, and social dislocations brought about by the Industrial Revolution. Whereas in earlier times workers might have had a range of actions to perform that called for significant amounts of calculation as well as collaboration with other workers, by about the turn of the century, the human scale of jobs had been lost:

> Ever increasing numbers [of workers] found themselves in a work environment crushing to any sense of individual mastery or even understanding. "The man working for the United States Steel Corporation," remarked a labor investigator after spending the year 1911 in the Pittsburgh district, "sees on every side evidence of an irresistible power, baffling and intangible. It fixes the conditions of his employment; it tells him what wages he may expect to receive and where he must work." And any effort to raise his voice would be "either ignored or rebuked." (pp. 8–9)

Not only was income and wealth being distributed more and more unequally, but the quality of one's work life in the factory deteriorated as workers' insights and capacities became less and less relevant for the kind of work that was required in the expanding factories and corporations. There was simply less opportunity to combine one's talents and personality with the increasingly specialized and fragmented tasks that needed to be done.

Compounding this sense of alienation was the development of new forms of management in the expanding industries of the United States. We noted in Chapter 1 the contributions of Frederick Winslow Taylor and his associates to the "scientific management" movement that often bears his name. Taylor sought to rationalize work as fully as possible, dividing it into its constituent parts and making the movements necessary to enact them as efficient as possible, ensuring enhanced productivity from workers. The effect was to make the operations of the workplace more regular and systematic, less subject to individual interpretation and initiative, and more centrally controlled through a system of hierarchical management. The need for oversight of this sort was even more important, as one writer put it in 1900, in order "to readjust the balance of responsibility disturbed by the expansion of industrial operations, and to enable central control to be restored in its central operations" (cited in Brody, 1980, p. 10). Thus an increase in the size and sophistication of industry—and its increased centralization—meant that work had to be more tightly supervised and controlled, first by people in an expanded hierarchy and then by the technologically sophisticated manufacturing processes themselves (see Edwards, 1979).

A further indication of the growing centralization of both work and wealth in the United States can be seen in the number of mergers that took place in the early twentieth century. The largest number of these took place in public utilities: in 1919, 22 mergers took place within this domain, while in 1926 this number totaled 1,029—an increase of more than 46-fold in that seven-year period (cited in Laidler, 1931, p. 6). Between 1919 and 1928, a total of 7,259 mergers had taken place in mining and manufacturing establishments. Moreover, between 1919 and late 1930, 8,003 such firms had disappeared altogether (Laidler, 1931, pp. 6–7). The centralization of economic power meant the elimination of competitive enterprises in many sectors of the economy.

New inventions modifying the techniques of production and distribution, altered forms of the division of labor, and hierarchical systems of management, later aided by more control through new technologies themselves, helped bring about an industrial revolution that increased efficiency and altered the economic and social landscapes for millions of people. The implementation of these new processes and systems was not, however, accompanied by a more widespread and equitable distribution of wealth and power. When we look at patterns of income distribution, we see part of the underside of capitalist expansion: a concentration of wealth in the relative few, growing poverty for many, and a loss in the social good. Capitalism generated new products and means for producing them, to be sure, but neither the wealth thus generated nor the products thus created brought about the reality of the good life for wage workers that classical liberals believed would spontaneously be generated.

Dewey (1935) put these realities in historical and conceptual perspective, noting that in their economic doctrines classical liberals failed to consider the possibility that productive activities within a capitalist economy could themselves become tyrannical and oppressive, requiring intervention by the state to maintain personal liberties:

> [Classical liberals] had no glimpse of the fact that private control of the new forces of production, forces which affect the life of every one, would operate in the same way as private unchecked control of political power. They saw the need of new legal institutions, and of different political conditions as a means to political liberty. But they failed to perceive that social control of economic forces is equally necessary if anything approaching economic equality and liberty is to be realized. (pp. 36–37)

Classical liberals were, of course, not much concerned with the creation of economic equality. For they believed that a "natural aristocracy," replacing older distinctions based on birth or inherited status, would respect the differences in talent and effort that generate meritocratic-based inequality. Yet the proposition that unrestrained economic activity can erode personal liberty must, modern liberals say, be taken seriously. The effects of capitalist expansion noted here document the concrete effects of the centralization of wealth and power, and the ways in which these deform human life and social prospects.

CREATING THE WELFARE STATE

Politics, Values, and Forms of Consciousness

If an unfettered market economy did not produce the positive effects that its adherents had promised, the solution according to modern liberals was not to abandon capitalism wholesale. Rather, they proposed the creation of various social safeguards, safety nets, and regulatory agencies. These would, adherents argued, curtail the excesses of capitalism while ensuring that everyone would be granted more widespread access to its productive powers and consumptive advantages. As two commentators have put this:

> The repercussions of the inability of the system of unregulated markets to provide individual stability, or even general economic advance, were far reaching. Although the population of many countries . . . remained remarkably quiescent, there was a widespread feeling among social commentators and "progressive" politicians that a "middle way" had to be found between the waste and irrationality of unencumbered capitalism and the loss of liberty and individuality imposed by "totalitarianism." This "middle way" entailed the *reintervention of politics into the social and economic order.* Markets had to be regulated ("planning" became the emotive word of the 1930s), and property could not be considered inviolable if its exercise ran counter to plans for orderly economic development. (Furniss & Tilton, 1977, p. 9; emphasis in original)

As we shall see in the next chapter, calls for the elimination of capitalism have been put forward by radicals who argue that ameliorative responses to the negative aspects of a capitalist economy are insufficient. For modern liberals, however, oversight of private enterprise through a system of state regulation would allow its productive contributions to continue, while saving us from the excesses of more communitarian social systems.

It would be a mistake to see the call for the regulation of capitalism as solely a matter of economic reform, however. Beyond attempts at attenuating the consequences of capitalism in economic terms, proponents of the welfare state argue that the kind of issues discussed in the previous section "present us with problems and perspectives that call for new concepts, and indeed demand a reconstruction of the entire theory of society" (Unger, 1975, p. 174). What modern liberalism must provide, then, is not only a critique of laissez-faire capitalism and a set of policy guidelines for its reform, but also a new social theory and epistemology that will move us beyond the evident shortcomings of unrestrained capitalism. New forms of consciousness, meanings, and value orientations are part of this reform.

Following Unger (1975), we may identify the following aspects of the "welfare-corporate" state:

> First, it is a state in which the government assumes a widespread and overt responsibility for the distribution of economic and social advantages, as a complement or a limit to the market. That is what makes it a welfare state. The firm distinction between formal equality of political or legal status and almost unlimited substantive inequality of social circumstance is abandoned as a premise of social policy.
>
> Second, it is a state in which bodies intermediate between the individual and the agencies of government—corporations, unions, associations—achieve an even larger place in the life of the society. This makes it a corporate state. . . .
>
> [Third, it] is often characterized by the importance of a process for the transformation of nature, technology, and by the preeminence of a bureaucratic class, the class of professionals, technicians, and managers who direct the welfare activities of the government and administer the corporate organizations. (pp. 175–176)

These attributes of the welfare-corporate state are undergirded by forms of consciousness that diverge from classical liberalism. Recall that in the older world view the center of human life is, in critical respects, the sphere of economic exchange. Dominant in this world view are the freedoms to produce, consume, and act as we see fit. This sets up something of an attitude toward nature focused on conquest—the view that the natural world, as a distant and somewhat alien force, exists to provide human beings with the opportunity of extracting resources that can be fashioned into products that will enhance human happiness. Natural resources are, therefore, instrumentally useful, as they become valued means to whatever ends we may as individuals value.

Part of the intellectual impetus for new forms of consciousness that would help mold the modern liberal agenda was provided by the romantics:

> The influence of romanticism, as exemplified in different ways by Coleridge, Wordsworth, Carlyle and Ruskin, is worthy of special note. . . . Wordsworth

preached the gospel of return to nature, of nature expressed in rivers, dales and mountains and in the souls of simple folk. Implicitly and often explicitly he attacked industrialization as the great foe of nature, without and within. Carlyle carried on a constant battle against utilitarianism and the existing socioeconomic order, which he summed up in a single phrase as "anarchy plus a constable." He called for a regime of social authority to enforce social ties. (Dewey, 1935, pp. 21–22)

With the appearance of modern liberal forms of consciousness, the kinds of instrumentalism and exploitation that had attended classical liberal practices were challenged. A concern for the interconnectedness of means and ends—an idea that arguably has been most articulately forwarded by John Dewey (1916, chapter 8)—was manifested in the writings of many modern liberals. This led to a more sustained focus on the value of ends that particular means are thought to procure, as opposed to an exclusive focus on the level of efficiency involved in procuring those ends. This, in turn, requires a framework of values and an emphasis on social planning with which public priorities can be articulated and accomplished.

The difference between this orientation and the one accompanying classical liberalism can be illustrated in the altered understanding of humankind's relationship to nature. Instead of perceiving nature as the plaything of human will, a fund of material for the satisfaction of our desires, there is an increasing interest in the preservation of natural surroundings and an increasing respect for the continuity between human beings and nature. Sometimes this interest proceeds to the point of the deification of nature and to the reassertion of a mystical religious union with the natural world (Unger, 1975, p. 178). More commonly, it led to altered social and governmental policies, seen, for example, in decisions to preserve wilderness areas and create a national park system (Ise, 1961).

More generally, modern liberals point to the inseparability of the individual and those familial, cultural, and social practices that help shape people's identities:

> Through the attack on instrumentalism, and particularly on the manipulative relationship to the natural world, [the welfare state] denies the discontinuity of nature and culture. Nature is to be conceived and treated as the totality of which social relations are a part rather than as a category of external objects whose value lies in their capacity to satisfy human desires. (Unger, 1975, p. 179)

In adopting what we might call an ecological consciousness, people's individual, productive strivings are no longer seen as "natural," with the surrounding social and physical environment only perceived as serving more or less well our independently defined utilities. The separation between self and others that is a central assumption within classical liberal theory is rejected as an illusion. As a result, both the instrumentalism and individualism of classical liberal theory are overturned by modern liberalism. The physical universe, social interactions, individual personalities and strivings, and community values are pictured as forming a seamless whole. Appeals to natural law or natural rights or a state of nature lose their force, replaced by social connections, community values and actions, and a more encompassing, holistic view of the world. Within this context, laws and rights must be justified through appeals to values that have human origins and that require human defense and legislative sanctions.

Individualism, Liberty, and the Social Good

Whether we take the rejection of classical liberalism and the appearance of the welfare state as a fundamental conceptual shift or not depends, in part, on our frame of reference. At one level, we believe there are changes beyond those associated with the New Deal or the Great Society that are needed in our economic, social, and educational arrangements. Yet, important shifts that accompanied the development of the welfare state did make a concrete difference in many people's day-to-day lives.

An alternative understanding of liberty surfaced that differed from that espoused by classical liberals. The older tradition pictured people as being essentially disconnected, atomistic individuals, with only tangential ties to other members of civil society. For modern liberals such as Dewey, however, this is to isolate, and in an important sense dehumanize, people. For we do not first form individual identities that we then "take out into the real world." Instead, those identities have an inescapably social origin. As Dewey (1935) put this, "effective liberty is a function of the social conditions existing at any time," and not a transcendent, natural reality applied to isolated individuals that mandates restraint from artificial/social institutions (p. 34). What liberty means, as a concrete reality, will be shaped by the particular customs, habits, laws, values, cultural codes, and forms of social and economic status that exist within a particular social order. This view is inconsistent with the classical liberal view of human existence. For, as a matter of fact:

> It is evident that while there are native organic or biological structures that remain fairly constant, the actual "laws" of human nature are laws of *individuals in association*, not of beings in a mythical condition apart from association. In other words, liberalism that takes its profession of the importance of individuality with sincerity must be deeply concerned about the structure of human association. (Dewey, 1935, p. 41; emphasis added)

John Rawls (1971) similarly claims that important forms of human sociability exist that run counter to the classical liberal emphasis on individualism. He says that human beings "value their common institutions and activities as good in themselves. We need one another as partners in ways of life that are engaged in for their own sake, and the successes and enjoyments of others are necessary for and complimentary to our own good" (pp. 522–523). When we value other people instrumentally, we cut ourselves off from a portion of our potential to be human; we fail to recognize that not only do we enjoy the company of others, but we become the people we are because of the talents, virtues, and abilities of those with whom we form a community, within which we *become* free.

A central problem in this context is that classical liberals equivocate between "formal liberty" and "real liberty." The former refers to contentions about what it is possible for people to do and become, given particular theories, principles, and proposals for how to construct some sort of social system. Within classical liberalism, formal liberties associated with people's freedom to participate in an economic arena within a political structure that is only minimally intrusive are said to allow us the freedom to purchase goods, to develop values, and to make choices free of constraint. Yet if we look at the "real liberties" associated with laissez-faire capitalism and a minimalist state, a quite different picture emerges. This involves going beyond the rhetoric and abstractions of classical liberal theory and looking at the real, day-to-day, material and social conditions in which people live. The actual economic activities and situations of workers, as outlined above, were not fulfilling, nor were they generative of personality traits and values that enhance liberty and dignity. The material goods made available under capitalism have not been, for many, an enduring source of satisfaction and meaning; indeed, they have fostered forms of consumerism that have been injurious, especially as they have led to malformed cultural and political realities (see, for example, Lasch, 1984). The economic inequalities noted earlier eroded personal freedoms and prohibited the exercise of autonomy. Many have argued, like Dewey (1935), that "servility and regimentation are the result of control by the few of access to means of productive labor on the part of the many" (p. 38).

For modern liberals, the servility and regimentation created by the new corporate order were to be eliminated by an expanded role for a regulative state that would generate real, as opposed to formal but ultimately hollow, liberties associated with classical liberalism. Such real liberties can only be understood and worked toward if we first acknowledge the historical and socially conditioned nature of human freedom, thus giving up pretensions to natural laws. Instead, the only form of enduring social organization that is now possible is one in which the new forces of productivity are cooperatively planned and controlled, in which they are used in the interest of the effective liberty and the cultural development of the individuals that constitute society. Such a social order cannot be established by an unplanned convergence of the actions of separate individuals, each of whom is bent on personal private advantage (Dewey, 1935, p. 54).

In the modern liberal view, the good society is itself founded on a notion of community. As human beings, we do not inherit a fixed nature that it is the business of individual actors to express. Not only are we unable to individually procure those things which we may desire (and thus use other people and various social institutions instrumentally, in order to accomplish those desires), but we become who we are—we "discover our nature"—when we engage with each other socially. The patterns of social interaction, the bonds we make with others, and the social practices in which we engage help create who we are.

The Welfare State and Social Justice

There are two general ways one could argue for the creation of the welfare state on the basis of its moral necessity. The first is what we call an accommodationist perspective, within which claims are made that accept some of the basic premises of classical liberalism. Within this perspective, we might argue that the provision of basic goods and services ought to be included among those fundamental rights of citizenship embraced by classical liberals. In this scheme, the provision of basic goods is a response to the right to welfare that is akin to our other "inalienable rights"—to life, liberty, and the pursuit of happiness, for example, as endorsed by Locke (1690/ 1960) and codified in the Declaration of Independence. It could be argued that this is a logical extension of those guarantees that have been recognized by classical political values and social policies.

The problem with this justification for the welfare state is twofold. First, it overlooks the vision of equality and responsibility that is central to the classical liberal world view. The individual liberties touted within this vision postulate precisely what modern liberals condemn: Each person must be allowed to pursue his or her own purposes, as these are individually defined. To rely on the assistance of others, especially through the auspices of some governmental agency whose actions are made possible only through compulsory policies and actions (such as tax collection and transfer payments aimed at redistribution of wealth), is to intrude on our liberties and unfairly burden the populace. Second, the extension of inalienable rights to include welfare provisions would, for the classical liberal, violate the naturalness of human difference. We might, out of charity or religious conviction, provide services or monetary support to individuals whose lack of talents or simple bad luck result in a life of poverty. But to mandate welfare and basic goods through the auspices of the state as a matter of inalienable right is to overlook the facts of difference in ability and striving that, within this tradition, are inescapable.

Against this charge, it could be asserted that what is natural is not necessarily right. We may, for example, provide evidence that any number of heinous activities, while apparently "natural," since they have existed from at least the beginning of recorded history, should not on that account be accepted or tolerated. Thus the alleged existence of a natural aristocracy, or of natural differences in ability, cannot by itself be used as a basis for protecting those differences.

This leads to a second, more promising set of ethical arguments in behalf of the welfare state. As noted earlier, one of the critical arguments of modern liberals is that there is no natural law to which we can appeal in determining political principles and social structures. This perspective implies two things. First, that our rights to life, liberty, and the pursuit of happiness are socially constructed ones, premised on some view of what we all deserve as human beings. The difference between one set of political principles and another is thus not a difference between what is natural (and therefore obligatory) and what is imposed (and thus optional). Second, a denial of natural law serves to remove the distinction between productive activities engaged in by individuals and associated with an economy, on the one hand, and civic activities associated with communities, civic institutions, and governments, on the other. Removing this distinction, adopting the view that all social proposals and activities require ethical justification, provides the modern liberal with an alternative way to justify welfare state initiatives: through the elucidation of theories of justice.

There may be no contemporary American philosopher who has done more to advance the moral case for some kind of redistributive welfare state than John Rawls. The views he develops in *A Theory of Justice* (1971) have been widely analyzed and critiqued (see, for example, Barry, 1973; Clark & Gintis, 1978; Daniels, 1975; Wolff, 1977).

Rawls attempts to develop a social contract–oriented theory of justice as fairness that takes this theoretical tradition to a different level of abstraction. In this, he is attempting to provide an alternative to the utilitarian conception of justice that played a key role in classical liberalism. Rather than seeing isolated individuals and productive activity as starting points around which a variety of moral values can be individually postulated, Rawls says, "for us the primary subject of justice is . . . the way in which the major social institutions distribute fundamental rights and duties and determine the division of advantages from social cooperation" (1971, p. 7). One of the primary purposes of a system of justice is to create guidelines for the distribution of goods and social benefits that acknowledge the "especially deep inequalities" into which people are born.

Saying that his theory "is not offered as a description of ordinary meanings [of justice] but as an account of certain distributive principles for the basic structure of society," Rawls aims to address the requirements for social justice (p. 10). These must be a central part of any social theory and corresponding set of practices. The orienting question for Rawls (1971) is, therefore, the contractual agreements that could be entered into regarding the most basic structures of society—the principles of justice:

> They are the principles that free and rational persons concerned to further their own interests would accept in an initial position of equality as defining the fundamental terms of their association. These principles are to regulate all further agreements; they specify the kinds of social cooperation that can be entered into and the forms of government that can be established. This way of regarding the principles of justice I shall call justice as fairness. (p. 11)

A hypothesized setting is constructed by Rawls that will short-circuit egoism and focus on what rational beings can agree to as providing the basis for a social situation that will be fair to all. Central to this setting is the insertion of a "veil of ignorance." People cannot know what their place in the resulting social structure will be, their intelligence level, their physical capacities, and so on. In stripping people of their physical and social characteristics, they are led to focus on *principles* that are rationally defensible and that promote fairness. The basic idea is to develop "first principles" of justice that can be defended apart from how their implementation may affect any individual or group.

Rawls concludes that in such a position we cannot assume that the aggregate of people's satisfactions justifies lesser life chances for others. Given the reality of equality and mutual ignorance in the original position, that is, it would not be rationally defensible for any person to choose to be a utilitarian, since his or her own life position might be harmed through a utilitarian-oriented calculation of social benefits. Instead,

> persons in the initial situation would choose two rather different principles: the first requires equality in the assignment of basic rights and duties, while the second holds that social and economic inequalities, for example inequalities of wealth and authority, are just only if they result in compensating benefits for everyone, and in particular for the least advantaged members of society. These principles rule out justifying institutions on the grounds that the hardships of some are offset by a greater good in the aggregate. (Rawls, 1971, pp. 14–15)

Movements to provide compensatory educational programs such as Head Start can be seen as responding directly to the view that social disparities are just only when they benefit the least advantaged. Such programs, and the commitments to justice that they embody, seek to diminish arbitrary and undeserved differences among people—even those that are said to derive from capacities that allow a "natural aristocracy" to flourish.

This theory of justice, then, requires an equal sharing of basic rights and responsibilities and a principle for the distribution of social and economic goods according to which disparities are tolerated only if they accrue disproportionately to the least advantaged. "It may," Rawls (1971) concludes, "be *expedient* but it is not *just* that some should have less in order that others may prosper. But there is no injustice in the greater benefits earned by a few provided that the situation of persons not so fortunate is thereby improved" (p. 15; emphasis added).

These concerns for justice must ultimately place limits on how society may be structured and lead to considerations of distributive justice—that is, how rights and duties, as well as social and economic advantages, are to be fairly allocated among the populace. Rawls's scheme sets out a theory of social values, grounded in a conception of justice, around which society should be organized. For Rawls, justice—not, for example, efficiency, or measures of economic growth, or individual happiness—is socially primary. Likewise, real, as opposed to formal, liberty is a more fundamental value than individual utility, or social advantage, or the production and consumption of commodities. Social advantages—wealth, power, and prestige, for instance—that erode the liberties of others, especially of the least advantaged, are, therefore, seen as unjust. As a result, an individual's desires that compromise the principles of justice, or whose satisfaction undermines those principles, would not be fulfilled. What we see here is a reordering of priorities, away from the classical liberal/utilitarian tradition, and another way to conceptualize human fulfillment.

In order for such a social system founded on justice to be stable and self-sustaining, "it must be arranged so as to bring about in its members the corresponding sense of justice, an effective desire to act in accordance with its rules for reasons of justice" (Rawls, 1971, p. 261). Thus social institutions must be "not only just but framed so as to encourage the virtue of justice in those who take part in them. In this sense, the principles of justice define a partial ideal of the person which social and economic arrangements must respect." In addition, Rawls says, "certain institutions are required by the two principles [of justice]. They define an ideal basic structure, or the outlines of one, toward which the course of reform should evolve. . . . This view [contains] the feature of setting up an ideal of the person that *constrains the pursuit of existing desires*" (pp. 261–262; emphasis added). Rawls suggests that his theory of justice and its social consequences will have the effect of limiting personal prerogatives and influencing functioning systems of political economy, setting up ethical standards with which all institutions, including economic ones, must comply.

Modern liberalism, to the extent that it sets limits on both individual actions and social practices, as well as economic exchanges specifically, articulates principles that, when embedded in the laws of the state, justifiably place limits on laissez-faire capitalism. Justice, as an orienting framework for human experience, replaces the classical framework of individual desires. There are values that when enacted constrain human conduct and institutional practices— even when they do not immediately impair the actions of others and even if they contribute to the greatest happiness for the greatest number. Whatever form of political economy is to be implemented in society, it must be consistent with the requirements of justice as fairness and with the prerequisites of political liberty and fair equality of opportunity.[4] These requirements impose restrictions on what is personally, socially, and institutionally permissible. If justice requires that resources be distributed so that the interests of the least advantaged are secured, and if these are to coexist with political liberty and fair equality of opportunity, an unfettered system of capitalist production cannot be tolerated. Political participation, occupational opportunities, and the fulfillment of human needs are sacrificed when an unregulated economy with its emphasis on efficiency and utility is allowed to trample on the prerogatives of justice. At another level, we see again an emphasis on community:

> The main idea is simply that a well-ordered society is itself a form of social union. . . . In much the same way that players [in a game] have the shared end to execute a good and fair play of the game, so the members of a well-ordered society have the common aim of cooperating together to *realize their own and another's nature in ways allowed by the principles of justice*. This collective intention is the consequence of everyone's having an effective sense of justice. . . . When everyone acts justly, all find satisfaction in the very same thing. (Rawls, 1971, p. 527; emphasis added)

The just society will help generate those forms of character and demeanor that are necessary for the establishment and continuation of that society. This entails new educational policies and practices that will go some way toward creating the necessary character types that accompany a new social, moral, and democratic vision.

EDUCATION AND SOCIAL DEMOCRACY

As we saw in Chapter 2, democracy within the classical liberal tradition is associated with a limited role for a constitutional government, founded with the intent of protecting the private, individual prerogatives of citizens and guaranteeing their natural rights. The work of politicians is to be limited to generating neutral procedural rules that leave open questions of distributive justice. A representative government composed, ideally, of those "natural aristocrats" elected to protect our individual interests is best suited to such a society. Following Novak (1982), political life may be bounded by "interest-group pluralism" in which politicians would work to "preserve the sphere of the person inviolable" (p. 65). The democratic state contained within this orientation, while providing a crucial shift away from older forms of aristocracy associated with inherited status, is thus rather limited. It allows the general population—or, in the early stages of its incorporation in the United States and elsewhere, a rather small portion of that population, restricted by class, racial, and gender characteristics—to elect people to office who will protect their interests. And all governmental activity would be restricted to a fairly narrow sphere, surrounded by productive life within a market economy—but an economy, as we have seen, that could hardly be called democratic or geared toward advancing the interests of the common good. This notion of democracy has been called "protectionist" by Barber (1984).

For modern liberals, whose platform is to some extent founded on eliminating the separation between the individual and the social, democracy cannot mean simply preserving the sphere of the isolated/atomistic individual. Since "the core of the collectivist view is the idea of the spontaneity of social bonds and of their priority over individual striving" (Unger, 1975, p. 83), there must be ways to supersede interest-group pluralism, through the adoption of shared values that allow for the development of communities (see also Selznick, 1992).

Through the efforts of John Dewey (1900/1956b, 1902/1956a, 1916, 1938) and others (for example, Bode, 1927, 1938; Kilpatrick, 1918), forms of progressive education emerged and developed during the establishment of the welfare state—though these had numerous historical antecedents, to be sure—that involved new conceptions of teaching, learning, and schooling intended to help further this communitarian orientation. These conceptions would assist in the development of individuals who could take their rightful place in a new democratic order, individuals for whom new social policies and programs were needed in order to enact the ethical and political obligations of the emerging welfare state.

For educational progressives, both a critical view of previous and current social and educational policies, as well as a new understanding of democracy and civic life, provided an important impetus for an altered system of schooling. Such a system might become part of a new, expanded state that would intercede between the demands and priorities of the economy, on the one hand, and the opportunities of familial life, professional advancement, and civil society, on the other. To be consistent with the outlines of the welfare state, such schools would have to value real—not formal—liberty, be founded in part on the importance of community and the social good, be committed to a notion of social justice, and offer a new conception of democracy.

Vying for influence over the direction of schooling and the formal curriculum was that group concerned with efficiency, scientific procedures and technical calculations, and social stability that Kliebard (1986) refers to as social efficiency advocates. As discussed in the introduction, it was this group that sought to tie schools more closely to the prerogatives of industry, while borrowing their commitments to efficiency, scientific analysis, and social functionalism. For many of the founding fathers of the curriculum field, the school became a "plant" to be used efficiently so as to make sure that its "products" were diverse and of high quality; the internal dynamics of classrooms were to be shaped by commitments to establishing concrete objectives that could be measured and for which teachers could be held accountable (see Bobbitt, 1918, 1920; Charters, 1924, 1927; Cubberley, 1929). It was such a "factory system" of schooling that modern liberals challenged.

As the welfare state developed a more regulatory orientation that sought to humanize and provide planning and oversight for the economy, it developed both new agencies for this specific purpose and a new conception of what democracy means and implies for the citizen. Formal components of an expanded state apparatus emerged over time in the United States. These included, for example, the Interstate Commerce Commission, the Internal Revenue Service, a broad social welfare system that included Social Security provisions for the elderly and dependent minors, the Occupational Safety and Health Administration, and the Equal Employment Opportunity Commission. Such agencies would regulate trade, collect taxes, enforce equal opportunity, and generally underwrite a minimum quality of life for Americans by providing a social safety net for all. In addition, government agencies would provide a means of planning or controlling social and economic affairs so that they would be predictable and responsive to social and human need. It was such predictability and responsiveness, as well as fairness, that had been absent in a society dominated by laissez-faire capitalism.

In addition to new governmental agencies that would serve to buffer the internal dynamics and social effects of a market economy, new or expanded civic organizations were generated that assisted in broadening the vision of democracy in U.S. society. Professional associations, trade unions, political interest groups, religious institutions, and other organizations were seen as having an important role to play in social life. They provided new opportunities for social participation and gave new meaning to civic life. Democracy then meant something more than the election of professional elites who would protect our interests. It might instead be seen as a process that had a range of applications beyond constitutional guarantees. Democracy as a way of organizing decision making and other processes might well include more, and more diverse, people, institutions, and causes.[5]

This more comprehensive orientation to democracy had a significant bearing on progressive proposals for schools and education generally. In part this is because of the extent to which schools are woven into the social fabric: Changing social and political dynamics have often resulted in the more or less direct reform of the school curriculum, approaches to teaching, and means of assessing teachers and students. Whatever else schools do as institutions, they provide environments within which the young will be socialized in one direction or another, along the lines of some value orientation or another. As Levin (1990) put this point, "most persons spend at least 10 of their early years in schools, so it is not surprising that schools must undertake much of the burden of political socialization for both the polity and the workplace" (p. 160). This socialization function of schools, as compulsory institutions in which young people spend the greater part not only of every day but the greater portion of the early years of their lives, is necessarily undergirded by certain assumptions and orientations. Those orientations may be related either to the current society in which they function and/or to some (implicit or explicit) alternative vision of social life. Given an expanded view of democracy and a wider range of sites and activities into which democratic values could be incorporated, it is not surprising that

> attempts have been made to enable the wider participation of those who have traditionally been underrepresented in the various levels of the educational system. Notable examples include ethnic and racial minorities. The struggle for egalitarian gender roles in the family and society and attempts to democratize the school and workplace are additional examples of a growing struggle to apply democratic principles and procedures to diverse social issues. (Ichilov, 1990, p. 15)

The attempt to include underrepresented people and groups among those who may enjoy the benefits of a society's productive activity has been a central concern for the modern liberal. Efforts to provide expanded access to social goods can be clearly seen in the commitment to provide compensatory education programs, based on the principle of providing equality of opportunity to all people.

The basic premise behind equality of opportunity is that accidental or irrelevant characteristics, such as those associated with race and gender, should not be used to discriminate against people. If groups of people have suffered from a lack of equal opportunity, they have a valid claim to special programs and forms of assistance that will create a level playing field. Regarding the dynamics of inequality and how it might be addressed, Strike (1982) says:

> The role of schooling vis a vis equality is to ensure that opportunity to succeed does not depend on irrelevant background characteristics. But what does this require of schools? Shall schools equalize inputs and allow outputs to differ in ways which will correlate with race and socioeconomic status, or shall schools attempt to equalize achievement and allocate resources unequally so as to compensate for the inequalities in students' backgrounds? Neither position seems satisfactory. (p. 209)

The basic argument for compensatory education programs is that some people have educational disadvantages that result from disadvantages in experience linked to poverty, race, and so on, for which the individual cannot be held accountable. Inherited disadvantages result in experiential deficiencies that culminate in poor school achievement. As a result of low achievement, students do not gain access to higher-paying jobs, and the cycle of poverty continues generation after generation.

To break this cycle, the state intervenes to establish a number of programs that will help children before it is too late—that is, before the cycle is re-created. What compensatory education attempts, then, is to provide equal opportunities by creating more than equal resources for those who have been historically disadvantaged through no fault of their own—an interesting example of Rawls's theory of justice. Yet Strike is dubious about society's ability to abolish injustice through compensatory education. There are a number of possible reasons for this, including the fact that good educational programs which benefit the disadvantaged are also frequently available to the more affluent. Since both groups benefit more or less equally from such programs, the inherited inequalities persist—even, perhaps, in exaggerated form. A plausible explanation for the apparent failure of early childhood compensatory education over the long haul is that its effects diminish as children enter the public schools, since the white, middle-class cultural norms and values that exist there undermine success for students who do not share those values. More expansively, compensatory education programs may fail to address social inequalities because they are premised on the belief that the inequalities they are designed to eliminate are not the result of overt discrimination. If this is the case, equalizing achievement outcomes in schools by providing programs aimed at redressing the disadvantages wrought by racial discrimination will not by themselves provide equality of opportunity. In other words, it may be the case that "our society generates inequalities of such magnitude that schools cannot be expected to overcome their effects on the distribution of achievement and social rewards in the next generation" (Strike, 1982, p. 222). Here Strike is suggesting that if the source of inequalities is not prejudice or other forms of overt discrimination, but something more endemic to social life, then liberal theories of justice—and the welfare state with which they are affiliated—may prove to be inadequate. This position, as we shall see in the next chapter, has been articulated by radical social and educational critics, who argue for more deep seated social changes.

Whether modern liberal theories of justice that argue for compensatory educational programs are sufficient to overcome inequalities remains for now an open question. This is partly because of the complexities of empirical research findings and sometimes conflicting interpretations of them, partly because of significant dispute about the causes of inequality and whether schools will ever be able to overcome them. A more promising aspect of modern liberalism, however, is its commitment to a conception of democracy that diverges from the protectionist version touted by classical liberals. Here the schools, as has been thought by many modern liberals, have a vital role to play.

If revised understandings of democratic values and processes are to become influential in social life, it seems they must be incorporated into the day-to-day dynamics of schools. Not only is the school an important social institution in its own right—as are the factory, the professional society, and the civic club—it also has the function of preparing students for some sort of future. As Dewey put this point, "with the renewal of physical existence goes, in the case of human beings, the re-creation of beliefs, ideals, hopes, happiness, misery, and practices. The continuity of any experience, through renewing of the social group, is a literal fact. Education, in its broadest sense, is the means of this social continuity of life" (1916, p. 2). Forms of knowledge, skills, ways of thinking, and so on are needed not just to get a job or gain access to consumer goods. They are crucial for the very re-creation and renewal of human and social life. Without some form of education, in short, social life would be not just less rich, but not possible.

It would be a mistake to assume that visions of democratic education that differ from those associated with the classical liberal tradition only appeared with the development of modern liberalism. Many educators and scholars advocated more participatory, democratically governed, and student-oriented schools long before a different kind of state came into being.

What might have made such educational initiatives more palatable and practic-able were the changing forms of consciousness and the changing set of ethical concerns that accompanied the development of the welfare state, as discussed above.

Just as modern liberal social theory elevates the role of human sociability in theories of justice and the civil state, educational spokespersons in this tradition highlight the importance of community and shared understandings. "Persons do not become a society," Dewey tells us, "by living in physical proximity. . . . Individuals do not even compose a social group because they all work for a common end." In addition to sharing common interests, people become members of a community when they are "all cognizant of the common end and all interested in it so that they regulated their specific activity in view of it." Under these circumstances, Dewey (1916) concludes, "they would form a community" (pp. 4–5). *Common*, *community*, and *communication* not only share a common linguistic root but are also practically interrelated in terms of people's everyday actions. We cannot develop common interests, or establish a widely held social good, if people are unable to effectively communicate with one another within a setting in which something beyond self-interested individualism dominates.

Education allows people to form genuine communities when they are brought together in a common setting where interests can be shared and attachments can be formed. Communities are strengthened when people with diverse backgrounds come together to share experiences that contribute to everyone's growth. As Dewey puts it, "the intermingling in the school of youth of different races, differing religions, and unlike customs creates for all a new and broader environment" (1916, p. 21). An expanded environment provides new avenues for expanded experiences, which in turn provide the basis for educative growth. Forms of communication that are necessary for the establishment of such communities develop as people share these experiences. A common purpose is advanced when we feel the significance of some problem, and when we develop shared understandings and some means of providing social direction that can solve it. This requires not only various forms of technical knowledge, but an emphasis on sociability that is denied in conventional forms of schooling. While in social life outside of school people often learn through the process of working through real problems requiring cooperation and communication, traditional teaching in the schools is often more abstract, less connected to problems of living in the world. As Dewey (1916) puts this, "formal instruction . . . easily becomes remote and dead—abstract and bookish, to use the ordinary words of depreciation. . . . There is the standing danger that the material of formal instruction will be merely the subject matter of the schools, isolated from the subject matter of life-experience" (p. 8). In complex societies, there is always the danger that something like becoming educated—a normal process of living and interacting with the physical and social world—will become stultified and artificial, especially as it is embedded in institutions that serve particular ends, such as the development of job-related skills. "Children doubtless go to school to learn," Dewey (1916) remarks, "but it has yet to be proved that learning occurs most adequately when it is made a separate conscious business" (pp. 38–39). One of Dewey's emphases is, accordingly, on recognizing and valuing the way people learn through experiences in everyday life, and reconnecting classroom and everyday life. Indeed, for Dewey (1916), "to make the conditions of life such that all will learn in the process of living is the finest product of schooling" (p. 51). Schools must accentuate both the organic qualities of living and the necessity of building communities within which common purposes and shared understandings form the basis of communication that can enhance the quality of human life.

In discussing different societies and the forms of interaction they allow and prohibit, Dewey makes a telling point about the kinds of activities that further or detract from genuine involvement and communication. The assembly lines, technical and managerial controls, and forms of disconnected activity that dominated the expansive and centralized corporation were antithetical to certain fundamental values. For Dewey (1916), "efficiency in production often demands division of labor. But it is reduced to a mechanical routine unless workers see the technical, intellectual, and social relationships involved in what they do, and engage in their work because of the motivation furnished by such perceptions" (p. 85). It seems all but impossible for workers on the tightly controlled and regulated shopfloor to engage in work for the reasons Dewey provides. The management techniques of industrial production consciously seek to divide workers rather than unite them in activities that serve a common purpose; the isolation and subordination on the job militate against the sort of sociability and open communication aimed at articulating the sense of common purpose with which Dewey is concerned. "Mechanical routine" seems the only outcome of work in the modern factory, as illustrated in the work situations described earlier in this chapter. There are no common interests that hold workers together, no sense of working for a common purpose that is productive of community. "Economic democracy" did not find a congenial home in the large-scale, centrally controlled enterprises that resulted from capitalist expansion. Beyond the economic disparities associated with such expansion, we see its cultural and social consequences.

The sharing of a common purpose that necessitates and enlivens forms of communication, the valuing of social relationships and the intellectual aspects of those relationships that provide work its real meaning, and the formation of communities of shared aims are all related to the dynamics of democracy. Rather than the narrow view of democracy that grows out of classical liberalism, Dewey (1916) prompts us to consider a more expansive view:

> A democracy is more than a form of government; it is primarily a mode of associated living, of conjoint communicated experience. The extension in space of the number of individuals who participate in an interest so that each has to refer his own action to that of others, and to consider the action of others to give point and direction to his own, is equivalent to the breaking down of those barriers of class, race, and national territory which kept men from perceiving the full import of their activity. (p. 87)

If democracy entails something like a form of life that is shared and that obliterates boundaries that have only served to keep people separated and disunited; if real learning involves people engaged in experiences within which they can grow; and if community is a central ingredient of human life—then there seem to be clear implications for the possibilities of education in a democracy.

One of these implications is that the separation of people in general, and in educational settings in particular, is injurious. Separating the privileged from the subjugated is harmful for both groups, though the material injuries are clearest in the latter class. But, for the more privileged who are socially isolated, "their culture tends to be sterile, to be turned back to feed on itself; their art becomes a showy display and artificial; their wealth luxurious; their knowledge overspecialized; their manners fastidious rather than humane" (Dewey, 1916, p. 84). Similarly, schools must not divide students by class or race or supposed ability; such separations are inimical to the kind of shared purpose within communities that leads to the kind of associated living that puts into practice the democratic and educative life. The movement to incorporate diverse forms of multicultural literature into classrooms derives some of its support from commitments to bringing together diverse voices that have often been denied entrance to the public schools (Wood, 1990).

Amy Gutmann (1987) provides a contemporary gloss on the development of democratic ideals and their relevance for schools. She says of the general functioning of a democratic system of education:

> A democratic society . . . must be constrained *not* to legislate policies that render democracy repressive or discriminatory. A democratic theory of education recognizes the importance of empowering citizens to make educational policy and also of constraining their choices among policies in accordance with those of principles—of nonrepression and nondiscrimination—that preserve

> the intellectual and social foundations of democratic deliberations. A society
> that empowers citizens to make educational policy, moderated by these two
> principled constraints, realizes the democratic ideal of education. (p. 14;
> emphasis in original)

What is important for democratic forms of education is that the basic
principles of nonrepression and nondiscrimination be followed in formulating policies and practices for schools. This perspective is consistent with "procedural justice" as outlined by Rawls (1971). While we cannot know the proper
outcome of educational decision making that is genuinely democratic, we can
place negative stipulations on the processes through which such decisions
are made—we can specify that it not be repressive or discriminatory.

Central to Gutmann's understanding of democracy and of democratic
education is the ineradicability of disagreement. People have, and will always,
disagree about what "the good life" consists of. The only way to eliminate
such disagreement is to enforce a kind of authoritarian moralism through
the auspices of a central government or other authority—a perspective alien
to welfare state proposals that seek to provide a certain minimum of security in accord with which real liberties can be acted on. Thus "a democratic
state must aid children in developing the capacity to understand and to
evaluate competing conceptions of the good life and the good society"
(Gutmann, 1987, p. 44). This capacity will be promoted by helping students
consider, analyze, and discuss competing perspectives, and by allowing them
to have both a stake and a voice in determining what values and orientations will be embedded in social life. In order for a society to be truly democratic, moreover, we cannot allow individuals or groups to be unfairly
excluded from developing the capacities that are necessary for rational
deliberation and choice. In other words, "no educable child may be excluded
from an education adequate to participating in the political processes that
structure choice among good lives" (Gutmann, 1987, p. 45). We have an
obligation not only to educate all children, but to educate them in ways that
allow them to take part in deliberations concerning the most important of
human questions, such as those surrounding what constitutes the good life.
Teachers and parents have a special claim on the education of children, as
does the state. Yet each of these groups must subordinate its concerns to
the more general interest of creating democratic citizens and people—that
is, people whose values and orientations are neither rigidly predetermined
nor subject to the uncritical acceptance of extant social institutions or
practices.

This makes clear why, for modern liberals like Gutmann, the views represented by Milton Friedman are so misguided. Advocates of a free market
system of education like Friedman fail to understand the legitimate stake

we all have in the education of our children to become democratic participants. In his 1955 essay, Friedman suggests that we might limit government
to "assuring that the schools met certain minimum standards such as the
inclusion of a minimum content in their programs, much as it now inspects
restaurants to assure that they maintain minimum sanitary standards"
(p. 127). As Gutmann realizes, "were our public interest in regulating schools
as analogous to our interest in regulating restaurants as Friedman suggests,
it would be hard to explain why we should subsidize schooling for every
child." Representing here the perspective of the modern liberal, Gutmann
(1987) argues that

> a necessary condition for justifying public subsidy of schools—but not of res-
> taurants—is the fact that citizens have an important and common interest in
> educating future citizens. By labelling that interest an "externality" of educa-
> tion, Friedman suggests that educating citizens is a side effect, rather than a
> central purpose or "internality," of schooling. (pp. 67–68)

Educating children so that they may become deliberative decision makers
in a democratic society in which alternative conceptions of the good life
can be discussed, debated, and acted upon is fundamental to modern liberal conceptions of education. Indeed Gutmann uses "deliberative" and
"democratic" interchangeably, with respect to the development of character in children.

This does not mean, however, that the enforcement of proper habits
and the exercise of authority with respect to behavior—especially that of
young children—are unwarranted. For children are not able to reason their
way through situations in a sufficiently open-ended and rigorous way, due
to their lack of experience with certain situations and a capacity for reasoning that is only partially developed. Therefore, "the earliest education of
children is not and cannot be by precept or reasoning; it must be by discipline and example" (Gutmann, 1987, p. 50). Parents are, in this way, the
first moral educators of their children, to be supplemented, and eventually
replaced, by other people, by social institutions, and finally by the development of autonomy in their offspring; young people "develop capacities for
criticism, rational argument, and decisionmaking by being taught how to
think logically, to argue coherently and fairly, and to consider the relevant
alternatives before coming to conclusions" (Gutmann, 1987, p. 50). During their early years, children learn through example and instruction; their
learning is subsequently broadened through acquiring more formal capacities for reason and reflection.

At the same time, teachers committed to democratic education cannot
embody a value-neutral perspective in their teachings. Partly, this is because

children are exposed to a number of value orientations simply by interacting with other children in schools, through the operation of a hidden curriculum of one sort or another, and because they bring with them to the
school, the playground, and the reading group values that have been instilled
in them already. Long before they enter kindergarten, they have internalized values that are embodied by the ongoing cultural realities and social
situations they have experienced. In short, children in and outside of schools
are engaged in activities and actions that necessarily embody some values
and not others. To treat every possible value that children bring with them
as acceptable—or as needing simply "clarification" and not "criticism"—is
to misunderstand the requirements for democratic participation. More
broadly, one of the essential differences between the kind of education
children receive through school-based experiences and the kind they receive
in the world beyond the school door is that the former is, and must be,
selective. Not every experience is equally capable of promoting intellectual
or social or moral growth in students, and some serve to actually stunt
growth in those areas. Dewey (1916) articulates this need for selectivity:

> It is the business of the school environment to eliminate, as far as possible,
> the unworthy features of the existing environment from influence upon men-
> tal habitudes. It establishes a purified medium of action. . . . The school has
> the duty of omitting [the undesirable, the trivial, and the dead wood from the
> past] . . . from the environment which it supplies, and thereby doing what it
> can to counteract their influence in the ordinary social environment. By
> selecting the best for its exclusive use, it strives to reenforce the power of this
> best. [An enlightened society] realizes that it is responsible *not* to transmit and
> conserve the whole of its existing achievement, but only such as make for a
> better future society. (p. 20; emphasis in original)

By selecting what is best from current social life, and omitting those aspects
of the current reality that are corrosive to community attachments, democratic practices, and personal and social growth, schools may serve to help
provide a better future—a point that educational radicals have often utilized
in their own educational proposals, as we discuss in Chapter 4.

The ability of school to focus on selective experiences that serve progressive purposes is related to Dewey's (1916) emphasis on education as
providing for the "social continuity of life" (p. 2). It is also a central aim of
democratic education for Gutmann (1987): the commitment of people to
"collectively re-creating the society that we share." We must provide the sort
of education that will allow young people, our future citizens, to engage in
"conscious social reproduction" (p. 39). This kind of engagement demands
of teachers that they cultivate a certain kind of character in order to enhance
particular forms of cognitive ability. The teaching of certain virtues, more-

over, does not rely for its justification on some future situation in which
children will later in life be involved:

> A democratic theory of education . . . requires us to challenge the propriety
> of some claims and distinctions: the claim, for example, that one race is inher-
> ently superior to another, or, to take a more controversial example, the claim
> that a woman's place is in the home. In admitting moral distinctions among
> lives and characters, we bear the burden of differentiating between legitimate
> and spurious moral distinctions. . . . Accepting freedom as the goal of educa-
> tion does not provide an escape from the burden of choosing (on some
> grounds) among the many possible lives that children can be taught to appre-
> ciate. (Gutmann, 1987, pp. 40–41)

While members of the new right, such as Milton Friedman, may espouse
the virtues of freedom unrestrained (at least of a certain kind, in theory), a
democratic society has the right, and the obligation, to choose among competing value systems for schooling. Accepting any value orientation for the
classroom, attempting to be value-neutral, could well have the effect of
socializing children into forms of thinking and feeling that do not allow them
to develop the sort of character traits and cognitive abilities required for
the "re-creation of society" for enlightened social continuity and for the
engagement in those deliberations over differences that define the nature
of democratic practice. Because we live in a democratic society, we must
be able to consciously rethink the directions and purposes of our society.
Because education is inevitably a process of socialization (whatever else it
may be), it must proceed by furthering not *any* and *every* value orientation
or depiction of the good life, but only those required for deliberation about
the nature of such a life—and its conscious social reproduction. In that context, teachers in democratic societies cannot be neutral with respect to, for
example, racism or gender stereotyping.

Modern liberals in this way reject some of the basic postulates of both
classical liberalism and the contemporary new right. It is not individual liberty, directed at any individually oriented end, that is foremost; because we
believe in broadly based participatory processes and practices, we must reject
those ideas and customs that are discriminatory and repressive. Further,
insofar as we are to have genuinely "public" schools, we must reject value
orientations and points of view that are corrosive to the operation of a
public—that is, to a situation in which we can collectively deliberate over
and make conscious decisions about the future direction of society. Affirming the importance of conscious social reproduction for all citizens, teachers must act and teach in such a way as to maintain and further develop the
underlying perspectives, abilities, and forms of character that are required
for democratic communities and actions. It is not that spokespersons such

as William Bennett and Chester Finn are wrong about the need for character education. Rather, it is that they favor the wrong sort of character and personal attributes, that they have the wrong set of values and operating principles in mind, and perhaps that they have misidentified the causes of the lack of character with which they are preoccupied.

Modern liberal views of democratic education are also at odds with one historical wing of "progressive education." In particular, some progressive educators have suggested that teachers have a predominantly negative role: to leave the child/student largely alone to "flower," since his or her "inner nature" will spontaneously develop. Perhaps the most famous contemporary example of this perspective is A. S. Neill's (1977) *Summerhill*, as well as certain kinds of child-centered projects that have been founded on the interests of children. Some forms of the child-study movement, as well as some proposals for the education of young children based on their interests, seem to reflect a "caretaker" or "gardener" metaphor of education (Kliebard, 1975b). But for modern liberals this is to make a mistake not unlike that made by members of the new right: to prize individually identified freedoms above all other values, in spite of their effects—personally and socially. To be consistent with the modern liberal's conception of democracy, we cannot "leave the circle of freedom bare," in schools or elsewhere. That is precisely the route to both amoral neutrality or emotivism, to political caprice and whimsy, to the denial of community, and to moral and social decay. In combination, such forces virtually assure the erosion of democratic values and ways of life.

CONCLUSION

For many people, especially those who worked in the expanding industries and corporations that were fueled by a wave of capitalist expansion, the opportunities to pursue liberty and enjoy happiness, to articulate and work to realize whatever vision of the good life they found most compelling, and to create that moral code they found most satisfying—while being protected by constitutional guarantees so that they would not be harmed or coerced by more powerful individuals—were hollow and without substance. Struggling to keep life and limb together and to take care of their families, many found themselves on the wrong side of a widening gap between the very wealthy and the very poor, subject to managerial directives on the shopfloor that robbed work of its meaning even as the promise of freedom was elusive. At a more global level, it became clear as the industrial age advanced that a commitment to furthering the social good—the sense that there is something vital about community and social life that cannot be judged by an individualistic, utilitarian calculus—could hardly be guaranteed through the unintended consequences of capitalist expansion.

In short, an unbridled economy became increasingly seen as part of the problem of the age rather than part of the solution to menacing social problems. In response, modern liberals sought to develop new social visions and policies, as well as altered conceptions of liberty, social justice, the state, and, more generally, human life. An emphasis on communal attachment as opposed to individualistic striving, participation in the public sphere rather than protection by an elected elite, planning and controlling the forces of production rather than allowing them to develop without benefit of human reflection and judgment, and an expanded role for a civic life that had been, at best, of secondary importance began to emerge and eventually became central ingredients of the welfare state. A reformed system of education, along with other aspects of a state that sought to redress the excesses of capitalism, might humanize social life, making it more predictable and less harsh. By incorporating regulatory and legal protections that enforced equal opportunities for all, in part through the abolition of overt discrimination, Americans might be more able to live out the promise of political freedom and economic abundance. In one sense we could see the development of the welfare state as giving more credence or significance to the political guarantees and protections that could lead to the good life, as opposed to the classical liberal emphasis on a market economy as providing a route to personal happiness. A school system that incorporated commitments to equal opportunity, democratic participation, an inclusiveness and openness to all groups, and the development of communal bonds might well help socialize American youth into the mores, norms, commitments, and attachments necessary for the reconstruction of social life along modern liberal lines.

Yet the changes advocated by modern liberals were in many ways conceptualized within the older liberal tradition. "Most contemporary liberals," Strike (1982, p. 176) says, "while still subscribing to the basic tenets of a free-market society, also believe that human beings deserve a minimal level of support independently of what they earn in the market." It is reasonably clear, as well, that Dewey believed that the harsher realities of economic life could be overcome by more communal attachments, more participation in decision making, and a more genuine sociability.

But a central question persists: What are the real causes of inequality, human misery, and alienation as they appear in the United States? Is it enough to reform the system of production that seems at least partly responsible for persistent social ills? What role might education play in alleviating those ills, and in restructuring society in ways that generate equality and an encompassing notion of social justice? Different perspectives on these questions—ones that offer clear alternatives to the classical and modern liberal views—have been developed that provide other, and quite distinctive, social and educational visions.

NOTES

1. The data reported below need to be qualified in certain ways: First, they discount the contributions of spouses; second, the actual number of deaths that took place during these periods far exceeded the number of probated estates; and third, "in some forty per cent of the cases, no inventory was filed and, hence, the size of the estates is unknown" (King, 1915, p. 66). This last qualification is especially important for our purposes. It is reasonable to assume that noninventoried cases will likely be of lesser total value than inventoried ones. If this is the case, the actual data reported by King (1915) are likely to understate the actual economic disparities among social groups. In spite of these qualifications, the data allow us to make some rough generalizations of social dynamics related to industrialization during the periods indicated above.

2. Some indication of the centralization of capital can be seen in the fact that the total value of manufactured products in the United States in 1860 was $1.9 billion, while by 1900 that figure had increased to $13 billion (Levine, 1988, p. 22). Whereas in 1859 the value of the product of each manufacturing firm was $13,429, by 1919 that figure had jumped to $125,157; the average number of wage workers in each firm had similarly increased during that time span, from 9.3 to 31.3 (Faulkner, 1951, cited in Levine, 1988, p. 24, table 1).

3. The changing nature of workers' jobs is reflected, for example, in the fact that in 1909 less than one-sixth of people working in factories were employed in businesses with 1,000 or more workers, while by 1923 almost 25% of workers were so employed. By that same date 70% of factory workers were employed in businesses having 100 or more workers, and only 20% of workers were employed in businesses with 50 or fewer employees. In addition, by 1923 less than one-half of 1% of all U.S. factories employed almost 25% of total factory labor, and no more than 9% of the factories employed 71% of the factory laborers, while 85% of the total number of factories employed less than 20% of the total work force (Laidler, 1931, pp. 4–5).

4. Rawls identifies fair equality of opportunity as, "a certain set of institutions that assures similar chances of education and culture for persons similarly motivated and keeps positions and offices open to all on the basis of qualities and efforts reasonably related to the relevant duties and tasks. It is these institutions that are put in jeopardy when inequalities of wealth exceed a certain limit; and political liberty likewise tends to lose its value, and representative government to become such in appearance only" (1971, p. 278).

5. The contributions of Mary Wollstonecraft in expanding the notion of democratic rights to include women have often been overlooked. For example, see, in this regard, Wollstonecraft (1982).

CHAPTER 4

Dominating Dynamics:
Radical Critiques of Class,
Gender, and Race

It is our conviction . . . that (1) any educational philosophy which is to be significant for American education at the present time must be the expression of a social philosophy and that (2) the social and educational theories and conceptions must be developed with definite reference to the needs and issues which mark and divide our domestic, economic, and political life in the generation of which we are a part.

—Kilpatrick et al. (1933, pp. 35–36)

Strictly speaking, the idea of laissez faire has not been carried out for a long time. Monopolistic ownership of land and of values socially created, privileged control of the machinery of production and of the power given by control of financial credit, has created control by a class, namely, control over production, exchange, and distribution. Hence general and public repudiation of the doctrine of laissez faire in behalf of the principle and practice of general social control is necessary. Education has a responsibility for training individuals to share in this social control instead of merely equipping them with [the] ability to make their private way in isolation and competition. The ability and the desire to think collectively, to engage in social planning conceived and conducted experimentally for the good of all, is a requirement of good citizenship under existing conditions. Educators can ignore it only at the risk of evasion and futility.

—Kilpatrick et al. (1933, p. 69)

These sentiments, published more than 60 years ago, convey some of the central tenets of radical educational analysis. Although not all of the authors (William Kilpatrick, Boyd Bode, John Dewey, John Childs, R. B. Raup, Gordon Hullfish, and V. T. Thayer) who penned *The Educational Frontier* would have accepted the radical label, most saw their task as the reconstruction of society and education. These early-twentieth-century "social reconstructionists" offered broad critiques of capitalism, focusing on the effects it had on schools, teachers, students, and a democratic way of life. Today's radical writers continue in that tradition, presenting critiques of how our social and political contexts affect our public schools, expanding the terrain to include focused analyses of gender and race relations.[1]

CLASS, GENDER, AND RACE

Class, gender, and race are the realms through which the dynamics of oppression, exploitation, and domination are said by contemporary radicals to operate. Class dynamics and the structure of the capitalist economy are condemned as the main contributors to a life that is increasingly partitioned into the haves and the have-nots—both economically and educationally. Patriarchy and sexual exploitation are seen as central components of the "air we breathe," an air that alienates and harms women and young girls both at home and in schools. Racial and ethnic forms of domination are viewed as deep flaws in our national character and as among the forces behind our urban slums, gated suburban communities, and devastated inner-city schools. American society offers a democratic promise, but, the radicals note, due to class, gender, and racial dynamics, it cannot keep it.

Radical Claims

Radicals hold the mirror up to our lives and ask us to see and comprehend the implications of the following portrait. Purportedly we are becoming a nation that impoverishes a significant portion of its population. In 1987 the official poverty line for a family of three living in the United States was $745 a month [Children's Defense Fund (hereafter, CDF), 1989, p.16]. In the late 1980s, one out of five children (18 years of age and younger) and one out of four toddlers and infants (children under 3 years of age) lived in poverty. Among black children, one out of two was poor; among Hispanic children, two out of five were poor (CDF, 1989, p. xvi). The distribution of our national income pie further highlights an expanding gap between the haves and the have-nots. The poorest fifth of Americans garnered 3.8% of the national income, while the richest fifth brought home almost 50% of it. In effect, "the gap between the rich and the poor is now wider than at any time since the Census Bureau began collecting such data in 1947" (CDF, 1989, p.17). And the poor, radicals note, are predominantly women and people of color, while those who are well-off are mostly white.

In this economically divided society, women are significantly more at risk. In the United States women earn 71% of the male wage. Sixty percent of all women employed outside the home work in "clerical, service, or professional positions, and more than 60 percent of these professional women are in female intensive fields such as school teaching and nursing" [American Association of University Women (hereafter, AAUW), 1992, p. 4]. In 1987 more than one-third of female-headed families were poor, compared with approximately 11% of all families (CDF, 1989, p.17). Twenty-five percent of children growing up today live with one parent, and 90% of those single parents are women—most of them the result of separation or divorce (Okin, 1989, pp. 4, 160). Divorce, it is also reported, does not affect men and women equally. "In the first year after divorce, the average standard of living of divorced men . . . increases by 42% while that of divorced women falls by 73%" (Okin, 1989, p. 161). In effect, "the economic situation of men and that of women and children . . . diverge after divorce" (Okin, 1989, p. 161).

This unequal economic picture directly affects the public schools and the students within those schools. In 1991, Jonathan Kozol reported that the resources supplied to schools differed vastly for poor minority and rich white school districts, even when located in the same geographic area. As an illustration of that point, he notes:

> A study, a few years ago, of 20 of the wealthiest and poorest districts of Long Island, for example, matched by location and size of enrollment, found that the differences in per-pupil spending were not only large but had doubled in a five-year period. Schools, in Great Neck, in 1987, spent $11,265 for each pupil. In affluent Jericho and Manhasset the figures were, respectively, $11,325 and $11,370. In Oyster Bay the figure was $9,980. Compare this to Levittown, also on Long Island but a town of mostly working-class white families, where per-pupil spending dropped to $6,900. Then compare these numbers to the spending level in the town of Roosevelt, the poorest district in the county, where the schools are 99% non-white and where the figure dropped to $6,340. Finally consider New York City, where, in the same year, $5,590 was invested in each pupil—less than half of what was spent in Great Neck. The pattern is almost identical to that which we have seen outside Chicago. (Kozol, 1991, p. 120)

This inequity in school funding has its effects on student performance. The National Educational Longitudinal Survey of eighth graders for 1988 shows that among "low SES students, boys are more likely than girls to have repeated at least one grade. This holds almost equally true for black, white, and Hispanic boys. . . . An extraordinary one-third of all low-SES boys are held back at least one grade. [And] in spite of the media attention placed specifically on black boys, 29 percent of low-SES black girls were held back at least one grade" (cited in AAUW, 1992, p. 35).

The curriculum is implicated in these inequities. The AAUW (1992) study entitled *How Schools Shortchange Girls* maintains that "the long-term combined message of both formal curricular materials and informal classroom inter-action patterns is a discouraging one for girls and young women" (p. 60).

Girls' self-esteem drops as they go through school, teachers focus more on male students, and competitive rather than affiliative skill building is the norm. In the arena of race and ethnicity, the curriculum is also a critical issue. Andrew Hacker (1992), noting that historically public schools have not served black children well, maintains that: "The question black Americans will deal with for themselves is how much attention they wish to give to African and African-American history and culture, and how much to mastering the skills needed to succeed in a highly technical world" (pp. 174–175). A curriculum of heritage and culture or a curriculum of technical skills is the choice outlined by Hacker (1992), a choice that he does not view in stark either/or terms but rather in terms of appropriate "doses." It seems to be a choice that once made will need to be pressed vigorously by the black community if it is going to become a reality for black children.

Such is the mirror that radicals hold for others to see. Although numerous conceptual and political differences exist among those who examine and condemn the dynamics of class, gender, or ethnic domination, what brings them together is a concern for the subordination of others; a recognition that this subordination is a patterned, structured reality; and an understanding that class, gender, and racial dynamics are frequently intertwined. Radicals argue that various forms of economic, gender, and racial domination significantly diminish and constrain the life chances of certain groups. Opportunities for rich and fulfilling lives among people of color, the poor, and women are drastically diminished. Capitalism, patriarchy, and racism—forms of structured and patterned modes of domination—create significant and unnecessary constraints on people's lives. Educational institutions, radicals say, are part of this process. Public schools, institutions that traditionally have been promised as preparation for participation in a democratic society, do not fulfill that promise. They end up preparing students for roles in an economically limited, racially divided, and gender-biased future. In effect, schools neglect their democratic functions.

Central to the radical orientation is the view that the dynamics of race, gender, and class are structural elements of our society. That is, the domination and exploitation that occur as a result of racist, sexist, or economic discrimination are the result of patterned practices, institutional rules, and regularities that exist in our lives and from which certain segments of society benefit. While some feminists maintain that patriarchy is "simply" the "air that we breathe," they also highlight the patterns and regularities that create this process of domination. Familial patterns of male dominance, women nurturing daughters and sons, the ever-present possibility of male violence, and the sexual auction block of late-adolescent heterosexual relations all contribute to experiences and expectations of gendered oppression. A growing service economy along with a shrinking production effort

create more low-paid service-sector positions and fewer "Detroit- era" production jobs. Students graduating from either high school or college face
the prospect of unemployment or underemployment. School professionals, in trying to meet the demands of their student and parent populations,
end up satisfying very few. And while de jure segregation has been outlawed,
de facto separations and discrimination persist. Early on, black children
learn that the standards of excellence and attractiveness are predominantly
white, that white children have what they desire, and that the property of
whiteness will always evade them. Radicals maintain that their analyses highlight the logic of particular forms of oppression, uncovering and exposing
them for others to see and work against.

The language radicals use to analyze the effects of these dynamics varies. Terms such as *oppression*, *subordination*, *domination*, *exploitation*, and
alienation are used, sometimes interchangeably and at other times dis-
criminately, with the intention of identifying a specific effect and a distinct
felt sense. And while the processes may be different and the felt phenomena distinct, the general claim is that capitalist, racist, and sexist structures
and practices effectively disempower their captive populations. Poor people
of color and women have less power and are, in a significant sense, turned
against themselves and not allowed the necessary freedom to flourish as
human beings. Due to these dynamics, certain groups of people are not
allowed access to the resources and freedoms that others have.

Radicals describe and explain the world, while condemning certain
features of that world. That is, they morally evaluate the effects of class,
race, and gender, maintaining that such dynamics are socially and individually harmful and morally intolerable. The nature of their moral claims differs. At times, race, gender, and class analysts share a sense that these
dynamics represent injustices that are inflicted upon groups; at other times,
distinct moral assessments are issued. In legal theory and in recent feminist moral theory, distinctions have been drawn between an ethic of justice
and ethic of care or virtue (Brenkert, 1983; Fuller, 1973; Larrabee, 1993).
Claims are made that the injuries of class, gender, and racial discrimination are matters of justice and fairness—how we treat other people with
respect to certain moral principles related to equality. Others argue that a
justice framework is too limiting and that an ethic of care and virtue is a
more defensible way to critique the existing harms. Generally this critique
is viewed as emanating from the feminist tradition, but the distinction has
also been drawn in the Marxist tradition (Liston, 1988). Here we will not
provide a solution other than to say that the controversy exists and ought
to be pursued. However, despite this controversy, radicals argue that harms
are inflicted in schools, through the curriculum, and that these harms are
morally unacceptable.

Whether the analysis focuses on gender, race, or class, another feature that is central to the radical perspective is the belief that the dynamics of oppression tend to be intertwined. Most radical scholars claim that the capitalist economy, while generative of social classes, also aids in the exploitation of young people of color and women. In an era with an increased need for consumption, young people of color become one of the target populations. When the economy seems to necessitate that both parents work outside the home, women tend to staff the growing need for service and clerical positions. Many radicals also maintain that patriarchy—the structured domination of women by men—is further fueled by the class structure of a capitalist society and that it operates differentially within distinct classes and among separate ethnic groups. As already noted, women earn 71 cents to the male dollar (AAUW, 1992, p. 4), and male violence directed at women is differentially manifested in the various economic classes. Radicals also maintain that racism is pervasive and that the need for a surplus labor force in capitalist economies augments the creation of an underclass of color (W. J. Wilson, 1990). Skin color and cultural markers "determine" what school and job slots will be filled. Most radicals accept the view that gendered domination and racist practices predate capitalism. While some radical analysts may want to identify one or another dynamic as the central form of oppression, most concede that they are intertwined.

Finally, radicals maintain that the dynamics of class, race, and gender affect students in schools and that schools act to reinforce these dynamics in the broader society. As a result, certain students' life chances are significantly diminished. Radical educational writers document how this occurs—by class, race, and gender—and call for transformed educational environments. They argue that strong correlations between student test scores and racial and economic background point to factors of differential monetary resources and cultural fit rather than features of academic or cognitive ability. Radicals maintain that the inequitable distribution of financial resources has to end. They also argue that by ignoring the assets and heritage that culturally diverse students bring to the classroom, schools end up alienating rather than educating these students. By offering a curriculum that is focused more on competitive than affiliative skills, students are constrained in significant ways; and male and female students are differentially constrained. Radical critiques are often accompanied by alternative suggestions; they frequently outline educational initiatives that follow from the critiques. Their educational agendas, however, vary significantly, depending, to a large extent, on the conception of the oppressive dynamic, the embedded notion of social change, and the perceived connection of these things to schools. When radicals call for educational change, they tend to envision an education that empowers individuals to overcome the deleterious effects of oppression and to critique the set of constraints and rules that support those oppressive systems. They also commonly call for the establishment of forms of solidarity and collective action against social ills.

Thus far we have highlighted, at a general level, the central, shared features of a radical orientation to society and schools. It is time to focus on each realm, noting the particularities of each approach and at the same time highlighting features that all three orientations share.

Capitalism and the Public Schools

> One of the major ironies of our time is that Marxist thought becomes even more relevant after the collapse of communism in the Soviet Union and Eastern Europe than it was before. The explosion of capitalist market forces on a global scale—concomitant with open class conflict, aggressive consumerism, rapacious individualism, xenophobic tribalism, and chauvinistic nationalism—makes Marxist thought an inescapable part of the intellectual weaponry for present-day freedom fighters. (West, 1991, p. xiv)

For many individuals neo-Marxist analyses of schools and society are antiquated academic exercises. Radical analyses focusing on the class structure of capitalism and schooling are said to be out of touch with the times. Members of the new right, having observed the dismantling of the Berlin Wall, argue that it represented the crumbling edifice of the radical-Marxist alternative. Others, operating from a more postmodern perspective, have maintained that class-based radical thought operates on certain illicit intellectual assumptions that are "terroristic" in nature. Despite these critiques, the radical focus on class is a persistent strand in educational and sociopolitical analyses, and it is one that will probably not disappear in the near future. Although the historical roots of this effort within education can be traced to social reconstructionist analyses, more contemporary authors have offered educational analyses rooted in this tradition. Individuals such as Samuel Bowles and Herbert Gintis (1976, 1987), Michael Apple (1979, 1986), and Martin Carnoy and Henry Levin (1985) maintain that in order to understand the inequities and injuries of our present system it is necessary to comprehend the structure and dynamics of a capitalist society. All have turned to the Marxist tradition as a source and impetus for their own educational analyses.

Traditional Marxist analyses maintain that in order to comprehend the structure of people's lives it is necessary to focus on their productive activities. People require food, shelter, clothing, and other objects for their very physical survival. The focus in Marxist analyses tends to be on the ways in which people use, or "appropriate," natural resources to produce the necessities of life. Though all societies must provide for their continued physical existence, the particular way this is accomplished—the relationships among the people engaged in production, the tools available for that purpose, the sort of consciousness and sets of values that go along with that process, in short, the type of economic formation that is dominant—not only creates the conditions of survival but also helps to create the people who engage in that productive life.

To be productive, people must somehow organize and establish relationships with one another. These relationships, of course, vary from one society to another and from one historical time to another. Different forms of production, then, create different types of individuals; different systems of production entail values and ideas that contribute to the formation of those individuals. At the heart of the capitalist mode of production is alienated (wage) labor, the division of people into social classes, private property, the production of commodities, and surplus value.

Fundamental to capitalism is the separation of people into those who control the "means of production"—what Marx (1848/1948) called the bourgeoisie or the capitalist class—and those who must work for a wage but do not control the means of production—what Marx called the proletariat or working class.[2] The means of production refers to (1) the ownership of the "stuff" of production, the tools, materials, resources, and access to some system of markets in which goods can be sold, and (2) control of the productive process itself—decision making about what goods are to be produced, how this is to be accomplished, the pacing of work, and so on. Thus we arrive at a crucial distinction within Marxism: the separation of "conception" from "execution." The bourgeoisie has the power to make decisions about productive activities that the proletariat must then implement. The former group enjoys the results of workers' labor in the form of profits without having to be involved in the physical work of production. Moreover, members of the bourgeoisie receive a salary for their involvement in the process that is considerably higher than that of the workers. They also enjoy a more secure position than do the proletariat, who can be fired from their jobs for any number of reasons. This basic pattern of social inequality, Marxists argue, is fundamental to capitalist modes of production.

Within capitalist production, the interests of the bourgeoisie are focused on accumulating capital or profit. Profit, within the capitalist mode of production, is the "surplus value" that represents the difference between the money paid to the workers and the amount for which goods are sold. The capitalist, to survive within that system of production, must extract more "labor power" from workers than they are paid for; it is this surplus that accounts for the profit of the company that makes it economically viable. The capitalist gains from this process, and it is in his or her interest to ensure the continued expansion of surplus value. The worker, on the other hand, is the victim of exploitation or alienation.

In Marxist analyses of schooling, the public schools are said to contribute to this pattern of social inequality in a number of ways. In their now-classic work on the topic, *Schooling in Capitalist America*, Samuel Bowles and Herbert Gintis (1976) argue that in the United States there have been two notable "correspondences" between capitalism and the schools: (1) between the historically changing structures of class and public schooling, and (2) between the social relations of work and education. They claim that each major change in the educational structure corresponds to a distinct transformation in the U.S. class structure:

> The three turning points in U.S. educational history which we have identified all correspond to particularly intense periods of struggle around the expansion of capitalist production relations. Thus the decades prior to the Civil War—the era of the common school reform—was a period of labor militancy associated with the rise of the factory system. . . . The progressive educational movement—beginning at the turn of the present century—grew out of the class conflicts associated with the joint rise of organized labor and corporate capital. At least as much so, Progressive education was a response to the social unrest and dislocation stemming from the integration of rural labor . . . into the burgeoning corporate wage-labor system. . . . The recent period of educational change and ferment . . . is, in large measure, a response to the post-World-War II integration of three major groups into the wage labor system. . . . (Bowles & Gintis, 1976, pp. 234–235)

According to Bowles and Gintis (1976), "the emerging class structure evolved in accord with these new social relations of production: An ascendent and self-conscious capitalist class came to dominate the political, legal and cultural superstructure of society. The needs of this class were to profoundly shape the evolution of the educational system" (p.157).

Michael Apple and Lois Weis (1983) add to these claims of correspondence by arguing that schools in the United States perform three economic functions. They produce effects that meet the accumulation, legitimation, and production needs of a capitalist economy. Schools produce a stratified and socialized work force, thereby enhancing the accumulation needs of U.S. capitalism. They provide students with a sense that the economic and social system is basically just, thereby helping to legitimate the existing social order. And educational institutions, especially research universities, aid in the production of technically useful knowledge, thus enhancing the production needs of the U.S. economy.

One of the main effects of living in a class-based society for the worker is the experience of alienation. There are several aspects to the process of alienation. First, it is important to note what happens in the process of production itself. Consider, as a case in point, the manufacturing of cabinets. In order for a cabinet company to thrive, it must sell cabinets. These cabinets then become a "commodity"—something to be produced, placed on a market, and sold. In the process of producing this commodity, the proletariat is paid a wage in exchange for a certain quantity of labor power. At the same time the worker, let us suppose, does one small repetitive job on a production line—say, putting the handle on the upper right-hand drawer of bedroom dressers. Note that the worker has little control over the nature of her or his work. Work loses its meaning for that person. Indeed "work" and "life" come to refer to quite distinct, even antagonistic, realms. As a member of the proletariat in capitalist society, workers may "earn a living" but they do not "create a life," at least not one worth living, through their labor. Through their daily work routines, workers become alienated from themselves. One possible result is the search for meaningful engagement in pursuits outside of work or, more negatively, for an escape from the alienation of work through alcohol and other drugs, violence, or sexual exploitation.

Second, when a product becomes a commodity, the worker is alienated from it as well. The commodity has an independent existence and value—namely, the price it will bring on whatever market it is sold on. Rather than containing something that represents the character or personality of the people involved in its creation, the commodity takes on the character of the market conditions that comprise its value within a capitalist economy. It may even become an alien force, opposed to the interests and values of the workers who produce it.

Third, people engaged in capitalist production become alienated from one another. Work within the factory, typified by the assembly line, becomes specialized and fragmented, with individuals assigned increasingly small responsibilities within the overall process. The person who puts the handles on the upper right-hand corner of bedroom dressers may stand next to a person who puts the handles on the upper left-hand corner, while the next person applies a finishing coat of paint, and so on. In compartmentalizing work in this way, people are discouraged from creating solidarity with one another, undermining their ability to see their plight as similar to that of fellow workers who are also "proletarianized."

Fourth, people become alienated from what Marx called our "species being." In urging us to develop our species being, Marx had in mind a normative category, a moral vision of what human beings are capable of. He had in mind a situation in which people freely create, in their own individuality and artistry, objects that capture and express their own identity, that may be freely appreciated by others. Such objects would be created in people's own image, instead of serving the interests of capital accumulation. These products would be encapsulations of their creators rather than commodities to be purchased, used, and then discarded.

In schools, alienation occurs in a variety of ways. If one accepts the picture portrayed by Bowles and Gintis (1976), one sees schools as the sites where students are sorted and selected for their future roles in a capitalist economy. Schools exist to legitimate the capitalist social order, not to enable students to flourish as human beings. The education that occurs in schools is portrayed as impersonal, decontextualized, skill-oriented, and in general lacking in meaning or connection for students. In a similar but slightly more differentiated sense, Jean Anyon (1980) has portrayed the public school system as serving up separate curricula for students from distinct economic classes. According to Anyon, as one progresses up the economic-class ladder, the curriculum becomes less regimented and impersonal and more complex, rich, and engaging. Anyon's picture is a picture of a class-specific education. Again the claim is that schools serve the needs of capitalism more than they serve the needs of their students.

Marxists also maintain that in capitalist classrooms the predominant modes of instruction further support this alienation. These claims tend to follow Paulo Freire's (1974) analysis in *Pedagogy of the Oppressed*. There he maintains that most instruction is governed by the "banking model" of education—a model that tends to be transmissive in its orientation to knowledge, docile in its expectations of students, and adaptive with respect to both student and teacher. For Freire (1974), the banking model helps create a situation that he describes as follows:

> In the last analysis, it is men themselves who are filed away through the lack of creativity, transformation, and knowledge in this (at best) misguided system. For apart from inquiry, apart from praxis, men cannot be truly human. Knowledge emerges only through invention and reinvention, through the restless, impatient, continuing, hopeful inquiry men pursue in the world, with the world and with each other. (p. 58)

This pursuit of knowledge does not occur in the banking model. Instead the banking model negates education and knowledge as a process of inquiry, encouraging students to accept a passive role and "adapt to the world as it is and to the fragmented view of reality deposited in them" (Freire, 1974, p. 60).

The picture of people who live in a capitalist economy begins to emerge. For the bourgeoisie, the activities of production are organized in such a way that they are in a position of power to make decisions, extract the labor power of others, reap the benefits of the profits attained through surplus value, and generally maintain a socially privileged position. The position of the proletariat, however, is quite different. As alienated individuals serving the interests of the capitalist class, workers become objects, means, or things within capitalist production. Working for wages rather than for life-production, exploited in the factories owned and controlled by the bourgeoisie, producing commodities that are in neither their personal nor economic interests, workers are constrained unduly by capitalism. The inequities of capitalism constrain individuals such that they cannot develop in communion with others or as more complete and full human beings.

This is hardly an optimistic or rosy picture of life as we know it: one class dominated by another, one the victim of alienation and oppression, the other caught in a web of self-indulgent attempts at power-mongering, with society as a whole worse off for the inequities that are an inevitable component of capitalism. But while some have viewed Marxist social theory as a "pessimistic" and deterministic view of history, others have highlighted it as a realistic theory of struggle and change, with a more nuanced picture of power and resistance.

Working men and women have resisted, and continue to resist, the dictates of the capitalist class and the dynamics of capitalism as a productive system. Through the formation of unions, working people's clubs, political and social groups, and even political parties, people have attempted to reverse the inequalities of social life and assert their own independence. Yet such efforts, thus far at least, have failed to overthrow the current social arrangements of most industrialized nations. Part of the reason for this is that the state, as a peculiarly capitalist state, is able to use its military and police powers to keep working-class organizations in check. The repressive arm of the state has often been used, in the United States and elsewhere, to break strikes by workers, allow others to be employed in workers' places, and keep the factories productive. In this way the state has helped to support and maintain capitalist domination. In addition, the welfare state has not only provided a safety net for the poor and jobless but has also created government initiatives resulting in economic and political policies being enmeshed. Frequently capitalist enterprises have benefited from such "corporate welfare" policies that allow tax breaks, depletion allowances, and special incentives (e.g., to develop "enterprise zones") for various industries and forms of production.

Recently Marxists have also highlighted a tension, an internal contradiction, within the democratic/capitalist state: In a capitalist democracy, the state is responsible for protecting both personal rights and property rights. In a capitalist society, these frequently conflict when the property concerns of corporate capital attempt to run roughshod over individuals and their rights. Conflict persists between property and profit *and* individual rights and prerogatives. This persistent contradiction is identified as one of the ever-present tensions in a democratic capitalist society.

In the Marxist literature on education, the school is frequently portrayed as a state institution or, as Althusser (1971) called it, an "ideological state apparatus." In this conception public schools are viewed as tax-supported institutions that serve particular functions in a capitalist economy and frequently operate as an arena of social conflict. Taking this view, Martin Carnoy and Henry Levin (1985) maintain that schools are part of the democratic state that attempts to adjudicate the inequities resulting from capitalism. In their schema, schools serve two functions: (1) "improving the social position of have-not groups by making relevant knowledge and certification available to them" and (2) "by their very nature" reproducing capitalist social relations of production (Carnoy & Levin, 1985, p. 27).

Another central tension within a capitalist society concerns ideology. While attempts are sometimes made to control people's actions through physical force and the use or threat of violence, there is also a focus on people's thoughts, values, beliefs, and dispositions. As we noted earlier, analysts in this tradition claim that any particular mode of production not only attempts to ensure physical survival but also helps create people with general points of view and commitments. This is the terrain of ideology. In order for capitalism to function effectively, it needs to maintain a certain mental control over what people think of themselves, others, and their respective roles in the world. "Capitalist ideology," then, refers to a set of beliefs and values that maintain the logic of capitalist production. Examples include the belief that people are "naturally" arranged into groups such that some are better (intellectually, spiritually, and morally) than others and thus deserve more, the assumption that competition is a force for good in the world, and the idea that individuals must accommodate themselves to the world as it is rather than change it. If such beliefs become widely shared and taken for granted as "common sense," they function ideologically to promote social stability in a capitalist framework, and they are much more effective than the use of physical force. But there is rarely a smoothly running and efficient "reigning" ideology. Features are contested and challenged so that tensions exist between the "ruling" ideas and alternative ideas. In the United States, ideologies associated with capitalism have been challenged by socialist, environmentalist, and religious groups. The rampant consumerism currently pushed by corporate capital is criticized by child advocate groups and those concerned with life in the inner city. Within adolescent culture one can find groups of students who embrace the commodity fetishism that is now being promoted as well as those who reject it. So while capitalist ideology is an important element in the social configuration, it is not an uncontested one. At its heart Marxist social theory is a theory of history, a theory of historical transformation and change, and a theory of how power is structured by the class antagonisms in capitalist society.

It should be evident that Marxist analysis is not a neutral endeavor. That is, Marxist analyses seem to be motivated and fueled by the conviction that we live in a historically and socially conditioned world that is morally unacceptable. It is a theory in the service of workers and any others who feel the effects of class-based oppression. Generally, Marxists condemn capitalism and schooling in capitalism as a form of injustice and alienation. Usually the ethical content of such descriptors as *alienation*, *domination*, and *exploitation* and their connection to justice are not rigorously analyzed (Liston, 1988, pp.122–164). It is assumed that these forms of social relations are unjust and that, therefore, capitalism is unjust and morally unacceptable. Marxist educators claim that the structure of the larger socioeconomic system is unjust and that schools contribute to the reproduction of that unjust system.

These moral claims are present in recent Marxist analyses. For example, Samuel Bowles and Herbert Gintis (1976) and Paul Willis (1977) criticize the inequalities of schooling in a capitalist society and, by implication, condemn capitalism for its injustices. In both of these analyses the apparent general and shared assumption is that schooling in capitalism subjugates individuals to an exploitative and unequal social system and that such forms of domination and inequality are morally reprehensible. There is a pervasive message in these authors' works: Capitalism is characterized by unequal, repressive, and exploitative social relations, schools help to reproduce these relations, and such a social/educational system is unfair and unjust. Michael Apple (1979) argues explicitly that a standard of justice is integral to the study of schooling in a capitalist society.

> To hold our day-to-day activities as educators up to political and economic scrutiny, to see the school as part of a system of mechanisms for cultural and economic reproduction, is not merely to challenge the prevailing practices of education. . . . The kinds of critical scrutiny I have argued for challenges a whole assemblage of values and actions "outside" of the institution of schooling. . . . It requires the progressive articulation of and commitment to a social order that has as its very foundations not the accumulation of goods, profits, and credentials, but the maximization of economic, social, and educational equality.
>
> All of this centers around a theory of social justice. My own inclination is to argue for something left of a Rawlsian stance. For a society to be just it must, as a matter of both principle and action, contribute most to the advantage of the least advantaged. That is, its structural relations must be such as to equalize not merely access to but actual control of cultural, social, and especially economic institutions. (pp. 11–12)

The commonly accepted basis for Marxist condemnations appears to be a mixture of a rather broad standard of social justice and an elementary conception of freedom.

Marxist Educational Agendas

Finally, we need to consider the educational prescriptions that Marxist educators outline. Marxist educators have identified a spectrum of educational programs ranging from the Dewey-like efforts of the liberal progressive movement, to the humanist efforts similar to the ones that dominate our small liberal arts colleges, to the more "revolutionary" efforts of Paulo Freire's educational praxis. While this variation and broad range of proposals exists, Paulo Freire's *Pedagogy of the Oppressed* has become one of the classic Marxist-inspired educational works. It is in Freire's educational agenda that we find the essential elements of a radical-Marxist pedagogy and curriculum. In Freire's educational effort one of the central notions is education as problem-posing, a problem-posing that focuses on the contradictions of social, political, and economic life so as to empower individuals to take action with others to change the world. Central to this concern for problem-posing and empowerment is the notion of praxis. Roughly, praxis is construed as a recursive movement between thought and action in which reflection upon an action is central to further guiding and informing both future thought and action. For Freire these contradictions emanate from, and the transformative praxis is frequently focused on, the structures and practices of capitalism. When workers are denied the right to conceive and direct their work in concert with others, they are dehumanized. Educational actions that uncover the roots of that dehumanization and then empower individuals to act must liberate both the "student" and the "instructor." According to Freire (1974):

> Problem-posing education, as a humanist and liberating praxis, posits as fundamental that men subjected to domination must fight for their emancipation. To that end, it enables teachers and students to become subjects of the educational process by overcoming authoritarianism and an alienating intellectualism; it also enables men to overcome their false perception of reality. The world—no longer something to be described with deceptive words—becomes the object of that transformative action by men which results in their humanization.
>
> Problem-posing education does not and cannot serve the interests of the oppressor. No oppressive order could permit the oppressed to begin to question: Why? While only a revolutionary society can carry out this education in systematic terms, the revolutionary leaders need not take full power before they can employ the method. In the revolutionary process, the leaders cannot

utilize the banking method as an interim measure, justified on grounds of expediency, with the intention of later behaving in a genuinely revolutionary fashion. They must be revolutionary—that is to say, dialogical—from the outset. (p. 74)

Freire's educational agenda was conceived and has been utilized as a revolutionary educational endeavor, one that treats people humanely and engages them in transforming the class-based oppression of their situation. While others have utilized it in a less than revolutionary fashion, its intent is clear.

FEMINIST ANALYSES:
GENDER, PATRIARCHY, AND SCHOOLS

Sexuality is to feminism what work is to Marxism: that which is most one's own, yet most taken away. . . . Work is the social process of shaping and transforming the material and social worlds, creating people as social beings as they create value. It is that activity by which people become who they are. Class is its structure, production its consequence, capital a congealed form, and control its issue. . . .

Sexuality is the social process through which social relations of gender are created, organized, expressed, and directed, creating the social beings we know as women and men, as their relations create society. As work is to Marxism, sexuality to feminism is socially constructed yet constructing, universal as activity yet historically specific, jointly comprised of matter and mind. As the organized expropriation of the work of some for the benefit of others defines a class, workers, the organized expropriation of the sexuality of some for the use of others defines the sex, woman. Heterosexuality is its social structure, desire its internal dynamic, gender and family its congealed forms, sex roles its qualities generalized to social persona, reproduction a consequence, and control its issue. (MacKinnon, 1989, pp. 3–4)

The parallels and the distinctions between Marxist and feminist analyses are many and varied. Catharine MacKinnon (1989) succinctly captures similarities between the two. But the differences are also crucial and important. In what follows, we highlight features of radical-feminist analyses, features that they share with the radical tradition writ large and that illuminate peculiarly feminist orientations.

Probably the defining feature of recent feminist analysis is that it is centrally concerned with understanding and ending the subordination of women. Patriarchy, construed as the structured domination of women by men, is perceived as the source of this subordination. Just what constitutes patriarchy—how it is structured, operates, and affects women—varies and depends, to some degree, upon the particular analysis. However, few feminists have attempted to delineate an overarching theory of gender/sexual oppression similar to the Marxist analysis of capitalism and class. Catharine MacKinnon (1989) notes the absence of this sort of structural rendition and in recent work attempts to fill this lacuna by developing the outline of a theory of sexual oppression. Hers is a theory that highlights the structured nature of the oppression and one within which a number of recent feminist works can be integrated.

In brief, MacKinnon provides a more fully articulated view of what Adrienne Rich (1986) has called the "understructure" of patriarchy. It is an elaboration that fits well with various feminist examinations of male violence, parenting and familial relations, and heterosexual romantic relations. Here we summarize her view and then move on to consider more specific sites of patriarchal practice. For MacKinnon (1989) a theory is feminist in that it

> centers . . . on the perspective of the subordination of women to men as it identifies sex—that is, the sexuality of dominance and submission—as crucial, as fundamental, as on some level definitive in that process. Feminist theory becomes a project of analyzing that situation in order to face it for what it is, in order to change it. (p. 128)

In order to understand MacKinnon's approach, it is essential to clarify her use of "sex" and "sexuality." Sexuality, in MacKinnon's orientation, is more than shared physical intimacies, sensations, or behaviors. It is, she writes, "a pervasive dimension of social life, one that permeates the whole, a dimension along which gender occurs and through which gender is socially constituted; it is a dimension along which other social divisions, like race and class, partly play themselves out" (1989, p.130). For MacKinnon, sex and sexuality are ineluctable and pervasive features of human existence. MacKinnon conceives sexuality as a very broad social phenomenon, integrally connected to the existing social and political hierarchies and to the pleasurable experience of power. In MacKinnon's (1989) theory, sex and power are intertwined:

> This approach identifies not just a sexuality that is shaped under gender inequality but reveals this sexuality itself to be the dynamic of the inequality of the sexes. It is to argue that the excitement at reduction of a person to a thing, to less than a human being, as socially defined, is its fundamental motive force. It is to argue that sexual difference is a function of sexual dominance. It is to argue a sexual theory of the distribution of social power by gender, in which this sexuality . . . is substantially what makes the gender division what it is, which is male dominant, wherever it is, which is nearly everywhere. (p. 130)

The ways in which this sexual dynamic structures, affects, and manifests itself in our lives is varied and has not been fully elaborated. MacKinnon has not developed a comprehensive theory, and we do not find an analysis of sex and sexuality that actually parallels class and work. And so while radical feminists maintain that gender dominance is a structured matter, the nature of that structure requires further exploration. In this section we highlight additional features of gender dominance. Below we explore briefly the sexual auction block theory of Dorothy Holland and Margaret Eisenhart (1990), Nancy Chodorow's (1978) and Carol Gilligan's (1982) difference theses, Jane Roland Martin's (1981, 1992) critique of standard disciplinary knowledge as male cognitive frameworks, and Sandra Bartky's (1990) and Ann Ferguson's (1989) views of domestic-affective production. We then highlight the alienating consequences of this dominance and discuss educational strategies within the feminist tradition.

In their book *Educated in Romance*, Dorothy Holland and Margaret Eisenhart (1990) argue that patriarchy operates through romantic relationships to curtail young women's career aspirations, in effect further subordinating them to men. In a case study that examines the lives of young women attending two colleges (one predominantly white, the other black), they highlight and underscore the sexual dynamics that occur within young women's college lives. They note that most young women who attended and graduated from college "ended up with intense involvement in heterosexual romantic relationships, marginalized career identities, and inferior preparation for their likely roles as future breadwinners" (p. 4). This occurs, according to Holland and Eisenhart (1990), because of the existing culture of romance. For many women, social and emotional life on campus was affected profoundly by their sexual attractiveness to men, and their perceived social worth depended on their attachment and appeal to particular "valued" men. They write:

> In the process of establishing romantic relationships women exposed themselves to the sexual auction block. On it they faced the possibility of, and in fact often experienced, having their social worth—their attractiveness—impugned. They encountered men who wanted physical intimacy too soon, who made them feel that they were only sex objects, who paid too little attention to them, who let it be known that they were taken for granted, and who spread their attention around to many women and thus cheapened the value of their attention as a sign of worth. (p. 152)

It would seem that the sexual auction block is one way, as MacKinnon phrased it, to reduce a person to a thing.

In feminist work the concept of "gendered differences" has received a great deal of attention and has been the focus of much theorizing. Nancy

Chodorow's (1978) work on the reproduction of mothering provides, we believe, a way to connect sexual difference with sexual dominance, and a way of construing one of the routes through which both sexual dominance and difference are reproduced.[3] Chodorow's thesis is basically this: The fact that it is women who mother affects girls' and boys' development differentially. In particular, the relational capacities of boys and girls tend to differ dramatically, and this affects the differential abilities of men and women to relate interpersonally. Chodorow (1978) states:

> Women's mothering, then produces asymmetries in the relational experiences of girls and boys as they grow up, which account for crucial differences in feminine and masculine personality, and the relational capacities and modes which these entail. . . . From the retention of . . . attachments to their mother, growing girls come to define and experience themselves as continuous with others; their experience of self contains more flexible or permeable ego boundaries. Boys come to define themselves as more separate and distinct, with a greater sense of rigid ego boundaries and differentiation. The basic feminine sense of self is connected to the world, the basic masculine sense of self is separate. . . .
>
> Masculine personality, then, comes to be defined more in terms of denial of relation and connection (and denial of femininity), whereas feminine personality comes to include a fundamental definition of self in relationship. Thus, relational abilities and preoccupations have been extended in women's development and curtailed in men. (p. 169)

The difference thesis is developed further in the work of Carol Gilligan and her associates. Gilligan (1982) has argued that women tend to reason morally in distinct ways, ways that are not captured by the "male" focus on duty, principles, and moral obligation. Women's voice is more concerned with care, nurturance, and maintaining the connection to others. Women speak with a different voice and care and judge in distinct ways. As Gilligan (1982) states:

> The psychology of women that has consistently been described as distinctive in its greater orientation toward relationships and interdependence implies a more contextual mode of judgment and a different moral understanding. Given the differences in women's conceptions of self and morality, women bring to the life cycle a different point of view and order human experience in terms of different priorities. (p. 22)

MacKinnon interprets Chodorow's and Gilligan's difference theses as liberal, and essentially misguided. According to MacKinnon (1989), "when difference means dominance as it does with gender, for women to affirm differences is to affirm the qualities and characteristics of powerlessness"

(p. 51). Supposedly Chodorow and Gilligan elevate differences that are the result of male dominance to the level of universal, ahistorical truths. In doing this they reify a socially constructed disposition, making it seem natural, inevitable, and essential. MacKinnon maintains that in this literature, "women are said to care. Perhaps women value care because men have valued women according to the care they give. Women are said to think in relational terms. Perhaps women think in relational terms because women's social existence is defined in relation to men" (p. 51).

MacKinnon (1989), while raising important points, might be creating a distinction that is too rigid and dogmatic. It is certainly possible, if charitable and flexible, to interpret Chodorow's thesis as an account of how relational differences are currently created and reproduced; further, it could be maintained that such an account can be integrated with a view that construes such differences as elements within a context of structured domination. Because it is women who have been expected to mother, we find that girls have more and boys have less of a relational orientation. If these girls grow up to mother, we will find the situation reproduced due to both psychological dispositions and more structural, familial relationships. Certainly a radical orientation needs to view psychological dispositions within a larger social and historical context. But such a view need not dismiss or denigrate the power of individual lives and dispositions when they are patterned and recur. Gilligan's (1982) work is explicitly psychological, but she is careful to offer an important caveat, one that seems to be a basic assumption in most of her work:

> No claims are made about the origins of the differences described or their distribution in a wider population, across cultures, or through time. Clearly, these differences arise in a social context where factors of social status and power combine with a reproductive biology to shape the experiences of males and females and the relations between the sexes. (p. 2)

Gilligan is aware of the limitations of her study, placing them in a larger context.

MacKinnon's materialist orientation seems to overlook what is entailed in the work, the structure, and the effects of mothering and parenting. Unless one takes a grossly simplistic and dangerously technicized view of parenting, it is clear that someone has to parent, nurture, care for, and attend to children as they grow up. Many of the differences now *ascribed* to women represent dispositions that seem integral to the labor of parenting. As active parents of five children, we sense that a materialist analysis of parental work would add to, not subtract from, the kind of analysis that MacKinnon is proposing. It would contextualize an activity that is in need of further analysis. But we cannot do that here. It would take us too far afield. Instead we will continue with our delineation of the ways in which gender domination is created and re-created. Next we describe Jane Roland Martin's (1981) critique of disciplinary knowledge as an education that denigrates women and the work of the home and then highlight Ann Ferguson's (1989) and Sandra Bartky's (1990) analyses of the household as a way to see the domestic front in a more contextualized manner. Martin's, Ferguson's, and Bartky's analyses underscore additional ways in which gender dominance is secured and maintained.

Jane Roland Martin (1992) has argued that the standard intellectual disciplines (mathematics, the natural and social sciences, history, literature, and the fine arts) "into which a person must be initiated to become an educated person *exclude* women and their works, *construct* the female to the male image of her and *deny* the truly feminine qualities she does possess" (p. 101). In fact, what some might normally think of as bodies of basically unbiased forms of knowledge are in reality forms that "embody a male point of view" (p. 101). Disciplinary knowledge, Martin argues, is male-biased not only in its methods, its canons of objectivity, and its ruling metaphors, but also in its support of a peculiarly spectator view of the world (pp. 90–92). What we have come to think of as a liberal education is, she writes, seriously deficient. The liberally educated person, according to Martin (1982):

> will have knowledge about others, but will not have been taught to care about their welfare, let alone to act kindly toward them. That person will have some understanding of society, but will not have been taught to feel its injustices or even to be concerned over its fate. . . . [The] educated person is an ivory tower person: a person who can reason yet has no desire to solve real problems in the real world; a person who understands science but does not worry about the uses to which it is put; a person who can reach flawless moral conclusions but feels no care or concern for others. (p. 104)

Furthermore, Martin (1992) claims that such a person and such an education are tailor-made for what traditionally have been considered certain high-status male roles in society and certainly not for what have been traditionally considered female roles. If Chodorow (1978) captures ways in which gender differences are created and reinforced in familial relations, Martin (1992) offers an analysis of the ways in which an initiation into forms of knowledge further reinforces gender differences and the high status of men in society.

Another way to see how gender dominance operates and is reinforced is to underscore the manner in which caregiving and relational capacities are utilized and exploited within the household. Ann Ferguson (1989) identifies a sphere of "sex-affective" household production akin to the commodity production of the market. She maintains that four "goods" are produced in this system of sex-affective production: domestic maintenance, children, nurturance (of both men and women), and sexuality. Central to her claim is the proposition that the economic domination of the household by men is analogous to the capitalist ownership of the means of production. Focusing on Ferguson's analysis, Sandra Bartky maintains that just as the ownership of the means of production allows capital to extract surplus labor from the workers, "men's privileged position in the sphere of sex-affective production allows them to appropriate 'surplus nurturance' from women" (Bartky, 1990, p. 100). The exchange is unequal. Commenting further on this situation, Bartky (1990) writes:

> All too frequently, women's caregiving involves an unequal exchange in which one party to this exchange is disempowered by the particular inequalities that characterize the exchange itself. This disempowerment . . . lies in women's active and affective assimilation of the world according to men; it lies too in certain satisfactions of caregiving that serve to mystify our situation still further. Such disempowerment, like the disempowerment of the wage worker, may be described as a species of alienation, i.e. as a prohibition on the development and exercise of capacities, the exercise of which is thought essential to a fully human existence. The capacity most at risk here is not, as in the traditional Marxist theory of alienation, the capacity for creative labor; rather it is the capacity, free from the subtle manipulation of consent, to construct an ethical and epistemic standpoint of one's own. (p. 117)

In this radical-feminist account, sex and power are inextricably intertwined; subordination and domination are bound up with our understanding and experience of gendered practices; and hierarchies of power and gender are meshed together. One central effect of all of this is, as Bartky notes, an experience of alienation—an experience that is similar to and different from the sense of alienation outlined by Marxists.

Bartky (1990) elaborates on this sense of alienation in her *Femininity and Domination*. Alienation, she says, is twofold: It entails the fragmentation of the human personality and a prohibition against the exercise of certain human capacities. Alienation is the process whereby whole human beings are split into different parts and allowed to express some, but disallowed to express other, features of themselves. As Bartky (1990) states: "Alienation occurs . . . when activities which not only belong to the domain of the self but define, in large measure, the proper functioning of the self, fall under the control of others. To be a victim of alienation is to have a part of one's being stolen by another" (p. 32). Marx's theory of alienation focuses on the fragmentation and dehumanization that results from the organization of production under capitalism; it speaks to the alienation that women experience as workers. But, Bartky argues, it does not apply to women as women.

Women undergo a special sort of fragmentation and a loss of being *as* women:

> Women suffer modes of alienation which are absent from Marx's account and which can be distinguished from the ways in which all workers, men and women alike, are alienated under the prevailing system of material production. (Bartky, 1990, p. 34)

One aspect of this alienation lies in the arena of cultural production. Bartky (1990) maintains that most routes for cultural expression, whether they be popular or high culture, are "instruments of male supremacy" (p. 35). The pictures and images that women see of themselves are actually forms of misrecognition:

> Women have little control over the cultural apparatus itself and are often entirely absent from its products; to the extent that we are not excluded from it entirely, the images of ourselves we see reflected in the dominant culture are often truncated and demeaning. Human beings begin to distinguish themselves . . . not only . . . when they start to produce their own means of subsistence, but when they begin to invent modes of cultural expression, such as myth, ritual, and art, which make possible the bestowal of meaning upon their own activity. If this is so, then the prohibition on cultural expression denies to women the right to develop and to exercise capacities which define, in part, what it means to be human. (Bartky, 1990, p. 35)

One consequence of this prohibition is that a woman comes to accept the "male" standard as her own standard: She has been "seduced by a variety of cultural agencies into being a body not only for another, but for herself as well" (Bartky, 1990, p. 41). In effect, Bartky (1990) argues:

> Woman has lost control of the production of her own image, lost control to those whose production of these images is neither innocent nor benevolent, but obedient to imperatives which are both capitalist and phallocentric. In sum, women experience a twofold alienation in the production of our own persons: The beings we are to be are merely bodily beings: nor can we control the shape and nature these bodies are to take. (p. 42)

In radical-feminist analyses, patriarchy is the structure and alienation is one of its prominent effects. While much has been written within the feminist tradition that examines this domain and much more could be said, we think that by outlining aspects of the structure of patriarchy and highlighting its alienating effects, we have emphasized features that feminism shares with the larger radical tradition. In this brief analysis we have not covered many of the important debates within feminism or between feminism and Marxism. Furthermore, we have brought together views (e.g., MacKinnon's and Chodorow's) that are usually regarded as antagonistic. But our sense is that it is a fair view of these aspects of the tradition. Before we move on to the examination of race, we need to bring together aspects of the feminist analysis of educational issues. Like the Marxist approach, feminists attempt to unite thought and action. Next we highlight some of the salient features of a feminist approach to education and pedagogy.

Feminist Pedagogies

For many feminists the "key to feminist theory consists in its way of knowing. Consciousness raising is that way" (MacKinnon, 1989, p. 84). Catharine MacKinnon, along with numerous other feminist writers, has identified consciousness raising as the quintessential method of educational and political progress. In this framework, consciousness raising operates on the assumption that women have experienced and, therefore, have access to the structure of the world. As Carol Roehrs (1994) describes it, consciousness raising is a process whereby women, talking with other women about their personal experiences,

> gradually came to realize that what they thought were individual episodes of oppression were actually part of a pattern of subjugation of women throughout the whole patriarchal society.
>
> Only by talking in depth with other women could this change in perspective occur, moving from the sharing of personal experiences of individual women to the analysis and understanding of the societal oppression of women that exists. Once that transition in thinking occurred, women's frame of reference was forever altered. The process came to be called consciousness raising and remains the essence of the women's movement. Its unique power arose from the confluence of three factors: content (analysis of women's oppression), interactive structure (reciprocity and equality), and epistemological premise (to start from subjective experience). (pp. 3–4)

By starting from women's own experience, interacting with one another so as to understand the dynamics of their oppression, the process of consciousness raising was intended to enable women to critique and transform their situation. It is viewed as one of the central methods for both personal and social transformation, as well as personal, social, and political education.

In addition to the emphasis on consciousness raising, individuals within a variety of feminist traditions have emphasized the importance of critiquing patriarchal presences within the current educational system (Luke &

Gore, 1992; Martin, 1982; Pagano, 1990), and some have argued for the
need to bring to public schooling an emphasis on the three Cs of care,
concern, and connection (Martin, 1992; Noddings, 1992). In *The Schoolhome*,
Martin (1992) maintains that the existing curriculum is outdated and injurious to children. It needs, she argues, to be supplanted with a curriculum
that is much more sustaining and nurturing, one that is focused on creating connections among people and between people and ideas. Martin pro-
poses that the elementary school curriculum be focused on integrative
projects, and she suggests that the endeavors associated with theater and
journalism are two key and potentially powerful ones. In *The Schoolhome*,
Martin conjures up images of students engaged in intellectual, practical,
and meaningful projects—projects that bring the students together as a
community around shared concerns. We need to teach children to care for
one another, teach them to be concerned about the ways in which our institutions demean us, and create places where people can maintain connections with one another and see the connections, not the divisions, in their
understanding of the world around them. Martin's framework offers an
education of both the head and the heart, the mind and the hand. We can
no longer pass off an ivory tower education as an education worth having.
In Martin's educational vision, the three Cs are offered as an essential means
to wed us together in an age that is tearing us apart.

In radical-feminist analyses, patriarchy is understood as structured male
dominance of women and the feminist project has as its goal the end of
that domination. Thus far, we have outlined a number of ways in which
gender domination occurs, including the sexual auction block, the creation
of gender differences, schooling as an immersion in male cognitive frameworks, and the home as the site of domestic-affective production. In each
of these domains patriarchy is created and re-created. Feminists have offered
consciousness raising and an education in the three Cs as avenues to combat,
curtail, and hopefully end this domination. Like other radical approaches,
the feminist tactic is to analyze and act, both educationally and politically.

RACISM, WHITE SUPREMACY, AND EDUCATION

Racial stratification [is] part of the structure of American society, much like
class division. Instead of being a remnant from the past, the social hierarchy
based on race is a critical component in the organization of modern American society. The subordination of people of color is functional to the operation of American society as we know it and the color of one's skin is a primary
determinant of people's position in the social structure. Racism is a structural
relationship based on the subordination of one racial group by another. Given
this perspective, the determining feature of race relations is not prejudice

toward blacks, but rather the superior position of whites and the institutions—ideological as well as structural—which maintain it. (Wellman, 1977, pp. 35–36)

I remember encountering white female insistence that when a child is coming out of the womb one's first concern is to identify gender, whether a male or a female; I called attention to the reality that the initial concern for most black parents is skin color, because of the correlation between skin color and success. . . . In other words to be born light meant that one was born with an advantage recognized by everyone. To be born dark was to start life handicapped with a serious disadvantage. (hooks, 1994, pp. 174–175)

Radical theorists of race maintain that in the United States race, hierarchy, and the economy combine to create systematic oppression for people of color, an oppression that is based in a structure of white advantage—what some call white supremacy. According to these writers it is a complicated tangle of individual attitudes, group advantage, institutional norms, and a market economy—it is much more than "discrimination."[4]

Radicals contrast their enlarged view with the one that most liberals hold. According to these critics, "liberal" talk about racism generally translates to a discourse focused on the views and attitudes that individuals in one group hold about another group based on prejudgment, misjudgment, and a systematic misinterpretation of the facts. Accordingly, racism is viewed as an emotional, unbending frame of mind that harms others. The antidote, within the liberal framework, is education. Summarizing this liberal view, Derrick Bell (1992), a legal scholar and law professor, writes that it is a perspective on racism that purports to solve the problem through education: "Education leads to enlightenment. Enlightenment opens the way to empathy. Empathy foreshadows reform. In other words, that whites—once given a true understanding of the evils of racial discrimination, once able to feel how it harms blacks—would find it easy, or easier, to give up racism" (p. 150). Radical critics argue that this view misses the complexity and complicity of whites in the structure and everyday enactment of white supremacy.

This complexity and complicity is underscored by bell hooks (1989) when she writes about the experiences that caused her to rethink the term *racism* and to replace it with the phrase *white supremacy*:

I try to remember when the word racism ceased to be the term which best expressed for me exploitation of black people and other people of color in this society and when I began to understand that the most useful term was white supremacy. It was certainly a necessary term when confronted with the liberal attitudes of white women active in the feminist movement who were unlike their racist ancestors—white women in the early women's rights movement who did not wish to be caught dead in fellowship with black women. In fact, these women often requested and longed for the presence of black women. Yet when present, what we saw was that they wished to exercise control over our bodies and thoughts as their racist ancestors had—that this need to exercise power over us expressed how much they had internalized the values and attitudes of white supremacy.

It may have been this contact or contact with fellow white English professors who want very much to have "a" black person in "their" department as long as that person thinks and acts like them, shares their values and beliefs, is in no way different, that first compelled me to use the term white supremacy to identify the ideology that most determines how white people in this society (irrespective of their political leanings to the right or left) perceive and relate to black people and other people of color. It is the very small but highly visible liberal movement away from the perspective of overt racist discrimination, exploitation, and oppression of black people which often masks how all-pervasive white supremacy is in this society, both as ideology and behavior. When liberal whites fail to understand how they can and/or do embody white supremacist values and beliefs even though they may not embrace racism as prejudice or domination (especially domination that involves coercive control), they cannot recognize the ways their actions support and affirm the very structure of racist domination and oppression that they profess to wish to see eradicated. (pp. 112–113)

Like Cornel West (1993) and David Wellman (1977), hooks argues that seeing the problem of racism simply as the misperceptions, misjudgments, and irrational claims of prejudice-based outlooks misses and misconstrues the problems that confront us. Certainly these sorts of prejudice and misperceptions persist, but they are neither the only source nor do they create the only consequences of racism. If we are truly to examine racism in U.S. society, radical-racial theorists argue, we need to cast a much broader conceptual net. We must see the connections between the dynamics of racism and the privileges and advantages that whites maintain. By examining some of the various ways recent commentators have looked at racial dynamics, by looking at the sources and consequences of racism and white supremacy, we should be able to understand better how they construe this complicated terrain.

Jennifer Hochschild (1984), in her work *The New American Dilemma*, describes two basic and irreconcilable ways—the anomaly and the symbiotic theses—to view the relationship between racism and liberal democracy. Proponents of the anomaly (what she describes as the liberal) thesis (e.g., Myrdal, 1944) maintain that racial separation and discrimination are odd but sadly understandable phenomena that have occurred in an otherwise healthy and defensible liberal democratic body. Purportedly the problem lies not in some structural or institutional nexus, but rather in the heart and soul of each American. Americans, according to Myrdal (1944), have always been caught in a conflict between the high ideals of a democratic civil society and the more base particularistic conflicts that they encounter in daily life, conflicts arising from jealousy, prejudice, and misunderstanding. According to this approach, white Americans can rise above these base determinations if they want to treat all equally and fairly.

In contrast to the anomaly thesis, there is the symbiotic view:

> Racism is not simply an excrescence on a fundamentally healthy liberal democratic body but is part of what shapes and energizes the body. In this view liberal democracy and racism in the United States are historically, even inherently, reinforcing; American society as we know it exists only because of its foundation in racially based slavery, and it thrives only because racial discrimination continues. The apparent anomaly is an actual symbiosis. (Hochschild, 1984, p. 5)

The symbiotic thesis is developed further when it is connected to Marxist understandings of capitalistic societies. Accordingly, Marxists maintain that U.S. capitalism is closely dependent on a liberal democratic state. A liberal democratic state helps to provide both the justification for and the instruments of a capitalist economy. Liberal democracies maintain that equality and fairness must prevail while facilitating economic development and growth. The task of elected state leaders is to enable and provide for the economic well-being of their constituents. Furthermore, a capitalistic economy thrives on racial hostility and economic discrimination. As Hochschild (1984) explains:

> Employment discrimination permits employers to hire some workers more cheaply and for less attractive jobs than others will accept. It also provides a cushion for economic fluctuations by keeping some workers unemployed or underemployed, reduces competition for scarce higher-level jobs, and creates a class of dependent consumers for the surplus goods of ever-expanding producers. (p. 7)

In short, in liberal democracies capitalism and racism are closely interwoven and interdependent.

Building on Hochschild's thesis of symbiosis, Derrick Bell maintains that these interconnections ensure that any perceived gains for blacks in U.S. society will be either temporary or illusory. White supremacy is able to maintain itself through this acclaimed symbiosis. Civil rights gains have been and will be lost. Color determines one's status and well being. Bell (1992) writes:

> In this last decade of the twentieth century, color determines the social and economic status of all African Americans, both those who have been highly successful and their poverty-bound brethren whose lives are grounded in

misery and despair. We rise and fall less as a result of our efforts than in response to the needs of a white society that condemns all blacks to quasi-citizenship as surely as it segregated our parents and enslaved their forbearers. The fact is that, despite what we designate as progress wrought through struggle over many generations, we remain what we were in the beginning: a dark and foreign presence, always the designated "other." Tolerated in good times, despised when things go wrong, as a people we are scapegoated and sacrificed as distraction or catalyst for compromise to facilitate resolution of political differences or relieve economic adversity. (p. 10)

In Bell's reading, racism is a persistent feature, an almost irremediable aspect, of past and contemporary American society.

The manner in which this racism benefits white Americans can be seen when one examines the issue of resource distribution. In most societies resource distribution is a difficult problem. Who gets what and how much is a perennial issue. David Wellman (1977) highlights this issue in his analysis of white racial advantage:

> If race is one of the basic divisions around which access to resources is determined and if institutional changes demanded by blacks are accommodated, then some groups of whites stand to lose certain advantages. The analogy of a zero-sum game is appropriate. For blacks to gain may mean whites will lose. White people thus have an interest in maintaining their positions of racial advantage. The issues that divide black and white people, then, are grounded in real and material conditions. (p. 37)

In the educational arena, the differences between the tax-based resources that are available for wealthy white and poor nonwhite school districts are part of those material conditions.

In the United States public schools are financially supported through a local property tax augmented by state funds. Very generally, the outline of funding is such that local school districts tax homes and businesses for the basic outlay of school funds. In wealthy and moderate-income districts, this provides sufficient funds for the schools, but in the poorer districts, since property values are lower, resulting funds are significantly lower and often insufficient. When the funds are deemed insufficient, state funds are frequently allocated so that the poorest districts in the state will meet a basic, foundational level of funding. And the problem arises here. For the basic foundational level of funding does not provide resources equal to what the wealthy districts can provide but instead provides a "level of subsistence that will raise a district to a point at which its schools are able to provide a 'minimum' or 'basic' education" (Kozol, 1991, p. 208). Throughout *Savage Inequalities*, Kozol (1991) underscores again and again the existing inequity of available school resources, differences that seem to be "determined by the social class, parental wealth, and sometimes race, of the schoolchildren" (p. 120). We noted earlier in this chapter the disparities among the towns of Long Island. Kozol found similar disparities in the Chicago and St. Louis areas, as well as in Texas and California.

These inequities in school resources have been challenged in state and federal courts by plaintiffs claiming that the funding system is unconstitutional given the wide differential between wealthy and poor districts. In numerous states and a variety of districts, lawsuits have been filed by parents and concerned others in an attempt to rectify these inequities. But, as Kozol (1991) notes, such attempts have generally not fared well:

> Attorneys in school-equalization suits have done their best to understate the notion of "redistribution" of resources. They try instead, whenever possible, to speak in terms that seem to offer something good for everyone involved. But this is a public relations approach that blurs the real dynamics of a transfer of resources. No matter what devices are contrived to bring about equality, it is clear that they require money-transfer, and the largest source of money is the portion of the population that possesses the most money. When wealthy districts indicate they see the hand of Robin Hood in this, they are clear-sighted and correct. This is surely why resistance to these suits, and even to court orders, has been so intense and so ingeniously prolonged. For, while, on a lofty level, wealthy districts may be fighting in defense of a superb abstraction—"liberty," "local control," or such—on a mundane level they are fighting for the right to guarantee their children the inheritance of an ascendant role in our society. (p. 223)

Again and again, Kozol notes, wealthy white districts oppose any distribution of resources that would provide poorer, nonwhite districts with anything more than a basic "foundation." But a "foundation" for what?

Students in those resource-poor schools, the ones located in resource-poor communities, discern the meaning of this situation. As John Ogbu and Maria Matute-Bianchi claim, the meaning that many urban black students discern is that school is not a way to get ahead. In effect they come to believe that "they cannot advance into the 'mainstream' of society through individual efforts in school and society or by adopting the cultural practices of the dominant group. The belief that they cannot 'make it' by following the rules of behavior and practice for achievement that 'work' for Anglos often leads [these students] to adopt 'survival strategies' to cope with the situation" (Ogbu & Matute-Bianchi, 1986, p. 93). Schools and the education therein become fragile options for many urban black students. They are extremely fragile options at a point in time when black civil society is weakened and becoming weaker. Radical-racial analysts argue that our resource-poor schools and resource-poor communities must be seen in the larger context—a context, Cornel West (1993) says, of corporate market institutions and market morality.

West (1993) maintains that "black people have always been in America's wilderness in search of a promised land. Yet many black folk now reside in a jungle ruled by a cutthroat market morality devoid of any faith in deliverance or hope for freedom" (p.16). Schools offer little and what the market offers, says West, is empty and seductive. In a rather telling analysis of the manner in which class, racial, and sexual politics intertwine, West (1993) argues:

> Market calculations and cost-benefit analyses hold way in almost every sphere of U.S. society. The common denominator of these calculations and analyses is usually the provision, expansion, and intensification of pleasure. Pleasure is a multivalent term; it means different things to many people. In the American way of life pleasure involves comfort, convenience, and sexual stimulation. Pleasure, so defined, has little to do with the past and views the future as no more than a repetition of a hedonistically driven present. This market morality stigmatizes others as objects for personal pleasure or bodily stimulation. Conservative behaviorists have alleged that traditional morality has been undermined by radical feminists and the cultural radicals of the sixties. But it is clear that corporate market institutions have greatly contributed to undermining traditional morality in order to stay in business and make a profit. The reduction of individuals to objects of pleasure is especially evident in the culture industries—television, radio, video, music—in which gestures of sexual foreplay and orgiastic pleasure flood the marketplace. (pp. 16–17)

He adds:

> Like all Americans, African Americans are influenced greatly by the images of comfort, convenience, machismo, femininity, violence, and sexual stimulation that bombard consumers. These seductive images contribute to the predominance of the market inspired way of life over all others and thereby edge out nonmarket values—love, care, service to others—handed down by preceding generations. The predominance of this way of life among those living in poverty-ridden conditions, with a limited capacity to ward off self-contempt and self-hatred, results in the possible triumph of the nihilistic threat in black America. (p. 17)

As in our analysis of class and gender dynamics, we have been forced to focus and limit our analysis of race and white supremacy. But it is clear that the effects of white supremacy are part and parcel of both schools and the larger social order.

Responses to Racial Oppression

Within the black community there are and have been numerous responses to this oppressive situation—ranging from separatist to integrationist destinations and calls for both peaceful and violent means. Two distinct but not unrelated responses can be discerned in the work of bell hooks (1994) and Derrick Bell (1992). bell hooks professes, as does Cornel West, the need to affirm the process of love as the practice of freedom. In their own respective ways, both West and hooks maintain the need for critical awareness along with an emphasis on an ethic of love. hooks (1994) writes:

> When I look at my life, searching it for a blueprint that aided me in the process of decolonization, of personal and political self-recovery, I know that it was learning the truth about how systems of domination operate that helped, learning how to look both inward and outward with a critical eye. Awareness is central to the process of love as the practice of freedom. Whenever those of us who are members of exploited and oppressed groups dare to critically interrogate our locations, the identity and allegiances that inform how we live our lives, we begin the process of decolonization. If we discover in our selves self-hatred, low self esteem, or internalized white supremacist thinking and we face it, we can begin to heal. Acknowledging the truth of our reality, both individual and collective, is a necessary stage for personal and political growth. This is usually the most painful stage in the process of learning to love—the one many of us seek to avoid. Again, once we choose love, we instinctively possess the inner resources to comfort that pain. Moving through the pain to the other side we find joy, the freedom of spirit that a love ethic brings. (p. 248)

hooks's and West's emphasis on an ethic of love, on a political movement of coalition building and "cultural" democracy, is met with cynicism by some. For example, Adolf Reed (1995) bemoans the academic posturing that he sees in West's and hooks's analyses and claims that they write for a white, not a black, audience. In contrast to hooks's focus on an ethic of love, Derek Bell offers what he likes to view as a rather realistic approach.

Bell points out that the civil rights movement has again and again failed to attain any lasting achievement. Seeing the history of race relations in the United States as an indication of the failure of our past policies and practices, Bell (1992) calls for what he terms a theory of racial realism, in which there are four distinct themes:

> First, the historical part that there has been no linear progress in civil rights. American racial history has demonstrated both steady subordination of blacks in one way or another and, if examined closely, a pattern of cyclical progress and cyclical regression.

The second theme is economic. In our battles with racism, we need less discussion of ethics and more discussion of economics—much more. Ideals must not be allowed to obscure the black's real position in the socio-economic realm, which happens to be the real indication of power in this country.

Third, we believe in fulfillment—some might call it salvation—through struggle. We reject any philosophy that insists on measuring life's success as the achieving of specific goals—overlooking the process of living. More affirmatively and as a matter of faith, we believe that, despite the lack of linear progress, there is satisfaction in the struggle itself.

Fourth, and finally, are the few imperatives implicit in racial realism. One is that those who presently battle oppression must at least consider looking at racism in this realistic way, however unfamiliar and defeatist it may sound, otherwise black people are bound to repeat with their children what their grandparents suffered. For over three centuries, this country has promised democracy and delivered discrimination and delusions. Racial realism insists on both justice and truth. (pp. 98–99)

Bell's racial realism theory does not offer set or predetermined avenues for change, but he does insist that a very real struggle against the economic and racial subordination of black people must occur.

While a variety of counterracist educational strategies have been proposed, Molefi Kete Asante's (1991/92) educational prescriptions underscore the advantages given to white students and the need to claim for the "African, Asian, and Hispanic child the same kind of experience that is provided for the white child" (p. 29). Central to Asante's Afrocentric curriculum is the notion that today's schools are suffused with white language, white culture, and a "white self-esteem curriculum" (p. 29). In today's schools white children are at an advantage while children of color are further disadvantaged by a curriculum that neither centers nor empowers them. Looking back to an earlier (segregated) era, Asante (1991/92) notes that in his own education he had been "nourished and nurtured by teachers who had mastered the nuances and idiosyncrasies of [his] culture" (p. 29). He goes on to note that in that era, "something was given to black children in those schools that was just as important in some senses as the new books, better educated teachers, and improved buildings of this era. The children were centered in cultural ways that made learning interesting and intimate" (p. 29). From all of this he surmises that children who are centered in their own culture and cultural information are better students, more disciplined, and show greater motivation for schoolwork. In a white culture, privilege is attained partly through the white-centered nature of the school and curricular experience. Asante argues that it is time for other children to receive that centered experience.

CONCLUSION

Whether we consider class, gender, or race, radicals maintain that particular and persistent social dynamics are oppressive and that schools further that oppression. In an age in which a renewed ethos of individualism seems to be growing ever stronger, in which a sense of community seems to be based on where people shop, and in which public schools tend to be viewed as drains on the "public" purse, a radical analysis and agenda seem anathema. But such is the predicament of our current situation. While we happen to think that the radical orientation offers many commendable features, it is an approach that many people find difficult to accept and one that has its own share of problems. Radical analyses and prescriptions are certainly not problem-free. At times radical solutions seem just as dogmatic and undemocratic as the problems they address. Frequently radical descriptive claims and causal analyses require further inspection. Radical analyses are, however, not without supporters or allies. While class may seem like an invisible element on the U.S. landscape, many individuals feel its pain (Rubin, 1976, 1994). The effects of gender and racial oppression are less hidden, and those affected by these dynamics are more likely to speak out. But despite these injuries, many individuals find the radical orientation much too structural or condemnatory. However, we find its descriptions and analyses helpfully pointed and, for the most part, morally defensible. We also think that the radical educational prescriptions aim in some very important directions. Radicals take seriously the interconnections between school and society. Their analyses highlight the ways in which our democratic aspirations are curtailed. Radicals, however, do not simply rely on analyses of our situation, for many maintain that forms of community connection and engaged action are necessary features for transforming our current situation. Their educational prescriptions attempt to weave together the head and the heart, theory and practice. These are, we believe, defensible and commendable directions. In Chapters 6 and 7 we utilize these analyses and prescriptions in formulating what we hope will be an attractive and defensible progressive agenda, while remaining mindful of the views and values of other groups, and of the attractions those views have for large numbers of people in the United States.

NOTES

1. Class, gender, and race are the "traditional" radical dynamics. Some analysts have included a much broader range. Here we focus on the classical trinity since they are the three most vigorously and rigorously analyzed. We hope that in

the next decade the dynamics of sexual identity and homophobia will receive the attention they deserve. Early developments seem promising. For example, see O'Conor (1993/94) and Unks (1995).

2. Traditional Marxist analysis has divided the world into two main classes—workers and capitalists. Here we utilize the dichotomy for heuristic purposes but want to underscore the empirical inaccuracy of such a gross division. Recent Marxist research recognizes the inadequacy of this division but continues to maintain the importance of class structure and class analysis. For an example of this more recent research, see Wright (1985).

3. Because of MacKinnon's criticisms of Chodorow's work, it may seem odd that we would attempt to incorporate Chodorow's thesis in a framework heavily influenced by MacKinnon's understanding of gender dominance. We will address this issue.

4. In this section we will focus on white–black race relations. Trying to take into account additional cultural and racial factors would complicate our task beyond this chapter's focus and probably beyond our ability.

CHAPTER 5

Postmodernism

The value of postmodernism lies in its role as a shifting signifier that both reflects and contributes to the unstable cultural and structural relationships that increasingly characterize the advanced industrial countries of the West. . . . Postmodernism raises questions and problems so as to redraw and re-present the boundaries of discourse and cultural criticism. . . . If there is any underlying harmony to various discourses of postmodernism it is in their rejection of absolute essences.

–Giroux (1991, pp. 17–18)

Postmodern analyses have appeared with increasing frequency over the last several years.[1] They have raised a number of important questions about the role of knowledge claims and forms of rationality (in general and with respect to schooling in particular); the relationship between individual, particularistic situations and larger social contexts; the predicaments of disenfranchised others; and the nature of discourse and meaning. Such questions are unavoidable for all those interested in educational studies. In helping illuminate, for example, the ways in which discourses are hegemonic, technical/rational modes of thought and analysis dominate educational life, and patterns of domination serve to deny authenticity to marginalized groups, postmodernism has contributed significantly to our understanding of the educational world (White, 1992).

In this chapter we examine the general tenets of postmodernism and the nature of educational theorizing as this has been informed by them. Our efforts here, similar to the analyses presented in previous chapters, center on the nature of postmodern social and educational theory, as well as their significance for daily life in and outside of classrooms. The postmodern literature certainly does not speak with one voice—indeed a central component of postmodern thinking is the celebration of divergent voices that deny unitary categorization. One result of this is that the implications for curriculum deliberation and decision making are not always clear. Still, we believe the postmodern perspective is central to the current social and educational debates, and thus we analyze here its major perspectives, ideas, and values as these have been identified by its adherents. We begin by analyzing the meanings of postmodernism and examining the possibilities contained within them. We also look at the assets and some of the problematic features of postmodern analysis. Following that section, we move on to consider some of the paradoxes of postmodernism and then on to consider the possibilities of moral and political action within a postmodern framework.

In contrast to earlier chapters, the tone of our discussion of postmodernism will be somewhat less charitable. This is not because we disagree more strongly with its claims than the claims of some of the previously discussed orientations. Rather, the difference in tone is attributable to three primary factors. First, perhaps because postmodernism has a shorter history than the other orientations we have analyzed, its specific meaning for some of the central concerns of this book is less clearly identifiable. Second, the postmodern literature seems inherently more committed to outlining what it seeks to move beyond rather than what it is moving toward. This detracts from the potential for substantive impact in charting new social and educational courses of action. Third, the forms of language and modes of discourse that typify much postmodern writing seem almost intentionally aimed at rendering dialogue more difficult. This tendency itself has political consequences that are disadvantageous for educational change. These three factors, taken together, serve to remove a good deal of the postmodern discourse from the sort of public debate and disagreement on which education depends, and which this book is aimed at illuminating.

POSTMODERN ANALYSIS

At times the term *postmodern* is used to designate a particular social condition, a historical juncture that is said to capture the fractured world in which we now live (Harvey, 1989; Jameson, 1984). At other times it designates a particular mode of critique or analysis. In what follows we focus primarily on the nature and possibilities of postmodern analysis, and to a lesser extent on the idea that postmodernism names a contemporary social condition.

We can begin by noting that the precise characteristics of postmodernism are less than completely clear. This observation is not meant as a definitive criticism. Indeed, the need to create an unambiguous, analytically rigorous, and precise set of parameters that result in objectively verifiable definitions and categories is often seen as a legacy of modernism and thus rejected by postmodern writers. That is, the search for precise, singular, definitive explications of bodies of thought is regarded as beholden to a spurious epistemology predicated on certainty, objectivity, and generality—qualities that postmodern writers have critically assessed and attempted to replace. A perceived lack of precision within postmodern thought is thus in keeping with one of its central thrusts. While the terms *postmodern*, *poststructural*, *post-Enlightenment*, *postrational*, and *postanalytic* have occurred with increasing frequency, they have been used in a variety of ways to designate new modes of intellectual and cultural criticism that, while often provocative, have multiple and divergent meanings (Dews, 1987; Harvey, 1989; Palmer, 1990; Waks, 1995). Given the multiplicity of writings that have appeared in the last decade, and the rather wide-ranging claims made on their behalf, some clarification of what is meant by postmodernism is necessary.

Postmodernism seems to denote several modes or strands of analysis, but modes that have, in many ways, become interrelated. What postmodern writings have in common is the claim that our current forms of intellectual activity and critique, both radical as well as more mainstream, liberal, and conservative, are fettered by an outmoded intellectual heritage. The bearers of this heritage, postmodernists say, can neither defend their reliance on universal reason nor deliver on their promises of incremental (or revolutionary) progress. Reason and progress—two elements of modernism—elude our practical activities. Our reliance on them has instead hampered our understanding of the social and natural worlds, as they have led us to think that we can systematically categorize and organize the natural and social worlds in ways that will make possible transcendent claims to knowledge and right conduct.

Rather than deal at length with the distinctions among various intellectual positions associated with postmodernism, we will focus on the literature that outlines some of its widely shared themes and concerns.[2] We believe it is possible to identify generally shared tenets that revolve around these views. Generally put, the claims are that: (1) the metanarratives that have typified modernist perspectives are misguided and ultimately futile; (2) knowledge claims cannot be based on a realism that promotes "the myth of the given" or "the metaphysics of presence," but instead are nonrepresentational; and (3) the crucial importance of a multivocal "otherness" makes communality in discourse and action infeasible and/or dangerous.

Against Metanarratives

An often-cited entrance to the domain of postmodernism is provided by Lyotard (1984) in *The Postmodern Condition*:

> I define *postmodern* as incredulity toward metanarratives. This incredulity is undoubtedly a product of progress in the sciences. . . . The society of the future falls less within the province of a Newtonian anthropology (such as structuralism or systems theory) than a pragmatics of language particles. (p. xxiv)

This rejection of metanarratives is related to the postmodernists' embrace of pluralism (in languages through which we create meaning and in interpretations of phenomena which can never be unambiguously known) and renunciation of realism. It leads, for example, to an undermining of the hope to discover or create a true theory or an accurate description of a just society.

The anti-metanarrative theme within postmodern literature is essentially the rejection of social, moral, political, or psychological theories, as well as any metaphysical or epistemological views, that posit a synthetic or natural/historical telos toward which we are inevitably heading or which we might prescribe. There is no "grand scheme" inherent in the natural or social world that is unfolding or capable of being enacted. This perspective, among others, is used to discredit the historical materialism of Marx and Engels, with its presumably determinist progression toward a communist society. It may also be used to undermine religious actions aimed at implementing a conception of brother/sisterhood, a just society, and equality in this world that resonates with the design of the Creator. Postmodern analysts maintain that all such theories are inherently totalitarian and symbolically terroristic in their efforts. For postmodernists maintain that while people have aspired to present a unified representation of the world, a world where particular actions and ideas are united by some broader organizing set of precepts or principles, such a representation is always partial and contingent. Social and physical reality, postmodernists say, is always particular, partial, and fractured.

Not only are substantive, generalized theories rejected for their metanarrative qualities; "reason," too, is subjected to a similar critique and rejected for its totalizing effects. According to postmodern writers, reason cannot deliver universal and valid claims about any alleged reality. Instead, reason, rightly construed, can only provide partial, locally determinate, isolated claims. The works of Foucault are often cited in this context, and his reflections on his own research are illuminating:

> A certain fragility has been discovered in the very bedrock of existence—even, and perhaps above all, in those aspects of it that are most familiar, and most solid and most intimately related to our bodies and to our everyday behaviour. But together with this sense of instability and this amazing efficacy of discontinuous, particular, and local criticism, one in fact also discovers something that perhaps was not initially foreseen, something one might describe as precisely the inhibiting effect of global, totalitarian theories. It is not that these global theories have not produced nor continue to provide in a fairly consistent fashion useful tools for local research: Marxism and psychoanalysis are proofs of this. But I believe these tools have only been provided on the condition that the theoretical unity of these discourses was in some sense put in

abeyance, or at least curtailed, divided, overthrown, caricatured, theatricalised, or what you will. In each case, the attempt to think in terms of a totality has in fact proved a hindrance to research. (Foucault, 1980, pp. 80–81)

Within educational theory, these views are echoed by, among others, Giroux (1988), who claims that "general abstractions that deny the specificity and particularity of every day life, that generalize out of existence the particular and local—that smother difference under the banner of universalizing categories are rejected as totalitarian and terroristic" (p. 14).[3]

With metanarratives and universal claims to reason rejected, postmodern writers claim further that moral deliberation and action cannot serve to generate a global project. Commitments to political revolutions, more gradualist cultural and social transformations, religious struggles, and ecological and social progress are all illusory, self-defeating, and oppressive. Instead, Foucault (1980) says that we must resist the centralizing tendencies of globalizing theories, substituting instead research into "subjugated knowledges" that combine "erudite knowledge and local memories" (p. 83). That is, we must be sensitive to the particularities of social, political, and economic life, as these have been smothered by the pursuit of universality and generalizability celebrated within the modern tradition. Many postmodern writers maintain that the only acceptable arenas are at the local level: "Action now felt to be acceptable [is] of a local, diffused, strategic kind: work with prisoners and other marginalized social groups, particular projects in culture and education" (Palmer, 1990, p. 32).

Postmodernism thus draws a sharp distinction between the immediate and the more distant, the particular and the general, the local and the universal. Consider, using these distinctions, the educational practices associated with Assertive Discipline. In incorporating a form of behaviorism that may successfully train students to act in ways that are desirable, given a particular conception of effective teaching, we may object to this practice on several immediate/particular/local grounds: It reinforces the role of teacher as behavioral manager rather than pedagogical guide; it disrupts the flow of classroom interaction; it provides a system of reinforcements and penalties that students quickly learn to manipulate to their own advantage; it stultifies student–teacher and student–student interaction, and so on. Other critiques of Assertive Discipline interventions, informed by more distant/general/universal moral and epistemological understandings, transcend the locality of those interventions. For example, there are serious ethical questions about treating people as ends rather than means, about emphasizing training rather than educational actions (Dewey, 1916), and about the ethical contours of personal interaction. Such questions and forms of critical analysis are rooted in a body of literature that is removed from the immediate reality of Assertive Discipline as this is practiced in local situations. Nonetheless, that literature can inform the immediate understandings and judgments of teachers who are immersed in those situations. A sharp distinction between the local/immediate and the more removed/abstract would obstruct those understandings.

Anti-Representationalism

Closely connected to the rejection of metanarratives and the preference for more local analysis is the postmodern disavowal of the view that knowledge of the social world can be representational or systematic. The pursuit of such claims to knowledge reflects a hubris of Western rational thought, which is partly to blame for the exploitation of those whose values, customs, and ways of life differed from those supported by purportedly genuine, transcendent knowledge. The postmodern orientation challenges

> notions of cumulative knowledge, scientific progress, and objectivity. The more characteristically postmodern theories of the intertwinement of the symbiotic relationship between power and knowledge amount to an outright rejection of the possibility of validating scientific method or knowledge, on independent, historical, gender- and race-free grounds: hence the dismissal of the time-honored aim of the sciences as the representation of an inviolate and unmediated cultural and natural reality. . . .
>
> Knowing can no longer be conceived as the mirroring of an independent reality or be reduced to the prediction or manipulation of psychic, cultural and natural phenomena. (Kiziltan, Bain, and Canizares, 1990, pp. 353–354)

Modern science has assumed that the natural world exists as an independent, objectively knowable reality that can be observed, analyzed, and categorized. By utilizing "the scientific method," it has been thought that we can construct, test, and confirm/disconfirm hypotheses. Further, through the incorporation of increasingly accurate empirical observations, we can produce incrementally derived generalizations that are verifiable, that cumulatively reveal the immutable laws of the universe. Thus we can generate a science that will allow us to know more and more accurately "the way the world is," through the use of observations, instruments, and generalizations that have a transcendent reliability.

Such perspectives are related to the development of empiricist natural science and to the development of positivism in the social sciences. Regarding the development of modern science, three general convictions were especially instrumental in articulating a view of the physical universe. As Toulmin (1972) puts it, these include the following:

1. The Order of Nature is fixed and stable, and the Mind of Man acquires intellectual mastery over it by reasoning in accordance with Principles of Understanding that are equally fixed and universal.

2. Matter is essentially inert, and the active source or inner seat of rational, self-motivated activity is a completely distinct Mind, or Consciousness, within which all the highest mental functions are localized.

3. Geometrical knowledge provides a comprehensive standard of incorrigible certainty, against which all other claims to knowledge must be judged. (p. 7)

Within these orientations, the natural world is seen as a vast system of interrelated mechanisms governed by fixed, complex laws. These laws govern the movements of physical objects and processes. In a similar way, some have assumed the human mind operates in accord with lawful principles. By incorporating these principles in the process of discovering the regularities of the natural world, we can obtain irrefutable knowledge of the universe.

For positivists, the route by which the social sciences and humanities may become more respectable and productive of genuine knowledge lies in their emulation of the methods and directions of empiricist science. By becoming more rigorous, less emotionally and evaluatively oriented, the social sciences may also issue statements and conclusions based on scientific procedures. The image of the sociologist, in this view, will be attainable by scientific discipline. As John Gillan said in his 1926 presidential address to the American Sociological Society:

> It will be necessary to crush out emotion and to discipline the mind so strongly that the fanciful pleasures of intellectuality will have to be eschewed in the verification process: it will be desirable to taboo ethics and values (except in choosing problems); and it will be inevitable that we shall have to spend most of our time doing hard, dull, tedious, and routine tasks. (cited in Bryant, 1985, p. 138)

The influence of empiricist science and positivism led to a reliance on statistical analysis, progress in knowledge about social reality, and a commitment to value-free inquiry. Such beliefs were thought to assist in the generation of a future that would in important ways be better than the past.

Against such presumptions, postmodernists maintain that with respect to all our worlds—physical, social, and cultural—we can only make interpretive judgments. These judgments are neither objective nor immutable, and they speak, again, to the contingent, particular nature of what we have come to call "reality." Such judgments are always attenuated through forms of language that create multiple interpretations, none of which are more real

or certain than any other. They do not "represent" the physical universe or
social realities but rather interpret them through forms of discourse that
are partial and variable. Postmodern projects involve, typically, narrative
accounts instead of statistical analyses or empirical findings.

In some postmodern accounts, however, the rejection of representational, objective knowledge and systematic accounts of the sociopolitical
world is accompanied by an important qualification. Giroux (1988), for
example, argues that if postmodernism rejects all notions of totality it will
run the risk

> of being trapped in particularistic theories that cannot explain how the vari-
> ous diverse relations that constitute the larger social, political and global sys-
> tem, interrelate or mutually deter and constrain each other. In order to retain
> a relationship between postmodern discourse and the primacy of the politi-
> cal, it is imperative that the notion of totality be embraced as a heuristic de-
> vice rather than an ontological category. In other words we need to preserve
> a notion of totality that privileges forms of analysis in which it is possible to
> make visible these mediations, interrelations, and interdependencies that give
> shape and power to larger political and social systems. (p. 16)

For Giroux the notion of totality needs to be retained for "heuristic" purposes. Yet, given the rejection of metanarratives and the renunciation of
reason as a source of nonparticular, nonlocal claims to knowledge, it is
difficult to see how postmodern writers could ground this commitment to
a totality, or what criteria might be offered to help us make choices about
competing heuristics, analyses, and calls to action. To label a commitment
to a particular social, political, and global totality a "heuristic device" is
problematic within the dimensions of postmodernism itself. In part this is
because it is difficult to see what case could be made, in concert with
postmodernist premises regarding the nature of knowledge, for the choice
of any particular heuristic route rather than some other one. What is there
to appeal to, absent more universal claims to knowledge and principles, that
would lead us to adopt the social, political, and global totality Giroux identifies? If no such appeal can be made, on what basis are we to act? Moreover, we agree that particularistic analyses entrap us in ways that deny the
interconnections and tensions among people, ideas, and social practices and
systems. Yet it is difficult to see why "a notion of totality" should be retained
as a heuristic device, unless there is something beyond this device (which
looks suspiciously as if it must represent something not exclusively local and
particular) that justifies its usage. If such a justification does exist, it is not
clear how it could be squared with the premises of postmodernism that deny
nonparticular knowledge and the possibility of progressive change, tied to
some teleology.

The antirealism emphasis in postmodernism is also related to a philosophy of language that has roots in the views of Saussure (1966) and Derrida (1976). Arguing that linguistics unites a concept (the "signified") and a "sound-image" (the "signifier"), Saussure saw the reality of language in relations between concepts and sound-images, not in what language might refer to in a nondiscursive world. The point, then, is to establish language as a system of signification where the only reality it has is its relation to other signifieds and signifiers. As Saussure (1966) put it, "the important thing in the word is . . . the phonic differences which make it possible to distinguish this word from all others, for differences carry signification" (pp. 117–118). Forms of language rely for their authenticity on other forms of language, for

> whether we take the signified or the signifier, language has neither ideas nor sounds that existed before the linguistic system, but only conceptual and phonic differences that have issued from the system. The idea or phonic substance that an idea sign contains is less important than the other signs that surround it. (Saussure, 1966, p. 120)

In a similar way, Derrida (1976) rejects the "metaphysics of presence" in favor of a system of signs that accentuate "differance." An experience of any kind can be understood as a text, which allows for an ensemble of readings that it and the reader make possible. New readings of texts/experiences are, in fact, often made possible by previous ones. Yet the point of interpreting or reinterpreting a text is not to discover some new knowledge about our social, cultural, or personal worlds, but to create new meanings through the play of signifiers/signifieds. For Derrida (1976):

> No engineer [who utilizes discourse from formal logic and the pure sciences, and aims at exactitude and the discovery of knowledge] can make the "means"—the sign—and the "end"—meaning—become self-identical. Sign will always lead to sign, one substituting the other as signifier and signified in turn. . . . The notion of play is important here. Knowledge is not a systematic tracking down of a truth that is hidden but may be found. It is rather the field "of *freeplay*, that is to say, a field of infinite substitutions in the closure of a finite ensemble." (p. xix; emphasis in original)[4]

Knowing is thus something like being able to interpret or provide meaning to a text/experience, within a system of signs that allows for new substitutions through a kind of intellectual playfulness. Yet taking part in this play of infinite grammatical substitutions will not enable us to more accurately perceive or understand the world, or to act in more insightful or morally compelling ways.

Discussing the inevitability of language as it always accompanies what we have mistakenly thought to be a separate, external world that has an independent existence, Richard Rorty (1989) highlights the importance of metaphor, alternative language games, and poetic imagery as routes to a changed human world. To suppose that there is a separate external world, Rorty tells us, is to be stuck within the linguistic frameworks of our philosophical predecessors. For Rorty, we have no prelinguistic consciousness to which language must be accountable, no deep sense of how things are. Rather, language in this view is the central, nontranscendent, human reality, generating a kind of aestheticism. The creation of new metaphors thus comes to replace the search for more adequate or true theories, insightful explanations, and defensible social actions.

Rorty is attempting to persuade us that our cultural and social worlds are inevitably mediated by the adoption of different languages, that it is through the creation of metaphors that new languages can come to exist, and that such creative acts replace the search for modernist theories and explanations. However, given the anti-representationalism of postmodernism, it is difficult to see on what ("nonplayful") basis we might come to approve one sort of language, on what basis we might choose to create or adopt one new metaphor instead of others, or on what basis such preferences should be expressed. Language is indeed a human creation, and changes in language may project new physical and social worlds. Yet if we lack access to alternative, teleological visions of what those worlds might become whose validity and value lies outside the domain of metaphorically and poetically suggestive language systems, why (on what basis, to what end?) should we adopt those new metaphors, those transformed worlds? If the basis for action is a system of signs and signifiers whose authenticity depends solely on an internal consistency and meaning, we are immediately confronted with a serious moral quandary. For social problems can be encoded in ways that have the effect of reinforcing patterns of social injustice, oppression, sexism, racism, and so on. If all possible encodings are to be judged by their internal/linguistic persuasiveness, with no appeal to moral or political principles that transcend such persuasive forms of language and suggest a world whose value lies in something other than its linguistic/aesthetic appeal, on what basis could we reject, for example, the messages of Mark Koernke, the Michigan-based right wing militia leader (Van Biema, 1995), or David Duke or Joseph McCarthy? To say that we would be "better off" to follow alternative metaphors or languages than the ones used by Koernke or his ilk is to beg the question, unless we can provide some substantive reasons that justify a different sort of world. The possibility of such a justification only makes sense outside the framework of aestheticism Rorty adopts. The alternative world to which such a justification could lead cannot be provided by appealing to the possibility of a new language without some kind of normative basis for the latter's superiority. It is just such a basis—one that is of necessity centered on more general social and moral properties—that postmodern writers reject as totalizing. It would require more than rejecting "the habitual use of a certain repertoire of terms," something in addition to superseding the "old tools which as yet have no replacements" (Rorty, 1989, p. 22).

The challenges to empiricist science and positivism that have been launched during the past generation have, we believe, been insightful and productive (see Bernstein, 1983; Bleier, 1984; Feyerabend, 1978; Harding, 1986; E. F. Keller, 1985; Kuhn, 1970, 1977; Williams, 1961; Winch, 1958). In disclosing the value-ladenness of all claims to knowledge, and in exposing the gender-related biases in the natural sciences, for instance, these critical analyses have created space for new ways of interpreting and responding to events in the natural and social worlds. Similarly, anti-representationalism as a component of postmodern analysis rejects "the metaphysics of presence"—the view that there is some sense in which reality is directly given, without mediation, to subjects. Dissenting from this naive realism results, as we have seen, in the postmodern acceptance of "textualism," a concern with texts as the only source of meaning. Every experience, then, becomes some sort of text, its meaning uncovered through the play of signifier and signified and the development of interpretations.

"Otherness" Versus Commonality

Postmodern writers repeatedly emphasize a concern for the "other"—those who have been oppressed or exploited. Women, people of color, prisoners, children, and the economically underprivileged have, in this view, been left out of reason's grand equation. According to Stephen White (1992), one of Foucault's most valuable legacies is exactly this focus and concern for the other. White (1992) captures one of Foucault's greatest contributions when he writes:

> If the underlying effect of our Western, cognitive machinery—political, philosophical, and psychological—has been to introduce clarity, metanarrational unity, and consensus into our lives, then Foucault's purpose can be described as that of elucidating how an Other is *always* pushed aside, marginalized, forcibly homogenized, and devalued as that cognitive machinery does its work. The other may be other actors, external nature, or aspects of our own physical or psychological life; but in every case, Foucault awakens in us the experience of discord as otherness is generated. (p. 19)

And in the educational arena, Carol Nicholson (1989) notes that once the postmodern orientation is brought into educational practice we must listen to those who are telling stories about what it means to be excluded from a conversation or community because their heroes or heroines are different from those of the dominant group. We need a "rainbow" coalition of postmodernists, feminists, and educators who are committed to the task of making sure that no serious voices are left out of the great conversation that shapes our curriculum and our civilization. (p. 204)

We are acutely aware, as detailed in Chapter 4, of how curriculum in particular and schooling in general have disempowered nondominant groups and of the need to alter curriculum form and content so that they are more expansive and liberating. Indeed, much of our work with students and teachers has been aimed at doing just that (Beyer, 1990; Liston & Zeichner, 1991). Both Nicholson's and White's comments need to be highlighted and underscored.

An emphasis on making sure that voices of the other become heard has led some postmodernists to become suspicious of or hostile to the notion of community. For some postmodern writers, community is necessarily oppressive, patriarchal, and limiting. In this view, the most that might be hoped for is the gathering of voices of the other, within which still more others might be located, themselves to generate discrete voices within increasingly small and homogeneous groups. Such voices will, it is feared by postmodernists, be lost or silenced within larger communities whose interests are opposed to those of the other, and whose commitments to more general principles and forms of reason work against inclusiveness (Ellsworth, 1989).[5]

The notion of community has historically been used by powerful individuals and groups to assimilate differences among people, to homogenize alternative perceptions, ideas, and feelings so as to protect their own power and interests (Welch, 1991). The movement toward a kind of pluralism that will support expressions of difference may lead to alterations in structures of differential power. Postmodern writers have argued that personal and social conditions need to be continually created, re-created, and reinforced so that differences will be valued and respected.

In her essay, "Why Doesn't This Feel Empowering?" Elizabeth Ellsworth (1989) deals with a number of issues that are pertinent to the postmodern emphasis on the other. Ellsworth provides a provocative description of efforts to generate antiracist activities as part of the course "Media and Anti-Racist Pedagogies" in the Department of Curriculum and Instruction at the University of Wisconsin–Madison. The goal of this course was to "define, organize, carry out, and analyze an educational initiative on campus that would win semiotic space for the marginalized discourses of students against racism" (Ellsworth, 1989, p. 302). Writing of the dominating tendencies she sees in the assumptions surrounding critical pedagogy, Ellsworth (1989) comments:

> It has been demonstrated that as a discursive practice, rationalism's regulated and systematic use of elements of language constitutes rational competence "as a series of exclusions—of women, people of color, of nature as historical agent, of the true value of art." In contrast, poststructuralist thought is not bound to reason, but "to discourse, literally narratives about the world that are admittedly partial." (p. 304)

A crucial aspect of genuine empowerment is a rejection of reason, as described in the previous section. Instead, we need to encourage narratives that are necessarily partial. Moreover, the goal of encouraging unfettered, open communication among the members of the course Ellsworth taught—as often celebrated by critical pedagogues—itself turned into a form of repression. This occurred, she tells us, because "open communication" actually denied the power differences between professor and students, white students and students of color, heterosexual and gay and lesbian members of the class, and so on. As she puts it, "Educational researchers attempting to construct meaningful discourses about the politics of classroom practices must begin to theorize the consequences for education of the ways in which knowledge, power, and desire are mutually implicated in each other's formations and deployments" (Ellsworth, 1989, p. 316).

Because of the need to acknowledge the differences that existed within this class—differences that are denied by critical pedagogues who value rational discourse and communal struggle for a fictitious "human betterment"—the participants formed "affinity groups" whose membership could be reshaped as the need to confront alternative forms of oppression arose. As a result, "the differences among the affinity groups that composed the class made communication within the class a form of cross-cultural or cross-subcultural exchange rather than the free, rational, democratic exchange between equal individuals implied in critical pedagogy literature" (Ellsworth, 1989, p. 318). Rejecting any universal characterization of appropriate antiracist activities, proposals for action were to be judged "in light of our answers to this question: to what extent do our political strategies and alternative narratives about social difference succeed in alleviating campus racism while at the same time managing not to undercut the efforts of other social groups to win self-definition?" (Ellsworth, 1989, p. 318).

The recognition of differences that transcend the usual search for commonality, Ellsworth tells us, is a strength, not something to be overcome. Such realization made possible, for members of this class, the fact of interdependency even while difference was not only tolerated but celebrated and protected. The "affinity groups" that formed eventually engaged in interventions to combat racism on campus. One of the conclusions Ellsworth draws from this experience is that there are realities that are unknown and unknowable. This is so because "the meaning of an individual's or group's experience is never self-evident or complete," and "no one affinity group could ever 'know' the experiences and knowledges of other affinity groups"; moreover, the author reports, "social subjects who are split between the conscious and unconscious, and cut across by multiple, intersecting, and contradictory subject positions [cannot] ever fully 'know' their own experiences" (Ellsworth, 1989, pp. 318–319). Yet while the author says that such (at best) partial forms of knowledge name an important reality and not a failure to be overcome or feared, what is genuinely frightening is the situation "in which objects, nature, and 'Others' are seen to be known or ultimately knowable, in the sense of being 'defined, delineated, captured, understood, explained, and diagnosed' at a level of determination never accorded to the 'knower' herself or himself" (Ellsworth, 1989, p. 321).

This discussion of some of what we take to be the central tenets of postmodernism may serve to orient the reader to what we believe are its common strands. They give rise to some complex paradoxes, which we explore in the following section; we conclude with a discussion of its relation to moral and political action.

SOME PARADOXES OF POSTMODERN ANALYSIS

"Standpoints Without Footings"

Postmodernists critique the totalitarian nature of the metanarratives present in modernist thought and offer in its place local, standpoint epistemologies. Having given up the belief that the social world can be understood in any systematic and nonparticular sense, postmodernists maintain that what we are left with is a world in which fragmentation, indeterminacy, and partiality are the defining features. The postmodern claim that knowledge of the social world can only be related through various, discrete, and unrelated standpoints has often been justified by appealing to the works of Nietzsche and Foucault.

In discussing the legacy of Nietzsche and its influence on postmodernism, Callinicos (1990) identifies four Nietzschean theses that are commonly invoked by postmodern writers. One of these is that

> the only attitude appropriate to the seething heterogeneity of the actual world is perspectivism, which recognizes every thought as an interpretation, valid only within a conceptual framework the grounds for whose acceptance lie not

in any supposed correspondence with reality, but in the purpose, construable ultimately in terms of the will to power, which it serves. (p. 65)

There is something clearly paradoxical in this view, especially since it under-lies the concerted efforts of postmodern writers to convince the reader of their claims about the poverty of modernism. As Dews (1987) argues, "if no perspective can claim ultimate validity . . . then the problem of the cor-rect philosophical standpoint is raised by Nietzsche himself" (p. 205). Dews indicates that Nietzsche's answer to this conundrum has two parts. The lack of an ultimate perspective "must be compensated for by a timeless varia-tion of perspectives, none of which lays claim to absolute validity" (p. 205). Further, Nietzsche argues that "there is only a perspective seeing, only a perspective knowing; and the more affects we allow to speak of one thing, the more eyes, different eyes, we can use to observe one thing, the more complete will our 'concept' of this thing, our 'objectivity' be" (p. 205). In other words, our conception of an object is more complete, more compel-ling, if we encourage multiple ways of seeing it, which create multiple interpretations. Though we can never know its "essence," we can develop multiple perspectives of the object—the only kind of "objectivity" that is possible.

According to Dews (1987), this multiple perspective approach is (for Nietzsche) merely preparation and training for the "true philosophical task of commitment and creation" (p. 205). The task of the philosopher is not to discover or uncover but rather to decree and proclaim truths. For Nietzsche, "authentic philosophers . . . are commanders and law-givers: they say 'thus it shall be!', it is they who determine the Wherefore and Wither of mankind. . . . Their knowing is *creating*, their creating is a law-giving, their will to truth is—*will to power*" (Dews, 1987, p. 205; emphasis in original).

This linkage of truth to power is characteristic of Foucault's (1980) work as well. For Foucault, truth is linked "in a circular relation with systems of power which produce and sustain it, and to effects of power which it induces and which extend it[:] A 'regime of truth'" (Dews, 1987, p. 210). Given that truth is related to some nontranscendent perspective, however, how can postmodernism, which offers only one among many possible interpreta-tions, be convincing? That is, what is the epistemological and ethical status of postmodernism as a particular perspective? As Dews (1987) puts it:

If one is interested in doing historical work that has a political meaning, util-ity and effectiveness, Foucault suggests "then this is possible only if one has some kind of involvement with the struggles taking place in the area in ques-tion." Indeed, it is clear that, behind this activist stance, Foucault never aban-dons his fundamental objectivism, since he immediately goes on to distinguish between truth and effectivity. "The problem and the stake was the possibility of a discourse which would be both true and strategically effective, the possibility of a historical truth which could have a political effect." But if Foucault is claiming truth for his historical theories, while insisting on an immanent connection between truth and power, he can only be claiming recognition for the particular system of power with which his own discourse is bound up. The fundamental question which emerges at this point, therefore, a question which is central to Nietzsche's thought, is whether it is possible to secure assent to a discourse by mobilizing a persuasive force entirely disconnected from considerations of veracity. (p. 215)

Unless we consider truth of any significant sort essentially illusory and reducible to power, we cannot escape considerations of veracity. In a world where truth is connected to a "will to power," throwing out concerns for veracity would amount to assured ineffectualness or the use of raw force. Even in the postmodernist flight from the metanarrative and from claims of "universal truth," a concern for the accuracy and veracity of a particular point of view cannot easily be escaped.

This issue arises in contemporary postmodern educational theory. For instance, Patti Lather (1991) is centrally concerned with assessing distinct modes of research. The need to adjudicate between distinct empirical accounts of educational phenomena is recognized by Lather when she explicitly states that even in a postpositivist age there remains a need for empirical rigor (Lather, 1991, Chapter 3). But her avowed concerns for validity frequently become transposed into a focus on the construction of meaning. For example, when she wants to explain existing structural contradictions she maintains:

> For theory to explain the structural contradictions at the heart of discontent, it must speak to the felt needs of a specific group in ordinary language. If it is to spur toward action, theory must be grounded in the self-understandings of the dispossessed even as it seeks to enable them to re-evaluate themselves and their situations. (Lather, 1991, p. 65)

Is offering a reasonable explanation of structural conditions the same as working for group affirmation? Certainly, for an explanation to be rhetorically sound and politically efficacious, it must speak to the felt needs of that group, but there are other methodological issues to be addressed. How does one identify, locate, and explain structures of oppression, much less structural contradictions? Throughout Lather's accounts her focus—consistent with postmodern premises and directions—tends to be on meaning and the construction of meaning, rather than on the analysis and explanation of material conditions or social structures. Even though she speaks of the need to come up with credible data, she does not discuss the ways in which we might investigate the social, material, and structural world.

Lather's preferred research orientation moves from a focus on meaning to the acceptance of regimes of truth. She states that research is "an enactment of power relations; the focus is on the development of a mutual, dialogic production of a multi-voiced, multi-centered discourse. Research practices are viewed as much more inscriptions of legitimation than procedures that help us get closer to some 'truth' capturable through language" (Lather, 1991, p. 112). Given Lather's preference for multiple voices, and assuming that these voices will at least sometimes conflict, we must confront the status and validity of these multiple views—or simply assume they are all equally true (or false), equally revealing (or opaque). Postmodern educational theory cannot fully address these issues inasmuch as it disavows a more comprehensive framework that might adjudicate empirical claims and their interpretation, and rejects a normative structure that might resolve value disputes.[6]

"Talking About Nothing"

Questions of nondiscursive veracity and empirical accuracy presume, to some degree, that our knowledge of the social world refers to a reality that exists, in some fashion, apart from us and our currently operant system of discourse. Such questions presume something very much like "the metaphysics of presence" that postmodernists reject. Of course, any "reality" may be described in various ways and may be more or less accurately rendered for particular purposes; further, such purposes are not necessarily equally valuable. What guidance can postmodernism provide concerning how to choose from among those purposes and descriptions and thus about how to act in the world?

One of the problems with rejecting the "metaphysics of presence" is that if discourses loose all connection to a world outside that particular language system, then "they remove the rational constraints that are supposed to shape discourse, when that discourse aims at nothing beyond itself" (Searle, 1990, p. 40). But even more than this is at stake. Without some sense of a reality beyond the language in use, postmodernists lack intelligibility. Searle (1990) is helpful here:

> The person who denies metaphysical realism presupposes the existence of a public language, a language in which he or she communicates with other people. But what are the conditions of possibility of communicating in a public language? What do I have to assume when I ask a question or make a claim that is supposed to be understood by others? At least this much: if we are using words to talk about something in a way that we expect to be understood by others, then there must be at least the possibility of something those words can be used to talk about. (p. 40)

Consider the very claims of postmodernists that meanings are derived from interpretive readings of texts/experiences, and that differences and the "other" need to be valued. These claims presuppose, for their intelligibility, "that we are taking metaphysical realism for granted" (Searle, 1990, p. 40). What is this text, and how can we value the other if he or she does not exist and cannot be more or less accurately (self-) portrayed and understood, granting the reality of multiple interpretations and portrayals? Without some assumption that our words refer to a world beyond the text, the postmodern stance is reduced to disconnected, literally unintelligible utterances.

Searle (1990) says it is not necessary to "prove" that metaphysical realism is true "from some standpoint that exists apart from our human linguistic practices" but rather that "those practices themselves presuppose metaphysical realism. . . . One cannot within those practices intelligibly deny metaphysical realism, because the meaningfulness of our public utterances already presupposes an independently existing reality to which expressions in those utterances can refer" (p. 40). He adds that, "metaphysical realism is thus not a thesis or a theory: it is rather the condition of having theses or theories. This is not an epistemic point about how we come to know truth as opposed to falsehood, rather it is a point about the conditions of possibly communicating intelligibly" (p. 40).

For postmodernists, then, without some sense of words and referents that extend beyond the signifier and the signified, their talk amounts to nothing or, if it does indeed amount to something, it undermines their own position. Without the possibility of utterances referring to something outside themselves, postmodernism is locked within a circular narcissism, which undermines not only the claims of modernists but postmodern writing as well. Such circularity is especially debilitating for those involved in education, who are confronted daily with choices that call for concrete action and that often carry long-lasting consequences.

Thus far we have identified a number of problems with and paradoxes within postmodernism. Our analysis suggests the following:

1. In spite of the postmodern repudiation of metanarratives, some writers have admitted the need for them, at least as a "heuristic device." Yet this seems contradictory, and the grounds on which to prefer one such device over others are not clear.

2. The rejection of noncontingent, nonlocal moral imperatives in postmodernism makes it difficult to determine how to choose among competing ideas and courses of action, especially given the aestheticism and textualism apparent in postmodern analyses.

3. Communities, especially as they currently exist, often promote

hegemonic practices that deny difference in their search for a homogeneity that will maintain disparities of power; yet it sounds as if the postmodern emphasis on the other can easily lead to the sort of individualism and moral relativism associated with the new right (see Chapter 2).

4. A concern for veracity cannot be avoided unless power is really only another name for truth; in that case, only the pursuit of the former will be efficacious and this will undermine not only postmodernism but all other forms of analysis and critique. If all knowledge is really a will to power, the status of postmodern knowledge is as suspect as any other.

5. While multiple interpretations of actions and events are always possible, our statements about the world must have some nondiscursive reference if our discourse is to be intelligible. It is not clear what postmodern words are being used to talk *about*, if indeed they have no connection to anything outside of discourse itself.

These issues raise important questions about postmodern discourse, since they identify internal contradictions that do not appear easily resolvable. Indeed, they seem to undermine key positions of that discourse itself. In addition to these issues, we need to inquire into the role and value of postmodernism as a force for moral and political action and as a basis for a social theory and an approach to education.

POSTMODERNISM AND MORAL ACTIONS

In 1983, Derrida contributed a piece of writing, "Racism's Last Word," to a catalog accompanying an anti-apartheid art exhibition in Paris assembled by the Association of Artists of the World against Apartheid (Derrida, 1985). His essay was criticized by two American literary theorists, McClintock and Nixon (1986), to whom Derrida (1986) in turn responded. The nature of this debate is relevant and illuminating:

> The main philosophical point at issue was whether or not Derrida's denial of the existence of the "[t]here is no outside-text" was responsible for his failure to attend to the evolution of racial domination in South Africa. Perhaps more interesting is the contrast he draws between apartheid, which he describes as a "concentration of world history" . . . and the opposition to it, which depends on "the future of another law and another force lying beyond the totality of the present." But it is impossible now to anticipate the nature of this "law" and "force." Commenting on the paintings, Derrida says: "their silence is just. A discourse would compel us to reckon with the present state of force and law. It would draw up contracts, dialecticize itself, let itself be reappropriated." (Callinicos, 1990, p. 78)[7]

The difficulty of postmodernism's pointing the way toward reconstructed social, racial, economic, and cultural realities is here crystallized. Locked into a kind of discursive presentism that accompanies the postmodern denial of the metaphysics of presence, future possibilities seem not only remote but beyond justification and construction, while present social realities appear to be beyond reconstruction. What we are left with is a kind of stasis and a resulting political conservatism that seems endemic to postmodernism; again, in reference to Derrida's reaction to the anti-apartheid art exhibit and the issues it raised:

> The resistance to apartheid must remain inarticulate, must not seek to formulate a political programme and strategy: any attempt to do so would simply involve reincorporation into "the present state of law and force" and perhaps even into the "European discourse of racism . . ." we can only allude to, but not (at the risk of "reappropriation") seek to know anything lying beyond "the totality of the present." (Callinicos, 1990, p. 78)

An alternative to apartheid is not nameable because there is no extant system of discourse into which such an alternative could fit without being homogenized and thus marginalized or destroyed. Moral judgments like those condemning apartheid are thus not analyzable outside the system of discourse from which it has presumably been generated; put differently, no alternative to apartheid can be offered because there is no set of extant discursive practices—no existing "pragmatics of language particles" (Lyotard, 1984, p. xxiv)—that will support it. Since relations of discursive practices are the only source of meaning and veracity, alternatives to apartheid must await new discursive practices—even when it is not clear what the source of those new practices might be, how they could be justified, or what enacting them might entail. In the meantime, silence [or what Jo Anne Pagano has referred to in another context as fear of being "exiled in the wilderness" (1990, p. 149)] seems to be the only available response to racial oppression; thus the silence of the paintings in the exhibition assembled by the Association of Artists of the World against Apartheid is "just."

Such a perspective undermines the importance of moral imagination and leads to a dubious role for social and political action. Such realities seem embedded within the postmodern turn. It isolates discourse and seeks to secure meaning through the relations of signs and signifiers, while focusing on the particularities that grow out of enclaves of shared experience. Within these enclaves, some people may decide at a given point in time that "the practice of dialogue . . . is not the most promising way to expend their energies and resources" (Leach, 1992, p. 262). Meaning for the people involved, in such cases, is in danger of becoming separated from political struggles, unable to influence social events.

Such emphases make postmodernism at best a problematic source of possibilities for social change. One of the prerequisites for any sort of social transformation is a moral and political vision of how things might be different and better—of how, for instance, a social formation in which racial equality and pluralism instead of oppression might be both justified and worked toward. Further, such a vision must be accompanied by a clear and accurate description of the current social reality, if we are to understand the importance of praxis in the process of its reconstruction. Postmodernists are correct in pointing to the multiple interpretations of any social or other reality, and in reminding us of the potential marginalization of others within a collective that homogenizes difference. But unless we want to replicate a social and moral relativism that mirrors the kind of moral perspective put forward by the new right, we must find ways to move beyond aestheticism and make judgments about competing normative possibilities. This means three things that are problematic for postmodernists: (1) a theory of language and meaning that moves beyond the world of signifier and signified, while avoiding the positivistic contention that there is a world of atomistic empirical events that allow for veridicality; (2) the development of values and practices that enact a moral vision that is not reducible to present realities yet are not simply idealist constructions; and (3) the articulation of alternative realities that are capable of being realized in a future that we can foresee, if not exactly predict.

Consider again Jonathan Kozol's (1991) *Savage Inequalities*. The author describes a set of fiscal, social, and political conditions that have kept poor and minority children from receiving their share of basic educational resources. Examining the legal, educational, and administrative practices in six urban areas, Kozol describes with particular detail the plight of urban children. He also relates how the financing of public education undermines attempts to reduce "savage inequalities." Kozol conveys with alacrity, outrage, and alarm a situation that is educationally and politically unacceptable. In a rather disarming use of poetics, he relates:

> In seeking to find a metaphor for the unequal contest that takes place in public school, advocates for equal education sometimes use the image of a tainted sports event. We have seen, for instance, the familiar image of the playing field that isn't level. Unlike a tainted sports event, however, a childhood cannot be played again. We are children only once; and, after those few years are gone, there is no second chance to make amends. In this respect, the consequences of unequal education have a terrible finality. Those who are denied cannot be "made whole" by a later act of government. Those who get the unfair edge cannot be later stripped of what they've won. Skills, once attained—no matter how unfair—take on a compelling aura. Effectiveness seems irrefutable, no matter how acquired. The winners in this race *feel* meritorious. Since they also

are, in large part, those who govern the discussion of this issue, they are not disposed to cast a cloud upon the means of their ascent. People . . . are left disarmed. Their only argument is justice. But justice, poorly argued, is no match for the acquired ingenuity of the successful. The fruits of inequality, in this respect, are self-confirming. (Kozol, 1991, p. 180; emphasis in original)

A postmodern perspective, in emphasizing the need for local action within determinate contexts, might well celebrate works such as Kozol's. For they movingly and poetically portray the plight of children caught within a local system of racial and social exploitation, producing narratives that are often submerged within the official rationality of an American capitalist hegemony that denies the authenticity if not the very existence of the other. In this sense we can see *Savage Inequalities* as responding to Foucault's (1980) call to conduct research into "subjugated knowledges" that combine "erudite knowledge and local memories" (p. 83). Such studies are indeed valuable and revealing.

Yet for Kozol, language must be tied in some sense to a reality that exists beyond itself. Moreover, our outrage at the conditions described by the author must be rooted in a moral condemnation of injustice and inequality. However, within the context of social and moral evils, postmodern premises foster an insularity and narcissism of discourse, a particularity of knowledge claims based on aestheticism and textualism, and a lack of substantial moral imagination. This leaves us stranded, without a clear direction to pursue in the alleviation of the inequalities Kozol describes—just as working for an alternative to apartheid seems beyond the grasp of postmodern analyses in the tradition of Derrida.

Given the interrelationships of educational and social theories and practices, it is clear that no substantive changes will take place through exclusively individual initiatives and isolated events. Moreover, the kinds of actions required for significant change must, as we argue in Chapter 6, be guided by genuinely democratic social relations, as part of the principles on which alternative worlds may be constructed. This makes the postmodern emphases on particularity, the local, and the specific problematic as sources of efforts that must be collaborative. While we recognize and concur with the need to create the conditions under which previously silenced voices can be heard, the segmentation of people into groups within which they speak primarily to each other undermines a broadly based, morally informed political project. The commitment must be to the sort of community that endorses solidarity and collaborative moral action even as it seeks to abolish power differentials that deny the authenticity of the other.

As educators we are always and necessarily moral actors—at whatever level we teach, in whatever subject matter we claim competence, with respect to whatever moral framework animates our actions. We are confronted daily with myriad choices that call for the development of reasons to support one course of action over another, the result of which may have profound and long-lasting consequences. It is not easy to see how a postmodern orientation could handle these deliberative features of daily educational life.

The defining question within curriculum deliberation, as outlined in the Introduction, is what knowledge is most worthwhile and what forms of experience are most worth having. Within the public schools, it has become relatively common for many to regard this as exclusively a technical or procedural question—to be answered by appeal to school district or state curriculum guidelines, textbook publishing house materials, tradition, or presumed experts outside the schools. Yet this fundamental curriculum question is at heart a moral, political, and cultural inquiry that can only be adequately dealt with by considering a host of allied questions that take us beyond the classroom door (Beyer & Apple, 1988). In any curriculum there are commitments regarding the kind of people we want students to be and become: how they will act with others, form their identities, shoulder social responsibilities, and exercise and act on their own choices.

Questions of curriculum deliberation are, it should by now be apparent, unavoidably normative in character, mandating political choices that require our most illuminating analyses, our deepest commitments to beneficial social relationships, and our most thoughtful and heartfelt moral imaginations. In the previous three chapters we have analyzed a number of bases for educational decision making that are based in social, moral, and cultural perspectives and assumptions. They present the educator with contrasting perspectives and differing priorities from which to draw in making educational and curricular decisions. Such proposals require, obviously, circumspect examination on their own terms. Equally important, they also must include analyses of present public school realities, examination of larger social and economic trends, and a real consideration of what types of knowledge, experiences, and dispositions are most educationally valuable. Postmodern premises leave us with a diminished capacity to deal with these crucial curriculum questions. They make it difficult to create community while valuing difference, to put forth nonlocal political and moral stances, and to examine the educational terrain for the ways it bestows benefits and injuries. The words and deeds of educators necessarily extend to a world beyond the text.

Consider another educational domain. While an oversimplified analysis, we may distinguish between two approaches to the preparation of teachers. One attempts to equip students with the skills, forms of knowledge, and personality traits that are necessary for the public schools to flourish in their present forms. Such programs place a premium on professional socialization into the patterns of work and meaning that now dominate, experiences in schools designed to ease the transition from college student to professional teacher, and courses that reflect a technical–vocational orientation. They center their efforts on adaptation by preservice teachers to a professional world that has already been defined and, to some extent at least, sanctioned. The other approach to teacher preparation construes professionalism, teaching, and the preparation of teachers quite differently. Instead of a technical–vocational orientation, these teacher educators take a critical, reflective, integrative approach that regards the current realities of schooling as important but not defining features of what the preparation of teachers might be. Emphasis may then be put on the development of critical reflection, a view of teaching as a moral calling, and the need to see the schools of our society holistically (Beyer, 1991; Beyer, Feinberg, Pagano, & Whitson, 1989; Liston & Zeichner, 1987). In either approach to teacher education (and in all others, of course), teacher educators take a moral stand on how the best interests of students, prospective teachers, public school pupils, parents, and larger social groups are served. The choices we make will, in important respects, affect the kinds of teachers we will have in our schools and the kinds of schools we will have in our society.

Both public school and college teachers confront moral and political choices that demand some form of reasoning, decision, and action. At its best, postmodernism has reminded us of the pretention to epistemological objectivity and certainty, as it has pointed out the connections between facts and values, interpretation and perception; the tendency for homogeneous communities to marginalize or ignore others who do not share their perspectives; and the importance of particular, local concerns and conditions. Yet it has also served to diminish the possibility of solidarity across differences, of connecting the local to the general and vice versa, and it has sometimes made all claims to knowledge—empirical or normative—seem equally problematic, as language, metaphor, signs and signifieds produce texts that appear independent of systematic forces and tendencies. More problematically, it is not clear how postmodernism—locked into a presentism that allows little or no room for moral principles or political forays informed by them—could generate the sort of future-oriented platform that could re-create the educational and social worlds. Such a reconstructed social world is, we shall argue, urgently needed.

NOTES

1. A previous version of this chapter was published as "Discourse or Moral Action? A Critique of Postmodernism"; see Beyer and Liston (1992).

2. There is always the danger in this sort of analysis that all postmodern literature will be treated as variations on a single theme. In what follows we attempt to identify common tenets and assumptions within postmodernism, recognizing that not every postmodern analysis will necessarily subscribe, especially with the same emphasis, to these tenets.

3. We would note here the clear use of "universalizing" claims made by Giroux regarding what he considers to be "general abstractions" used by "modernist" writers. Such ironic or self-contradictory claims are, we believe, not an anomaly within postmodern literature.

4. This quotation is from "Translator's Preface" to Derrida (1976); the quote within this citation is from Derrida (1976).

5. For a critique of this view, see Burbules and Rice (1991).

6. For a similar critique of "social moral relativism" as this sometimes is embodied in critical educational theory, see Beyer and Wood (1986).

7. The quotation within this citation is from Derrida (1985, p. 299).

CHAPTER 6

Our Social
and Democratic Vision:
Toward a New Progressivism

Politics is not simply about the manner in which power adjudicates competing claims for resources. It is also a contest over who we are to become, a contest in which identity, interests, and solidarity are as much the outcome as the starting point of political activity.

—Bowles and Gintis (1987, p. 8)

In previous chapters we considered a number of social, economic, political, and educational traditions and agendas that outline the major schools of thought in what have come to be called the "culture wars" (Graff, 1992; Shor, 1986). One of the persistent claims of this book is that educational policies and curriculum proposals necessarily contain at least implicit appeals to what is considered socially necessary or good. Some preferred way of life, some world view and set of values, inevitably accompany educational judgments and interventions. We have tried in the preceding pages to identify both the social views and educational positions of the new right, modern liberals, radicals, and postmodernists. So that readers can draw their own conclusions about the positions of these groups, we have tried to outline their points of view fairly.

We have our own perspectives, of course, on which social views are most compelling, what educational agendas most promising; readers familiar with our previous work are aware of that fact and may recall at least the outlines of those perspectives. In this chapter we explicitly develop and defend our social vision. We do more, however, than elaborate our positions and explain how they differ from those articulated by the other groups we have discussed. In considerable measure the current chapter relies on, and responds to, the ideas that have been forwarded by the groups we have analyzed.

As will be clear in what follows, we disagree fundamentally with the central ideas of some of the groups we have taken pains to understand and analyze; predominant among these—because of their current dominance and because of the depth of our disagreements—are the ideas and propos-

158

als of the new right. We reject many of their points of view and policies, just as we regard some new right proponents as engaged in demagoguery. However, we want to remain sensitive to the concerns, fears, and hopes that have motivated many people to pursue social and educational solutions we find wanting—even dangerous and unethical. In constructing alternative social directions and moral guidelines, we acknowledge the real concerns and fears that serve as catalysts for positions with which we strenuously disagree. To fail to appreciate the undergirding anxieties that give voice to those positions is to be politically ineffectual and morally self-righteous.

This chapter, therefore, often returns to issues raised by advocates of the groups we have analyzed, in an effort to respond to important themes and ideas. We build on these, positively and negatively, in creating our own vision. A central portion of this vision deals with the meaning of democracy and democratic values, as we articulate an understanding of social life that can be integrated with particular educational reforms. Those reforms occupy us in Chapter 7.

A SOCIAL VISION

Freedom, Moral Discourse, and Individualism

On the morning after the congressional elections of November 1994, Newt Gingrich was pleased to announce that the electorate had "chosen freedom" in ushering in a "Republican Revolution" that included a "Contract with America." Against the picture of a bloated, ineffectual, costly, and largely indifferent federal bureaucracy, the new right claimed, voters had made clear their commitment to privatization, budget balancing, more local governmental control, and a reduction in the welfare state generally. Familiar themes in classical liberalism as well as in the rhetoric of the contemporary new right, the promise of greater freedom and enhanced personal autonomy once again took a significant portion of the political center stage.

A central concept in the current political climate, and one deeply embedded in the history of the United States, is the nature of freedom and its centrality for everyday life. The ability of people to express themselves without fear of reprisal, to undertake actions based on freely chosen ideas and commitments, and to have others engage us in ways that respect our individual autonomy are central ideals for most Americans. In some sense, and in different ways, the freedom to "be left alone"—a message prominently displayed on a Fourth of July float in Bloomington, Indiana in 1995—is often important. Yet the new right's advocacy of "negative liberty," their commitment to at times vicious forms of moral relativism, and their individualistic orientation render their understanding of freedom inadequate as a basis for social life. A similar form of individualism can be seen in the postmodern valorization of "the other" and the centrality of difference. Indeed, we believe there is an interesting commonality between the positions of the new right and those of the postmodernists in terms of their embrace of individualism. Both have implications for the nature of freedom and human association. The recognition by liberals of the importance of the material conditions of life, on the other hand, and how they frequently erode personal liberties for poor and oppressed groups, provides an important corrective to the ideology of the new right and the dominant discourse of individualism. But a concern for the moral and structural causes of those material conditions must be acknowledged and acted on. This concern is central to the development of a new, progressive social vision that goes beyond liberalism while acknowledging its benefits.

Only in the most intellectually hollow and politically uninteresting senses can liberty be understood as allowing people to undertake whatever actions they have the capacity to envision. "Freedom of action," while in many situations obviously indispensable, tells us nothing about what *sort* of action we ought to undertake as a result of the freedom that is sanctioned. And this is precisely the sort of freedom members of the new right hold dear: *freedom from* governmental interference, *from* an organized, centrally planned and developed economic system, and *from* other individuals who seek to coerce us in one way or another. An emphasis on negative liberty is silent on the question of what we are supposed to do with the freedom thus created. And again, for the new right, that is precisely the point: free to do whatever it is that we find meaningful—as long as it does not infringe on the liberties of others—we are not to be constrained by our fellow human beings or by the power of the state. Yet, as Barber (1992) insightfully points out:

> Although we may use the imagery of laissez-faire as the key to our liberty, most people simply do not conceive of liberty in practice as being tied up with solitude, and endless choice. People feel free concretely not simply when they have choices, but *when their choices feel meaningful*; not when there is chaos and disorder in which anything is possible, but when what is possible is a set of life choices *ordered by ethical or religious values* they have chosen for themselves; not when they are left alone, but when they *participate in the free communities that permit them to define common lives autonomously and establish common identities freely*. (p. 25; emphasis added)

Beyond these observations concerning the meaning of liberty in social practice, there are two general problems with the new right's alleged commitment to negative liberty—one conceptual and the other normative.

First, at a conceptual level, it is not clear that a commitment to negative liberty is now, or indeed can ever be, consistently maintained within an even minimally complex social setting. Beyond the ethical dictum against infringing on the liberties of others, there are values, priorities, perspectives, norms, and so on that are indispensable for a group of people who are to live together in any kind of socially interactive environment and that therefore must engender some form of positive freedom. Simply being left alone—psychologically if not literally—allowing "the circle of freedom [to be left] bare" (Novak, 1982, p. 51), leads to ways of life that only the most anarchistic social isolates among us would find tolerable. Indeed, the new right acknowledges this when it consistently recognizes the need for some form of social cohesion—often seen by them as one of the primary functions of education. Given the new right's own individualistic tendencies, there is no obvious sense in which the kind of social feeling they advocate is natural. Therefore, some shared value framework in accord with which people can develop the particular kind of social cohesion they desire must be created and implemented. This framework necessarily extends beyond a bare negative liberty, outlining what people "shall" do and be as well as what they "shall not."

More specifically, the development of a free market economy requires certain kinds of social collaboration. Consistent with that collaboration, the social order envisioned by the new right stipulates certain ways of interacting with one another that will support a market economy. A system of capitalist production requires workers who have particular habits, commitments, states of mind, and character traits—workers are not to be allowed the "freedom" to develop whatever habits or character traits they may find individually or socially meaningful. These habits include, for instance, responsiveness to the demands of supervisors or managers who conceptualize work and outline the steps necessary for production, an ability to separate one's interests and personality from the productive tasks at hand, an efficiency of movement and action, a level of dedication to the purposes of the factory or corporation generally, and so on. These must be operant if work activities are to further the efficiency and profitability of the company or corporation. The same observations apply to the traits that are necessary in order for people to participate at a political level. For the new right, this level of participation is quite minimal, as already discussed. Thus the development and reinforcement of productive and civic habits cannot be left to chance or taken for granted, in either economics or politics. If such habits are not properly instilled through an educational system, they will be developed and reinforced through the productive relations mandated by the economic apparatus and by the culture more generally.

The inevitability of value-laden perspectives that go beyond negative liberty can be seen in the new right's understanding of the current social crisis. The very social criticisms provided by people like William Bennett (1989, 1992), Edward Wynne (1985/86), and Chester Finn (1991) are pointedly aimed at the lack of moral character, especially among poor and minority children. It is those traits of character they want to reestablish through a reformed public school curriculum. Such attempts at "character development" hardly "leave the circle of freedom bare." Instead, they outline an implicit ideal for the student and citizen. The issue here is not whether the new right's analysis of the perceived social crisis and response to it are accurate or insightful. Rather, our conceptual point is that new right spokespersons—like all of us with some social agenda and vision for a good life—cannot consistently maintain the supremacy of negative liberty and at the same time argue, for example, for state-imposed character education. The debate we join is one over conflicting conceptions of what ways of life made possible through positive freedom are most worthy, not over how to constitute a social order that leaves such freedom to be defined as each individual sees fit.

Consider, second, the actual normative claims made by the new right. We believe that the substantive moral precepts and social values they at least implicitly advance are ill considered, thinly developed, and at times repugnant. They are undertaken to support a political agenda at the expense of a sustained analysis, for instance, of the plight of the people whose individual characters they seek to uplift, and without fully considering the causes of social crisis and how they might be dealt with. The character education program of Bennett (1992) and Wynne (1985/86) demonstrates this substitution of political ideology for moral inquiry. Their views do not support a sustained concern with moral deliberation, since they do not reflectively examine the worth of the traditional values they proclaim or the alternative values they ignore. Their analysis also forgets the fact that we frequently find ourselves in situations where moral goods conflict. Instead, the new right imports other values, specifically values connected to particular conceptions of gender, inquiry, and democracy, that are inimical to a morally meaningful, communal life.

An example of this tendency toward truncated, morally insensitive analysis aimed at supporting a political agenda can be seen in the proposal by Edward Wynne (1987) that he believes provides a positive way to approach a morally meaningful education. As we noted in Chapter 2, many new right advocates, including Wynne (1987), want schools to teach both cognitive and moral lessons. He approvingly discusses the process by which an inner-city elementary school staff attempted to alter the allegedly deviant behavior of young female students. In this school, girls who were considered discipline problems were encouraged to take part in the school's "charm class"—a class that stressed proper dress, makeup, poise, good grooming, posture, and etiquette. Wynne (1987) states that "such activities need to be a part of the academic program because academics are an important part of the business of any effective school. If collective activities are segregated from academics, a critical message is being given: Academics are the really important thing for ambitious students" (p. 110).

At one level, the "charm class" example again serves to belie the supposed commitment of the new right to negative liberty, as it attempts to inculcate "problem students" with the "appropriate" values. More crucial for our current purposes, the particular norms taught through the charm class that is applauded by Wynne represent important elements of the substantive political orientation and social vision of the new right. In this specific case, these norms constitute an invitation to young African American girls to become accustomed to a future of being treated as sexual objects whose worth is based on their physical appearance. It is an invitation to a future of domination in a sexually and racially exploitative society, not an exercise in and exhortation for self-enhancement rooted in these girls' inherent worth or grounded in their participation in a morally defensible community. These "problem girls" need to have their character improved, according to this new right message, even if this means asking them to see themselves as "charming young things" in a society that exploits, degrades, and abuses charming young things. Far from a minimalist conception of liberty, this and other value-laden perspectives of the new right serve to ground their social vision within a particular understanding of *positive* freedom. It is precisely that vision, as well as a certain pretense to neutrality, that we find wanting.

Yet we agree that there is a social crisis in the United States that needs urgent attention. Many people seem to feel a sense of resignation or worse about the current state of life in the United States—from the bombing in Oklahoma City in April 1995, to threatened cutbacks in federal spending for programs in health care, the arts, and education, to the horror of parents abusing and even killing their infant children. We even agree with some of the particulars of this social crisis that the new right has identified as problems. Where we part company with them is in the way they explain the crisis and how they propose to deal with it.

Members of the new right misidentify the causes of the social crisis they perceive, as well as the routes toward its alleviation. These shortcomings can be traced in part to the embrace of individualism that forms an elemental component of new right ideology. In their view people are first or "naturally" isolated, atomistic individuals. We do, seemingly for reasons of necessity or convenience, form some kind of social bond from time to time. But such bonds have little value or place outside family life. Instead, we form larger social collectives primarily to avoid, as Thomas Hobbes put it, "that condition which is called war, and such a war as is of every man against every man" (Hobbes, 1651/1958, pp. 104–106). We do not, in this view, form communal bonds to become virtuous, fully developed, humane people. Given this commitment to individualism, and their presumed (or perhaps feigned) allegiance to negative liberty, the new right is unable to grasp the social sources of moral decay and how we may enhance the moral value of communities. They refuse, for example, to examine how the disparities of income and wealth documented by liberals, and the systemic inequities of class, race, and gender documented by radical critics, have themselves been partially responsible for the loss of communities. They are unable to consider how the very development of a free market economy is implicated in this process. Yet it is clear, whatever else we may think about a market economy, that capitalism requires a hierarchical division of labor and is built on economic inequality. Recall that Adam Smith (1776/1910b) himself recognized that "for one very rich man there must be at least five hundred poor, and the affluence of the few supposes the indigence of the many" (p. 199). Dealing with the roots of the current social crisis demands looking at the sources of inequality themselves—including the dynamics of a market economy. While the inequalities of race and gender predate the appearance of capitalism, as noted in Chapter 4, capitalism has been able to utilize those inequalities in furthering its expansion. Members of the new right are unable to recognize or respond to such realities, inasmuch as they are caught up in an untenable individualism and in either a posture of moral neutrality or a commitment to moral conservatism. They bemoan any substantial attention to larger social realities because such attention would allegedly undermine individual responsibility.

Contrary to the presumptions of the new right, a society dedicated to creating moral principles by which citizens can live, and through which they can attain the communal identity necessary for the development and exercise of liberty, must not focus simply on so-called characterless students. As Dewey, for example, noted, all education is both psychological and social. It is the *social* quality of experience, and the values people acquire *by virtue of living within particular social institutions*, that the new right overlooks. As Bowles and Gintis (1987) put it:

> in rejecting the premise of exogenous interests, we argue that an adequate conception of action must be based upon the notion that people produce themselves and others through their actions. According to this conception, action is neither instrumental toward the satisfaction of given wants nor expressive of objective interests, but it is an aspect of the very generation of wants and specification of objective interests. Individuals and groups, accordingly, are not merely to *get* but to *become*. The politics of becoming, we believe,

provides a central corrective to both the normative and the explanatory dimensions of traditional political theory. (p. 22; emphasis in original)

We become who we are, develop character and virtues of one sort or another, in the daily experience of living in social settings. We *become* free through the creation of robust, challenging social circumstances. Schools and other institutions therefore have no choice but to exhibit and encourage the adoption of perspectives deemed morally worthwhile and defensible. The society in which they function must be supportive of moral communities of a sort that have been eroded by the consequences of inequality, individualism, and discrimination that are in significant part the effects of the economic system the new right seeks to defend and further.

In addition to exposing the duplicity in the new right's claim to embrace negative liberty, then, it is important that we see the social vision that undergirds their understanding of positive liberty as ill formed, divisive, and at times morally reprehensible. For example, the moral relativism espoused by writers such as Milton Friedman (1982) offers us a view of racism as equivalent to different "tastes" in music, since extra-individual perspectives that can morally ground or critique our actions no longer exist. (See Chapter 2.) Morally meaningful debate and social sanctions are, then, replaced by personal expressions of preference.

This retreat from moral discourse and judgment does not result in actions (or inaction) that are value-neutral. Rather, as we saw in the "charm class" example, what happens when an emotivist stance is taken on moral issues is that the dominant norms operating in the larger social order provide the moral basis for what will be considered acceptable actions. Just as extant norms of beauty, sexuality, and so forth dominate in that classroom, norms of racism and social inequality become unchallenged and therefore continually infused into actions when we regard them as "matters of taste" rather than as realities requiring moral scrutiny. The dominant moral values that are embedded in social life become reinforced by the kind of withdrawal from moral discourse advocated by Friedman (1982), as well as by the absence of sustained and critical moral analysis by other members of the new right.

The fundamental problem with the perspective of members of the new right in conceiving individual freedom and moral autonomy, in short, is not that it embodies a conceptual incongruency in attempting to embrace a minimalist, negative liberty that is in reality impossible within the confines of any ongoing social life. Rather, it is that in hiding behind a posture of moral relativism, or in seeing moral decay as only a matter of individual character and culpability, it tacitly accepts whatever moral principles and normative structures have in fact become woven into the social fabric. This may be especially true now, at a time of conservative restoration.

Thus our claims regarding freedom, morality, and individualism are multifaceted:

1. That members of the new right are either simplistic or disingenuous when they claim a posture of moral neutrality
2. That negative liberty does not provide a sufficient grounding for any social, political, and economic system, including the one advanced by the new right
3. That the substantive social and moral framework offered by the new right is inadequate to deal with the problems we face as a society because of the individualistic nature of that framework
4. That the emphasis on individual character as the cause of moral decay, as well the route for its improvement, overlooks the social causes of that decay and what is socially required for its elimination.

In sum, we reject the new right's emphasis on negative liberty, moral relativism, and ontological individualism.

Reviving Community

We agree with Bennett (1988), Wynne (1987), and others representing the new right that we are living in a period of daunting social problems. For instance, the crisis in health care and health care insurance, the fiscal problems of many states as well as the federal government, the lack of voter participation even in major elections, the racism especially evident in urban areas, and the actuality of wars and the threat of nuclear arms being used in them even with the end of the cold war document the domestic and international circumstances that make the future problematic.

As already indicated, and in opposition to the new right, we see people as forming identities within determinate social situations—a position affiliated with the modern liberal perspective. In and through engagement with other people, institutional structures, cultural practices, and political situations, people become who they are, and sometimes become other than they used to be. Individuals do, of course, need to be held accountable for their actions—from corporate executives who engage in leveraged buyouts that result in workers losing their pensions, to government officials who break the laws of Congress, to gang members who commit drive-by shootings as a part of their initiation rites. But members of the new right are unable to see that a lack of character is more than an individual failing, that it is related to the ways of life, cultural values and goods, economic patterns, and so on that people engage in and that in significant measure form their character.

Members of the new right are unable to entertain the possibility that the very system of economic production, and the cultural values and practices associated with it, are among the important sources of the moral decay they bemoan. Further, when members of the new right call for a reemphasis on initiation into a larger, more traditional moral order, they also fail to consider the reasons for the collapse of the sort of community that could sustain moral discourse and action. The new right emphasis on individualism and the consumerism growing out of a free market economy are centrally at fault here.

To the extent that we regard people as forming collegial and social attachments only to avoid the perils of living among other individuals whose greater power may overwhelm us, it is not surprising that any notion of a common or social good will wither. And this is how classical liberals and contemporary members of the new right regard people. Further, in embracing a utilitarian ethic, within which the social good is seen as the aggregate of individual utilities, we are led to see social bonds as peripheral or secondary. The postmodern emphasis on "difference," concern for the "other," and dedication to "local" and "particular" situations and forms of knowledge also run counter to any sort of transcendent, extra-individual, or extra-group commitments. We should expect the notion of community to suffer, given these emphases. Against such ideas, we believe rehabilitating a notion of the common good is essential both as a political and moral force if we are to deal with the social and educational problems that confront us.

Apart from a group of people who happen to occupy a particular space at a particular time, the notion of community must include other key features. In order to become a community, people must see that there are interests and priorities that are held in common and that decisions can be reached and actions undertaken jointly. This does not mean that we all agree on every detail of social, economic, and political life, or that there is some overarching sense of uniformity that crushes intellectual and cultural diversity. We agree with those feminists, multiculturalists, and postmodernists who argue that a homogenization of difference has led to the exclusion of people and values. We acknowledge that hierarchical structures have placed a particular set of priorities at the top with which the rest of us must comply. In recognizing the need to develop some notion of a common good, we do not mean to suggest that all meaningful differences must be abolished. On the contrary, we believe that any community remains vital and genuine only when there is continual encouragement to develop, support, and openly express different perspectives and ideas. A community, that is, must actively encourage the expression of alternative perspectives, points of view, and priorities. As we shall see when we discuss our own commitments to democratic values and their place in the social and economic spheres, dissent, debate, supportive environments for the expression of difference, and so on, are vital for communities in which decision making is shared. Far from undermining a notion of a common good and a community identity, we believe that expressions of difference and public discussion of them are constitutive elements of such a notion.

The imperative for dissent as a constitutive element of community is often more difficult to implement than many recognize. We might suppose that simply allowing discrepant views to flourish, as well as providing equal access to public discussions and efforts at shared decision making, are sufficient to encourage the forms of dissent we are recommending. But the notion of a "level playing field" here is specious. For it overlooks precisely those dimensions of unequal power that radical critics have identified and critiqued. That is, when we suppose that we guarantee an open and critical arena for the discussion of ideas and courses of action merely by providing "freedom of speech," we confuse, again, substantive liberty with real liberty and promote a formal equality that is in some ways counterfeit. Challenges to the status quo must recognize that almost always in a hierarchical society like ours there are powerful vested interests—whether of an economic, political, or cultural sort—whose perspectives often define the constitutive "rules of the game" or "common sense." The implicit dynamics of power inscribed in such common sense often reinforce the interests of the most powerful. As we suggested earlier, in discussing the new right posture of moral relativism and an emphasis on negative liberty, remaining aloof from normative disputes does not lessen the value-ladenness of dominant practices and interests. When Wynne (1987) suggests a charm class is the appropriate repository for "disruptive" African American female students, and that charm class embodies particular norms and assumptions related to gender and sexuality, he at least implicitly furthers those norms. When people refuse to acknowledge the value-laden nature of dominant perspectives and ways of interacting that may be unchallenged and taken for granted, and thus invisible, we must reject any pretensions to neutrality. As Barber (1992) puts this point:

> Where is there genuine neutrality in a society riven with differences in power and status? And if apparent neutrality is always belied in the real world by power relations that privilege some speakers before they open their mouths—theirs are the dominant paradigms, they belong to the groups that make the rules, their speech is already part of the background for all speaking, they are privileged by previous education and eloquence—then how can there be genuine equality? (p. 96)

To create genuine, participatory communities that not only allow but value dissent and challenge, we must do more than simply provide a forum for those who disagree. For the constitutive rules, cultural codes, forms of language, modes of analysis, and so on often, by themselves, stifle dissent and create or reinforce hierarchies of one sort or another. This fact necessitates a greater attention to broadly pedagogical issues, specifically to the development of a pedagogical sensitivity that may not be a part of "business as usual," given the power dynamics of contemporary social life and many people's lack of experience with a notion of the common good. This perspective is also of central importance in the ongoing debate concerning "political correctness" in our schools and universities (Barber, 1992, especially chapter 3; Beyer, 1994).

An emphasis on dissent and on the development of pedagogical sensitivities leads us to believe that one of the things that holds people together within genuine (democratic) communities is an openness to the other, to debate, to intellectual conflict, to challenges and responses, and to the kind of empathy that permits us to see the world through others' eyes. This kind of openness is undermined by those (on the left or right) who lack a kind of epistemological humility and interpersonal sensitivity. In this context we recognize the importance of a number of writings affiliated with postmodernism that have undermined the assumptions of certainty that have been a part of the natural and social sciences; they have convincingly criticized the various methodologies that have been thought to offer irrefutable claims to knowledge (Feyerabend, 1978; Foucault, 1980; Gadamer, 1985; Kuhn, 1970; Rorty, 1979). Indeed, these writers, in identifying the need for a more pragmatic epistemology, point to the need to develop communities within which social practices become a primary means for determining the viability of claims to knowledge (Beyer, 1988b; Cherryholmes, 1988; Whitson, 1990).

This is related to a number of provocative ideas raised by Jean Bethke Elshtain (1995) in *Democracy on Trial*. She recognizes and understands the mistrust contemporary Americans have expressed in their elected leaders, in governmental institutions, and indeed in democratic practices as these continue to be lived out. She suggests as a response to this cynicism that we undertake to construct "a new covenant." The terms of this covenant recognize the need for some form of common good while simultaneously valuing disagreement. As Elshtain (1995) puts this:

> Unless Americans, or the citizens of any faltering democracy, can once again be shown that they are all in it together; unless democratic citizens remember that being a citizen is a *civic* identity, not primarily a private sinecure; unless government can find a way to respond to people's deepest concerns, a new democratic social covenant has precious little chance of taking hold. . . . The social covenant is not a dream of unanimity or harmony, but the name given to a hope that we can draw on what we hold in common even as we disagree. (pp. 30–31; emphasis in original)

This sort of openness to disagreement and collegial discontent, however, is not sufficient to establish community bonds of the sort that can support a new commitment to a common good. In addition, people must see that they have interests in common and, more importantly, that there is the possibility of joint, collaborative actions that will further those interests and through which they will attain freedom and personhood more generally. This necessitates creating a set of political and social possibilities through which the intellectual and moral openness already described can be realized in practice. Here there is a sense in which one of the rhetorical messages of new right spokespeople may be of some importance. As they decry the alleged heavy-handedness of the federal bureaucracy and argue for more local decision making, they offer a possible beginning for thinking about reviving community. For given the virtual collapse of a common good in the United States, and the resurgence of an individualistic ethic, it may well be necessary for people to see the potency of communal bonds at a neighborhood or local level before acting in more global, comprehensive ways. The sense of political efficacy that grows out of ventures undertaken by smaller groups may, in short, be necessary before we think about it in larger contexts. Thus we need to start thinking about rebuilding a sense of the common good in less "glamorous" or grandiose terms than we might ideally prefer. If this is so, then our neighborhoods, our workplaces, our schools, our civic groups, and our religious institutions may provide fertile ground for the sort of practical/political work that is necessary for rebuilding community and a commitment to the common good.

Also central to reviving community is the development of normative frameworks and support for forms of moral discourse that can serve as a valuative center for practical action. This valuative center must itself be open to reinterpretation, critical appraisal, and alteration. In part because of a loss of moral discourse in the United States, keeping such a valuative center open to reconsideration will likely be among the most difficult of the responsibilities we will have in re-creating communities. As already suggested, one of the central values that must be respected is the need for difference and conflicting points of view, along with an epistemological humility that tempers claims that are often, in the context of value disputes especially, quite heated. Yet there are examples of this re-creation of communities in which a moral center has been influential. Consider the activities of environmental groups to stop the contamination of drinking water, efforts to reform schools through parental and community involvement, and neighborhood organizing to "take back the night" and make the streets safer, especially for women and girls.

The difficulties inherent in this reassertion of collective, reciprocal discourse and action are compounded by the very reasons for the collapse of moral discourse in the United States. Beyond the assumption of individualism that denies a common good, many members of the new right, as well as others, have tended to regard value disputes as essentially relativistic.

The rejection of authoritative traditions, in different ways, by both modern and postmodern thinkers has affected our understanding of moral disputes and choices. As societies moved from older, aristocratic traditions to more open, human-based and human-defined ones, the way we saw the moral world changed. Whereas before the natural and social worlds were seen as imposing limits, the new human-generated world instead became increasingly regarded as offering opportunities that could be individually chosen and exploited:

> If the world is made rather than received, it is plausible to suppose that there is no limit to human inventiveness. If moral judgments are leaps of faith or expressions of personal identity, we can and perhaps should make our own moralities. If law is nothing more than the will of a legislature or judge, it becomes a brute manifestation of power, available for any purpose, unconstrained by any inner morality. If democracy is the "will of the people," how is that will to be governed? (Selznick, 1992, p. 15)

As political, religious, social, and moral traditions were increasingly challenged and disrupted, people became the arbiters of a range of decisions. These decisions became the province of the individual, disconnected self. In a sense, as Selznick (1992) says, the creation of self-awareness was "purchased at the price of moral disengagement. . . . We fashion our own conceptions of the good; we rely on ourselves, ultimately alone; no safe harbor is to be found in biblical or other unquestioned authority" (p. 15). This displacement of authority is in some important sense a progressive shift in focus: away from totalitarianism of political and intellectual sorts. It offers the possibility of redefining and refashioning human ends and means, undermining authoritarian doctrine and forms of social and political tyranny. Yet in part because of a lack of any other operant standards or institutions to shape the subjectivity that was made possible, we came to regard "sovereign will and freedom of choice [as] expressions of selfhood, and as such . . . self-justifying." Given that perspective, "only *restrictions* on will and choice require justification" (Selznick, 1992, p. 15; emphasis in original). Absent any constraints on what is good or morally obligatory, we have come to see moral judgments as self-defined and self-justifying, contingent on what we like or "turns us on."

We would not suggest here anything like a return to moral and social traditions whose injunctions are to be followed blindly by people helplessly caught within derivative rules that they must mindlessly follow. Indeed, such a picture rejects the importance of dissent and difference that we have already said is central to our notion of community. Such traditions also undermine the kinds of participation in the public sphere that is central to democracy as a way of life, as we shall see in the next section. We are, instead, arguing that something other than self-referential contexts must provide a basis for moral choices as we rebuild community. Such contexts must be provided by democratic, open, egalitarian communities where public debate, reason, and analysis flourish. Equally important is the need to develop empathy, nurturance, caring, and concern, as discussed by a number of important feminists (Larrabee, 1993; Martin, 1992; Noddings, 1984) and by those concerned with the interpersonal dynamics of cultural and political change (hooks, 1989, 1994; West, 1993). (See Chapter 4.)

The Cultural Manifestations of Capitalism

In addition to the kinds of intellectual and social shifts that led to regarding moral judgments as matters of self-definition and expressions of personal taste, we need to keep in mind the dynamics of a free market economy themselves and their cultural consequences. Recall that for many people, from Adam Smith to contemporary "supply-side" economists, the social good is automatically generated through each person pursuing his or her own individual interests. Through the operation of Smith's (1776/1910a, p. 400) "invisible hand," the social good will in fact tend to be more readily attained by the acts of disinterested market players than when we intentionally attempt to promote it. This itself provides a sort of license to distance ourselves from moral concerns and discourse within communities and to allow self-interest to reign. Even in his earlier (1759) work, *The Theory of Moral Sentiments*, Smith (1759/1804) provided a significant emphasis on self-interest. He suggests there that the actual pursuit of wealth is not, in reality, worth the costs it exacts. He does, however, see that self-interested drive as socially *useful*, even as it expresses a sort of illicit aim, in forming people's habits and demeanor. Thus, even in Smith's treatise on moral sentiments, "self-interest is put forward as the driving force of human behavior, and self-interested activity is happily thought to serve the general utility" (Crittenden, 1990, p. 219).

Consider the actual dynamics and effects of capitalist production and expansion, and the social and cultural consequences of those dynamics outside the actual workplace on the formation of community. Liberals noted the deterioration of both work practices and the quality of life of poorly paid and socially vulnerable workers during the Industrial Revolution. Wealth became more and more centralized, while conditions in new corporate structures robbed work of its dignity and meaning. With the increase in economic power came the opportunity to exercise increased political power, whether through legal means (e.g., contributing to political campaigns) or extralegal influences (e.g., intimidating those who would vote for the wrong candidate, hiring influence peddlers to cajole reluctant politicians). The avowed commitment to liberty and opportunity in that context rings hollow indeed.

In addition to these kinds of situations, the moral consequences of the consumptive ethic that infuses capitalist economies must be critically considered as an impediment to moral reflection and action. As more and more products are generated and available, "the good life" becomes increasingly associated with what we are capable of purchasing and consuming. Our social status becomes increasingly tied to the kind of automobile we can afford, the sort of house we have, the number of televisions and appliances we "benefit" from, the technologically cutting-edge computers and related equipment we own, and so forth. Our identity and our worth thereby become associated with these commodities and our ability to purchase them. This makes it seem as if our value as a person is intimately connected to our purchasing power, to the kinds of things we can buy and presumably enjoy. A cult of consumerism is developed as a part of the commodification process that erodes larger claims to moral imperatives. Similarly, a vast array of choices and actions tend to be "marketized" as they become seen as commodities to be produced, inserted in some kind of market, consumed, and then discarded. The culture of capitalism, accordingly, tends to generate a sense of temporariness, a belief that both things and commitments are there for the taking (and then, just as readily, for the "consuming"), after which we move on to the next consumable item or position. When we see even matters of moral choice as equivalent in some ways to options concerning what clothes to try on and, if they satisfy current desire, to "put on" and to subsequently discard when our tastes change, those choices become debased and misshapen. Both material things and valuative decisions become tangential, surface-level "goods" to be tried on, perhaps worn for a time, and replaced by newer, more fashionable "goods."

Consider as a case in point the current trend toward favoring capital punishment as a deterrent to crime. Many governors, legislators, and presidential hopefuls have embraced the death penalty as virtually a cure-all for violent crimes. An advocacy of capital punishment has become almost a badge of honor that demonstrates one's opposition to violent crime, as well as a strategy that is alleged to justly punish offenders. In appealing to public outcries, and perhaps our darkest natures, some politicians take stands that will presumably serve their interests in obtaining or maintaining political office. Yet the actual ability of capital punishment to deter crime is seldom considered or even debated in the public arena. Nor is the moral effect of capital punishment on the society that employs it reflectively considered. Instead a rhetorical appeal to "do something"—even simply to grab the latest headlines—is substituted for moral deliberation and social action. As sound bites take precedence over sustained reflection and debate, moral discourse and deliberation loses out to attractive slogans, to a thin surface reality that treats moral actions (or inactions) as virtually equivalent to advertising gambits. In a sense, "capital punishment" comes to be seen as a kind of "quick-fix" cultural commodity that will deal effectively with social problems by making them disappear.

This is related to another quality of capitalist ideology: the ability to provide immediate satisfaction through the purchase of appropriate goods. Virtually everything that we think contributes to the good life—from electric can openers to swimming pools—can be immediately obtained in a capitalist economy by those with the requisite economic means. Consider the range of items available through "shop-at-home" television channels, programs that promise a healthier, longer life if you only purchase the right home exercise equipment, the opportunity of purchasing by credit card a new car or a vacation trip to Europe. Many people can, by pressing the appropriate series of numbers on a telephone, have delivered a stunning array of goods and services that promise virtually unending happiness and immediate gratification. In a rush to purchase happiness, we tend to lose sight of less tangible, more distant forms of human contentment and satisfaction; "happiness," then, replaces "virtue" in our sensibilities. This sense of happiness is not only transitory but also corrosive of the sort of moral deliberation on which genuine communities rest. It is no wonder that many segments of society are dominated by a personalistic, me-oriented ethos. The shaping of character brought about through the potency of cultural values encouraged by a consumerist society is traceable to the dynamics of capital accumulation.

Beyond Individualism and Consumerism

If we are to challenge and replace the new right's emphasis on individualism, if we are to establish moral discourse and action as something more than expressions of personal preference, if we are to counter a consumerist ethic and drive, we must revive a sense of community, of shared commitments that are open to alternative forms of discourse and understanding. Part of the value of such communities is that they provide opportunities for positive actions in the world. They provide avenues for acting in ways that go beyond freedom as merely the absence of constraint and for considering virtue as something more than the purchase of the latest commodities. One of the difficulties in reviving such communities is that, as a culture, we have lost a sense of historical consciousness.

Modern technology, which seems to make everything available to us at the press of a computer key or the push of a button, actually contributes to a loss of historical sensibility. It also makes it seem as if the future can be captured, retained for replay at some more convenient time down the road, and accessible as our present whims dictate. For example, consider the ways in which technology allows us to videotape events—real or televised—that we can then enjoy at some more convenient time. Arriving back home after a two-week vacation, for instance, we can watch episodes of the television series we missed while away. This rearrangement of time sequences accentuates the tendency to live in a kind of presentism in which, perhaps ironically, both past and future lose their meaning. Able to control time seemingly as we wish, we lose a sense of historical continuity as well as the possibility of change. Further, with the assistance of technological "advances," we seem to be carried along on a wave of events that are largely outside our control. This contributes to a sense of powerlessness that is the very antipathy of what is required in a society committed to democracy. As Barber (1992) suggests, "we no longer travel in time propelled by imagination; we drag past and future into our own time, where they can be imbibed without time's assistance. Television is an insistent present's self-regarding eye, fixed stupefyingly on itself" (p. 32). When technology blends past and future into a self-enclosed present, and numbs us to the realities of social justice and the requirements of participation and social change, we become immobilized in a way that undermines the quest for democracy.

We do in some ways live in a different world than that which fostered, for example, what Bellah and his colleagues (1985) refer to as biblical and republican traditions. And there is no unproblematic way to return there, even if we as a society came to understand more fully than most of us now do what those communities consisted in. Whether we regard the "postmodern" as a part of the internal unfolding of the modern or as its renunciation, the uncertainty in which we now live seems sometimes suffocating, at other times liberating.

We would suggest, as outlined above, that the attempt to revive the notion of community be based on political actions and moral principles that can be worked toward in local situations and institutions, and connected to more encompassing social, economic, and cultural practices. Rebuilding genuine communities is vital if we are live out the promises of a democratic way of life. Democratic practice is, in a reciprocal way, impossible outside of genuine communities. Both require the reassertion of moral reasoning, discourse, and action in the world that makes a difference in the social space, for a common good.

DEMOCRATIC VALUES AND PRACTICES

Conflicting Conceptions of Democracy

America, we are fond of saying, is the greatest example of democracy in the contemporary world. Its constitutional freedoms (of speech, the press, and so forth) and its open-ended opportunities, we like to believe, make the United States the model of democratic freedom. There are a number of issues surrounding the meaning of democracy, however, as well as problems concerning the social and cultural conditions that are necessary for its existence, that make such claims problematic. One of these is that, given our own history, economics and politics are often seen as comprising different domains and as serving qualitatively different functions. This perspective can be traced to doctrines in classical liberalism as well as to the contemporary new right. It is easy to overlook, as a result, the way productive life shapes personal and social behavior, as if a capitalist economy is only a source of markets and a system of production. Yet, as Bowles and Gintis (1987) note, "capitalism, more than a system of resource allocation and income distribution, is a system of governance" (p. xi). It is important, therefore, that we recognize the political and cultural effects of capitalism as a system of governance. Further, it is important to consider the possibility that other systems of productive governance might prove more socially just because they provide a location for the enactment of moral discourse and action.

Another reality must be faced as we clarify our conception of democracy. Virtually all of the participants in the current social and educational debates espouse a commitment to democracy, though they typically mean quite different things. One way to clarify the meaning of democracy is to note the differences between, and the different requirements for, what Mansbridge calls unitary and adversary democracy. In what she refers to as the major conclusion of her work, Mansbridge (1983) says, "the model of democracy unconsciously adopted by the participatory democrats of the late 1960s and early 1970s [unitary democracy] . . . was in essence and in form directly opposed to the model of democracy that I, like most Americans, had grown up with, a model I shall call 'adversary' democracy" (p. ix). Unitary democracy is founded on feelings of friendship or solidarity, supported by a set of interests held in common and a respect for members of the group. It seeks to develop, through the process of face-to-face dialogue and discussion, a consensus on questions it takes up. Adversary democracy, on the contrary, assumes a conflicting set of interests among people who are, as the name implies, adversaries. At least in theory, it attempts to provide protections for these differing interests, but not through arriving at a broad-based consensus. Instead, adversary democrats attempt to resolve conflicts through debate, ending in a secret ballot in which majority rule is the deciding calculus. Interestingly, Mansbridge argues that the notion of equal power is less central to unitary democracies, since in those situations a shared set of interests allows those with more expertise to speak on behalf of others who share those interests, especially since the group embodies a form of solidarity based on mutual friendship. In democratic practices guided by the adversary model, it is more important for equal power to be developed. This is because individuals would be able to disregard perspectives with which they disagreed when they are made by those with less power than themselves and with whom they feel no kinship. Thus there is a need for some form of control over power in adversary democracies—embodied, for example, in the "one person, one vote" principle: In unitary democracies, such equality through voting procedures is at best secondary, even irrelevant, given the emphasis on consensus. Summarizing the older version of participatory democracy, Mansbridge (1983) says:

> People who disagree do not vote; they reason together until they agree on the best answer. Nor do they elect representatives to reason for them. They come together with their friends to find agreement. This democracy is consensual, based on common interest and equal respect. It is the democracy of face-to-face relations. (p. 3)

In outlining these differing conceptions of democracy, and providing case studies where each operates, the author takes pains to say that she is not advocating one over the other. Instead, she points to the need to be clear about the conditions that obtain in particular circumstances and how these are related to the dynamics of the kinds of democracy she outlines. The primary question about such conditions is whether or not the interests of those who must make decisions conflict. Accordingly, Mansbridge (1983) says, "the most important single question confronting any democratic group is . . . whether its members have predominantly common or conflicting interests on matters about which the group must make decisions" (p. 4). Clearly, since interests often do conflict, adversary democracy is essential. Given an inability to even conceive of a common good, as outlined above, it will often be the case that conflicting interests will be expressed, so that the adversary form of democracy will often be appropriate for resolving such conflicts.

The reason for the appearance of conflicting interests is not taken up by Mansbridge. We would argue that the differential in power that is endemic in the United States virtually guarantees conflicting interests and adversary democracy. If this is the case, and if we seek to extend the range of sensibilities that make participatory (unitary) democracy appropriate, we must work to diminish the inequalities of wealth, status, and power that are a part of the social structure—in large part through the dynamics of capitalism. There are—to underline one of the central themes of this chapter—incompatibilities between capitalism and democracy, especially of the unitary sort outlined by Mansbridge.

For members of the new right, democracy has a particularly limited range of meanings within the adversarial model outlined by Mansbridge. The role of a democratic government is largely to protect that negative freedom made possible by allowing the private, individual prerogatives of people to flourish, as well as to guarantee those inalienable rights specified in our country's founding documents. They emphasize the need to protect the individualistic domain of private choices against the intrusiveness of governmental actions such as those associated with the welfare state. Politicians in such a democracy are elected to represent our interests and to generate neutral, fair procedural rules that leave questions of distributive justice to a disinterested market economy.

For modern liberals, on the other hand, the often-touted opportunity to pursue happiness through the personal liberties provided by political and economic opportunities is empty for those who are discriminated against or are simply the victims of bad luck. Equally shallow and disingenuous is the democratic rhetoric of business and political leaders whose policies often stunt the lives of working people. Struggling to keep their heads above water, many continue to find themselves on the bottom end of a widening gap between the very wealthy and the very poor that makes a sham of democratic values and the hope of opportunity. As a recent article in the *Chicago Tribune* pointed out, "during a year when corporate profits and the stock market soared, American workers' inflation-adjusted compensation dropped 2.7 percent in the 12 months ended in March, the largest decline since the government began keeping track in 1987" ("Workers' Pay Drops," 1995, p. 11). An unbridled economy, liberals argue, is part of the problem rather than part of the solution to menacing social problems and the absence of liberty. Instead of the individualism and relativism of the new right, liberals emphasize communal attachment; rather than protection by an elected elite, they favor participation in the public sphere; rather than laissez-faire approaches to economic development, they advocate planning and controlling the forces of production; and rather than extolling the virtues of privately held wealth, they argue for an expanded role for civic life. By incorporating regulatory and legal protections that enforce equal opportunities for all through such actions as abolishing overt discrimination through the development of affirmative action plans, Americans might be more able to live out the promise of political freedom and economic abundance in the welfare state.

As we said in earlier segments of this book, we believe the liberal agenda has often provided necessary social guarantees and "safety nets" that have been of significant, often life-and-death, benefit to their recipients. They have provided health care, educational, and work-related guarantees that have enriched the lives of millions of people. Central problems, however, remain unresolved in the liberal perspective. These problems deal with a number of social/structural issues that liberals have not addressed at their roots. For example, in thinking about the economy as requiring reform rather than reconstruction, liberals fail to consider the deeply embedded structural sources of inequality and their relative permanence in spite of reform efforts. Nor do liberals deal adequately with the sources of human misery and what it might mean to live in a society that genuinely values democratic practices in all segments of social life.

We want to move beyond the understandings of democracy evidenced by the new right as well as by liberals. Because of our commitments to dealing with the structural causes of social misery and various forms of inequality, we find much to support in the radical tradition. Yet here, too, we have differences with significant portions of that tradition. One of these concerns the route by which transformative change may be implemented. We reject the notion that, at least in the United States and other industrialized nations, violence of any sort will be effective or morally allowable. If structural change is possible, it must be through processes that are public; that are based on argumentation, evidence, and persuasion; that lead to civic actions. This necessarily implies that any such changes will be slow and often frustrating. Second, we believe that such change will be facilitated not only through direct intervention in the productive dynamics of the workplace and the larger economy but also through cultural avenues. What we need to generate, in short, are not only social and economic alternatives but also cultural, spiritual, and civic ones (Elshtain, 1995; hooks, 1994; West, 1993; Williams, 1961). This requires a theory and practice of social interaction that allows a wide range of cultural realities and processes (forms of consciousness, works of art, intellectual analyses, and so on) to become aspects of social change. Third, it has become all too common for some segments of the radical contingent to develop arcane, and often inaccessible, linguistic and conceptual structures. Such structures serve to alienate people who might be more open to alternative ideas if they were presented in less intimidating ways. This, in turn, reinforces our earlier call for a sensitivity that acknowledges the perspectives and backgrounds of others, even when we disagree with their points of view and vice versa. It often seems to be the case, however, that the more abstract and convoluted (and even impenetrable) one's language and forms of analysis are, the more they will be seen as on some cutting edge or other. Such a perspective is both intellectually condescending and politically counterproductive. Instead, we must develop a more populist-style sensitivity to those whose lives are being exploited, even when the result of that exploitation is, understandably, the articulation of sentiments that belittle a radical perspective. We need to be more sensitive pedagogues, to talk to one another with greater understanding and sensitivity, even across differences (see Pagano, 1990). Elshtain (1995) suggests that as we engage in a common civic enterprise we are obligated to assume that our "fellow citizens are people of goodwill who yearn for the opportunity to work together, rather than continue to glare at one another" (p. 35). Given our commitment to structural change illuminated by radical analyses and perspectives, on the one hand, and our commitments to populist sensitivities and initiatives, on the other, we believe democratic values play a central role in structural changes that will take us beyond reforms.

In *Democracy and Capitalism*, Bowles and Gintis (1987) argue that while the classical liberal and Marxist traditions have each been influential and progressive in their own ways, considering the context in which each developed, neither forms the basis for thinking through the radical potential of democracy. Liberalism, while celebrating the importance of individual liberty and the need to protect ourselves from the autocratic potential of any state, has narrowed the range of activities over which individuals and communities can make choices. In celebrating property rights of the sort that are central to a market economy, they have allowed personal rights to diminish in influence. In addition, a limited role for democracy through appeal to its weak (adversary) form in which we elect representatives to protect our interests, within the minimalist state promoted by members of the new right, gives "politics" a constrained sphere of influence. When as a nation we seem skeptical of our elected representatives—and when *politics* is seen as a dirty word—we lose the sense in which people's lives are affected by a host of institutions and daily practices that shape them and that are thus political in a broad sense. If we think about politics as involving the interplay of power and decision making in arenas where public choices must be made, we may rekindle a radical democratic tradition that classical (and to some extent modern) liberals have undervalued. Marxist theory, on the other hand, according to Bowles and Gintis (1987), in focusing exclusively on class relations and related forms of exploitation, as well as class struggle, underestimates the importance of personal liberties and the other forms of action through which people may be empowered (e.g., feminist, racial, environmental, and sexual identity struggles). By breaking down the walls that liberalism has constructed and attending to all forms of exploitation that offer avenues for political action, the radical potential of democracy may be reasserted.

Understanding democracy in a rather narrow sense of embedded activities associated with electoral politics (voting, seeking or supporting others for political office, participating in candidate forums, keeping abreast of political issues and proposals, and the like) is too limited for these purposes. Instead, we see democracy as providing a moral and broadly social framework that has implications for interpersonal as well as institutional actions and decisions that must be made on a day-to-day basis. Here we agree with Dewey (1916) that democracy is "more than a form of government; it is primarily a mode of associated living, of conjoint communicated experience" (p. 87). The way we live with each other, the way we treat one another in our daily interactions and relationships, is central to this perhaps more homely understanding of democracy and its implications. Thinking about democracy as only a way of making narrowly political decisions allows undemocratic practices such as those associated with a capitalist economy to seem outside the pale of democratic inquiry—as if a democratic critique of the economy involves making something like a category mistake. As a way of life, a process that has application in many domains, a more comprehensive conception of democracy outlines how we are to regard and treat others, how we are to make choices, and how we can foster more widely shared decision making, in the process diminishing inequalities of power and status. As a moral and social force, democratic values provide frameworks and guidelines for how we live. "Democracy," Elshtain (1995) reminds us, "is not simply a set of procedures or a constitution, but an ethos, a spirit, a way of responding, and a way of conducting oneself" (p. 80). Again, this perspective is related to the emphasis on developing an ethic of care, even a capacity for love, as discussed in Chapter 4 (see Martin, 1992; Noddings, 1984; West, 1993).

The sort of participatory democracy we advocate is only possible, though, if we adopt something like the proposals sketched in the previous section that may reinvigorate a sense of community. This, in turn, requires, and is supported by, a grasp of the possibilities for a common good, collectively decided on by people engaged in open, moral discourse with others, within which a commitment to equality is central (Bastian, Fruchter, Gittell, Greer, & Haskins, 1985). Thus what we are proposing is a broadly based cultural vision for democratic practice in which daily activities and interactions, a search for the common good, the reinvigoration of community, and an openness to dissent and difference mutually support one another and allow for new forms of life and decision making to emerge.

These ideals resonate with Freire's emphasis on "integration" with the world, rather than "adapting" to it. As Freire (1973) puts it, "integration results from the capacity to adapt to reality *plus* the critical capacity to make choices and to transform that reality" (p. 4; emphasis in original). To become an integrated person is not only to understand the social, physical, and political worlds in which we live and work, but also to develop the attitudes, forms of consciousness, and outlooks that will allow people to take part in shaping and reshaping that world. This emphasis on critique of current realities, and on participating in the re-creation of our worlds, is a central part of our understanding of democracy.

A democratic community must, accordingly, enable people to develop values and ideas that outline alternative possibilities. Equally important, such a community must generate concrete practices that enact a moral vision— a vision not reducible to any set of present realities and yet not simply an idealist construction. A democratic community encourages its members to become participants in civic discussions that require concerted, collaborative actions in the name of social justice and structural change. This makes, at a political and social level, the postmodern emphases on particularity, the local, and the specific problematic as a source of efforts that must be collaborative, just as the new right's individualism is an obstacle to significant structural change. While we recognize and concur with the need to create the conditions under which previously silenced and oppressed voices can be heard, the segmentation of people into groups within which they primarily speak to each other undermines any sort of broadly based democratic project. If we are to avoid fragmented and even contradictory efforts at alleviating oppression, it would seem that we need some way to provide a measure of solidarity even across differences. This, postmodernists say, requires agreement of some sort among people whose own' experiences— much less those of others—may be unknown and unknowable. This substitution of otherness for commonality promoted by Ellsworth (1989), and generally celebrated by postmodern writers, makes the creation of coalitions seem quite difficult if not impossible. This difficulty is exacerbated by the postmodern rejection of metanarrative principles or commitments that transcend discourse and by the trends toward aestheticism and textualism discussed in Chapter 5.

Such protected havens make sense if we think about identity as a more or less individual matter, to be developed either in isolation or with others with whom we share some essential trait or characteristic. What is sometimes overlooked in postmodern writing on this topic—just as it is in the ideas of the new right—is that identity itself is worked out in some context, some social setting in which it is given shape and meaning. As Charles Taylor (1992) puts it, as I come to have an identity, it is not that I "work it out in isolation, but that I negotiate it through dialogue, partly overt, partly internal, with others" (p. 34). Even the "difference" celebrated by postmodernists has a social face. While some maintain that "we all are radically different"

(Welch, 1991, p. 89), we agree with Elshtain's poetic comment that "we cannot be different all by ourselves" (1995, p. 66).

Among the most important institutions for the revitalization of democracy are our public schools and universities. These sites, as the radical literature makes clear, are not narrowly determined by the constraints and influences of capitalist ideology and culture. We explore the possibilities of rethinking education in general and curriculum in particular in the final chapter. Beyond educational initiatives, and keeping in mind the contradictions between democratic practices and economic tendencies, we also believe that changes in the way we structure work and economic decisions must be undertaken. For these are the very places and activities in which the undemocratic nature of a capitalist economy are perhaps most strongly felt.

Beyond Market Mechanisms to Economic Democracy

The subject of how to reform or cut back the welfare state has, with the apparent political strength of the new right, taken on a new urgency. Advocates from this group have been adamant about preventing the alleged dependency created among welfare recipients and about the extent to which we need to see welfare as at best a temporary, locally sponsored initiative. Better, says the new right, that these people be taken off the welfare rolls and given "real," "meaningful" work that will help develop a sense of satisfaction and of real contribution.

We agree, at least in one sense, with the new right's emphasis on the importance and value of work as preferable to welfare—at least for those who are physically, emotionally, and intellectually capable of such work. Everything else being equal, meaningful, significant work is indeed morally preferable to receiving support from the state. But again, what is missing from the new right's perspective on welfare and work is an ability to critically look at the realities of economic life in the United States—that is, the actual meaning and value of work in a capitalist economy. For example, the inadequate wages and meaningless routine that accompany jobs in the service sector hardly make them the source of pride and satisfaction that the new right would have us believe. Working for a fast-food restaurant, for instance, provides neither sufficient income (especially for working, single parents for whom day care is a necessity) nor a sense of purpose that will prove uplifting for those now on welfare. As we discussed in Chapters 2 and 4, work in a capitalist economy often not only lacks meaning but also becomes separated from and even alien to our own personality and character; it also promotes a sort of alienation that erodes self-fulfillment and a sense of social contribution. Far from allowing welfare recipients (and employed workers as well, of course) to develop a sense of pride and character, jobs in our capitalist society often dehumanize and degrade people, adding to the social problems that the new right has highlighted.

The liberal response to these realities is also, in the long run, wanting. It is true that unions have done much to increase workers' salaries, provide health care insurance, promote safety on the job, guarantee a 40-hour work week, and so on. As people who have been engaged in attempting to create unions, and who also have struggled to preserve their influence, we recognize their value and support their development. The benefits brought about by the welfare state in regulating industries, providing a minimum wage, stipulating minimum health and safety standards, and so on have been of great importance historically as well. In many instances, the nature of the workplace would be much more oppressive and dangerous were it not for such liberal reforms. But the actual work that is performed, as well as its compensation, has not in our view changed enough to see productive activity as providing the kind of meaning and significance that it ought to, and can, have.

We believe that one way work can itself contribute to genuine self-development and to the genuine social good, as well as to the development of local communities bounded by moral precepts, is through a democratization of the workplace. We are calling here for the infusion of democratic values—ostensibly a part of our political rhetoric and practice since the founding fathers—into the decision making and day-to-day practices of the factory, the corporation, the school, and the university. By making workplaces themselves crucial sites for the practice of democracy through giving power to those to whom it has been denied, we promote a sense of efficacy. Moreover, given that most people spend eight or more hours per day in some work site or other, the salience of democracy for day-to-day life (not only for electoral processes such as voting and political office holding) would become more meaningful and practical. It might even have the effect, along with other necessary changes in civic life, of making clearer the meaning of democracy within a more conventional political context. While the advocates of a free market economy often tout the advantages of the purported democratization of consumption (a notion that is itself problematic, given the continued and growing inequalities of income and wealth [Friedman, 1989; "Workers' Pay Drops," 1995]), allowing democratic practices to dominate within production seems at least as important—provided we are serious as a society about the notion of participatory democracy.

Whether we are as serious about democratic values as we often claim, however, needs to be critically examined. For, again, there is an unbridgeable gulf between two of our most vital social structures: the economy and the realm of politics. The former is based on hierarchical arrangements, various indices of material and intellectual inequality, competitive forms of interaction that are often quite vicious, and lack of involvement in decisions affecting our daily lives. Democracy, in our view, involves some basic commitment to open, unencumbered participation, an ability to control our near as well as distant futures, equality, and an openness to new ideas and practices. As Bowles and Gintis (1987) argue this point:

> Capitalism and democracy are not complementary systems. Rather they are sharply contrasting rules regulating both the process of human development and the historical evolution of whole societies: the one is characterized by the preeminence of economic privilege based on property rights, the other insists on the priority of liberty and democratic accountability based on the exercise of personal rights. (p. 3)

Thus, when we say we are a democratic nation, we express at best a half truth, since economic practices and policies are infused with autocratic, unequal, hierarchical modes of operation based on property rights. And at the level of political matters, there are obvious nondemocratic components—for example, the inability of people without significant financial support to run for and win political office, and the lack of genuine opportunity that reality describes. To the extent that educational institutions are about preparing students for some sort of future or other, and to the extent that our economic and political inclinations diverge to the extent they do, we cannot adequately (or equally) prepare students for civic participation and economic productivity. At least part of the ambiguity about the ends of education is the result of the incompatibility between political and economic norms and values.

Our response to that incompatibility is to link economic decisions and practices more closely to democratic values and ways of life, as well as to generate a progressive social vision centered on incorporating democratic ideals throughout the social order—including those that affect our day-to-day work activities.

Given the evidence provided by both liberal and radical perspectives, we must recognize that there is no "invisible hand" that inexorably works toward the social good. The dynamics of social-class, gender, racial, ethnic, and other forms on inequality as discussed in previous chapters make any reliance on such an evanescent property at best wishful thinking, at worst an apology for the status quo that protects the interests of the powerful. We need instead to provide a moral framework that identifies and provides avenues for the creation of social justice and the common good, through the workings of democratic practices that recognize common interests.

As applied to the dynamics of capitalism themselves, there are moral and ethical principles that grow out of a commitment to democratic values that can serve to reorient the nature of work and thereby the nature of economic policies and practices. By replacing the hierarchical, alienating structures of capitalist work with the egalitarian, communal values that nurture democratic practices, we make available new structures that provide avenues for the renewal of community where they are perhaps least expected.

In *Individualism Old and New*, John Dewey recognized many of the central problems with dominant forms of production. Economic activities, Dewey said, are

> fixed in ways which exclude most of the workers in them from taking part in their management. The subordination of the enterprises to pecuniary profit reacts to make the workers "hands" only, their hearts and brains are not engaged. They execute plans which they do not form, and of whose meaning they are ignorant—beyond the fact that these plans make profits for others and secure wages for themselves. (cited in Wirth, 1983, p. 92)

In securing profits at the cost of human development and liberty, capitalist production denies human agency for most workers and prevents the sort of social attachments and search for a common good that are required for genuine communities.

The alternative to this state of affairs is not state socialism but the incorporation of democratic decision making into productive life. There is a long tradition of democratic socialism in the United States and other nations that needs to be reclaimed as we alter the nature of economic life so that it may be governed by the values and practices of democracy. One of the ways this may be accomplished is through worker councils and other teams working together, making decisions about conceptualizing and planning work (see Wirth, 1983, especially chapter 9). A division of labor might still be necessary and beneficial within such democratic work structures. Complex and varying activities may be more effectively done by those with specific skills; and in the process, the actual work to be completed may be more satisfying. But decisions about when and how activities are conducted, about the best way to complete the overall job, must be done through cooperative, open decision-making practices that provide a forum for all workers involved in that activity. Instead of decisions being hidden in the actual procedures and machinery that are a part of the process of manufacture, workers would be provided a voice in making such decisions.

Mansbridge (1983), in her analysis of democratic possibilities, provides case studies of attempts to put into practice a radical workplace democracy. Helpline was an urban "24-hour crisis intervention center, providing counseling and referral information for people with emotional, legal, medical, drug, or life-support problems, plus access to ambulance services, emergency shelters, short- and long-term counseling [and] special programs for teenagers" (Mansbridge, 1983, p. 140). As with other agencies that were popular in the 1960s and 1970s, Helpline services were free of charge, with support being provided by local philanthropic and religious organizations as well as by the federal government. Describing her dealings with this organization, Mansbridge (1983) notes, "from its inception, Helpline had always had the characteristics of a unitary democracy. It was dedicated to the common interest; it made its decisions by consensus, face-to-face; and it affirmed equal respect among its members" (p. 142). Like other attempts to introduce democratic decision making into work sites, the Helpline participants went through various stages of organization: "a first period of innovation . . . marked by administrative chaos, by deep commitment but widely varying amounts of work from the members, and often by the leadership of one or two hard-working, visionary, sometimes charismatic figures." This was followed by an abandonment of one or a small number of leaders, "and the institution of town meeting democracy in which the community made all important decisions in assembly." Problems of time and a lack of representation led to a third phase, which combined "representation and direct democracy—decentralizing most decisions to small groups . . . , arranging some form of representation to a coordinating committee, and meeting in assembly periodically to hash out difficult problems and to reaffirm a sense of community" (pp. 146–147). Throughout these periods of transition at Helpline, there was an evident commitment to the values of participatory decision making. Mansbridge is quick to point out that there were several features of this organization that differentiate it from a more typical place of work (the age of the workers, the equal salaries they received, the relative homogeneity of the workforce, and so on). Perhaps the central sustaining characteristic of the workers at Helpline was their idealism; as Mansbridge discloses, "the most important function of the time-consuming democratic procedures established at Helpline was . . . to meet the staff's ideals of the way their world should work." This idealism, she concludes, "makes Helpline, Inc., a dubious prototype for the worker-controlled organization of the future" (p. 147).

We understand, at one level, Mansbridge's cautions in this regard. Expecting all workers to be as idealistic as the relatively young, inexperienced (some might say naive) participants involved with Helpline requires some imagination. Given the deadening quality of much of the work that now takes place in American society, and the ways in which it blunts enthusiasm and imagination, to expect experienced workers to be as idealistic as the Helpline participants were may be naive. On the other hand, we need to consider how the very structure of work in contemporary America socializes workers so that they lose their idealism and are numbed by the activities of the workplace itself. As a "system of governance" (Bowles & Gintis, 1987, p. xi), capitalism expects and reinforces character traits and personality types that may well be at odds with the kind of commitments required for democratizing the workplace. But if we move too quickly to the conclusion that economic democracy is therefore impossible or that its costs are too high, we give current practices and tendencies too much legitimacy.

We are not naive about the wide-ranging alterations in the workplace that a commitment to democracy would entail, as well as the cultural values and priorities that would have to be changed in order for democratic socialism to become viable. But structural changes of the sort it necessitates, and would help generate, are never easy or quick, and the social, economic, and political problems that face us are of considerable magnitude. We hold out the possibility of hope, at one level, that such transformative practices may be worked toward. At another level, we see these proposals not only as embodying the promise of America that at least rhetorically has been central to "the American experiment," but also as materially and substantively improving the quality of day-to-day life.

CONCLUSION

Our social vision rejects the limited notion of freedom, the moral lapses and denials, and the individualism that are central to new right ideology. While recognizing the value of liberal causes and perspectives, we believe that reforms of current economic, political, and cultural practices are not sufficient. The sense of the social and natural worlds as malleable, of knowledge as constructed rather than found, as discussed by postmodern writers, is helpful even as their valorization of the other, of difference, and of textuality corrodes a political project that sees transcendent ideas and values as at least possible.

Our vision is guided by a commitment to radical democracy as it may provide avenues for reconceiving social institutions and practices, guided by a populism and humility in form and dedicated to structural change. Such change may be brought about by a reinvigoration of communities in which genuine participation, moral discourse, and the common good fuel actions in the world. Basic elements of our vision include seeing the various components of our world as susceptible to alteration through collaborative actions that build on our sociability; articulating moral values in open settings in which dissent that can guide those actions is expected and valued; and altering hierarchical structures and inequalities that demean and disempower, from which liberty and opportunity can become a reality. Like any vision, this one stresses certain priorities and commitments, specific values and obligations, while downplaying or denying the legitimacy of others. It necessitates, as well, a particular kind of framework for education and schooling.

CHAPTER 7

One Progressive Agenda

It is important to remember that the decision of what to make the basics of education, like every major curriculum decision, depends not simply on the way the world is but on the way we think it should be, on the kind of life we believe to be worth living, and on the kind of society we believe to be worth living in.

—Martin (1994, pp. 197–198)

In their attempts to assert a new right educational agenda, Chester Finn and William Bennett readily employ martial and medical metaphors. Finn (1991) speaks emphatically of the need to "take charge," to battle for and demand a curriculum of "substance." Bennett (1992) analyzes the body politic, raising the fearful specter of rampant viruses that invade and infirm our will, our abilities, and our virtues. As antidotes to this weakened condition, Bennett offers character education and an education rooted firmly in the "disciplines." Finn and Bennett are certainly not alone in their use of these rhetorical ploys. Other educationists have employed (and it seems almost certain that many others will utilize) martial and medical metaphors. The language of the fight and bodily images are powerful "weapons" in a rhetorical endeavor to convince policy makers and the public at large. At times these images help to demarcate understandings of what is at stake, but frequently the "grammar" of these rhetorical claims is more likely to illuminate the proponents' concerns and motivations. Looking back at our earlier analyses, it is evident that the new right fuels their claims and laces their charges with fear—fear of viruses in an age of AIDS, fear of civic dissolution through "acquiescence" to diversity in an era of ethnic rivalries, fear of economic and cultural deterioration, and fear of chaos when order seems desirable. Conviction through fear seems poorly founded, inadequately supported, and forever susceptible to those who are more vocal, strident, and powerful. While we disagree with the substance of much of the new right's educational arguments and its rhetorical strategies, we are convinced both that our educational, economic, political, and cultural "orders" are in turmoil and that curricular agendas offer one important terrain for a much-needed discussion of the current situation, our attempts to deal with it, and the values that ought to guide us. We are convinced that schools, while perhaps not providers of the much-heralded new right social glue, are important arenas in which children, knowledge, understanding, justice, moral vision, and compassion can come together. And we are convinced that if we follow the vision of the new right we will become traitors to our democratic heritage, increase the likelihood of class, racial/ethnic, and gender conflict, and fall further away from the values and concerns that we believe ought to guide democratic public education.

In what follows, we neither outline nor establish a curricular plan or courses of study. Instead, we offer a set of values and concerns that can and we believe should guide the curriculum deliberation process. At its best, curriculum planning is an activity that engages and utilizes many sources. It is our view that curriculum plans need to be informed by the concerns of students, parents, and community members and to be guided by the professional deliberation of teachers and other educators. Ours is not a linear or strictly organizational view of curriculum deliberation, but rather one that combines a number of guiding values and contextual analyses with a firm commitment to children, learning, and a better world. We outline the values that should, and the conditions and constraints that could, guide this deliberative process.

Viewed broadly, we see the progressive agenda (one that combines insights and understandings from the liberal, radical, and postmodern orientations) as offering a more sustained and defensible analysis of the turmoil that confronts us and a more humane delineation of the values and educational goals that are worth pursuing. In this final chapter we offer our view of one progressive agenda—one that not all liberal, radical, and postmodern proponents will accept but one that highlights what we believe are the positive and progressive formulations of these orientations. As we noted in earlier chapters, there are conflicts within each group and conflicts and inconsistencies among the three orientations. But a positive formulation cannot be constructed from one group alone, and a progressive agenda demands a collaborative, democratic, and sustaining vision. We venture here to articulate and offer possibilities that work toward such a vision.

We construe curriculum deliberation as a practical deliberative process that should be mindful of certain conditions and constraints: the need for professional collaboration; appropriate educational work conditions; a commitment to all students' learning through focusing on and balancing the student, knowledge, understandings, and contextual influences; and a recognition that curriculum deliberation entails choices, compromises, and trade-offs. Certain values and commitments are not only requirements in this process; they are also necessary presences in the final progressive curriculum exchange that takes place in schools and universities. The curricular route for public school and college students must be one that brings together the curriculum of the "father" and the curriculum of the "mother," recognizes the richness of our ways of understanding and viewing the worlds we inhabit, and attends to the meaning created by students in a way that acknowledges the worlds in which they live and the obstacles in their futures. While much of this is still, of necessity, somewhat abstract, in the next three sections we elaborate a progressive agenda based on the liberal, radical, and postmodern perspectives; discuss features of curriculum planning as a deliberative process; and identify what we think ought to be the guiding and embodying values of the enacted curriculum.

THE BROAD CONTOURS

If we were to take the new right approach and employ medical metaphors, we could certainly claim that antidotes are needed for our social ills. In a society that all too often views children as consumers of products, construes adequate public funding for all schools and attention to all student learning as perniciously "socialist," and understands attention to diversity as un-American, it seems that antidotes, if not triage followed by major surgery, are required. But the medical metaphor assumes that some sort of agreement about what constitutes our "health" and how to achieve that health are available. While some minimal consensus about human physical health might exist within the medical community, it is much more difficult to achieve an educational definition and then to devise the appropriate curricular and pedagogical interventions. This is, of course, due in large part to the political, social, and ideological disagreements that underline curriculum conflicts, as the preceding chapters have made clear. This "definitional" problem is compounded by the sense of uncertainty and urgency that frequently accompanies educational discussions. Differences regarding what our children ought to learn are wedded to views about our children's vague futures, as well as to our past and current practices. The former discussions, especially, inhabit terrain that is characterized by a large degree of uncertainty. This uncertainty can bring with it a sense of urgency that distorts considerations of what is truly important. Recognizing the uncertainty that attends such deliberation and the inability to gain a "secure" direction through any sort of anchored definition, Martin's (1994) admonition to be mindful of the kind of lives that we want to lead while we carry on our curricular discussions seems to be the best advice available. We think it is in the community of shared concerns represented by the liberal, radical, and postmodern orientations that some sense of that kind of life can be initially articulated.

Liberal Contributions

Recalling our earlier discussion of John Dewey and Amy Gutmann's liberal approaches to education, a number of telling features stand out. They (together or individually) emphasized the "corrective" influence of education through the selection of curriculum and school experiences; the importance of a democratic school community and a shared classroom ethos; and the need to see the child and the curriculum as conjoined, not separate, elements in the educational endeavor. We believe that all these elements are important features in the broadly construed progressive educational agenda. We begin with the emphasis on the child *and* the curriculum.

In his now-classic statement, *The Child and the Curriculum*, Dewey (1902/ 1956a) stated that we need to reconceive one of the most persistent educational problems. For too long, he argued, we have kept the child and the curriculum apart. He maintained that there are those who construe the problem of schooling as either the need to focus on the child, letting loose the natural forces of growth unencumbered by social forces, or the need to emphasize the knowledge to be acquired, highlighting the initiation of the young into these established bodies of knowledge. Dewey argued that we need to see the child and the curriculum as two points on the same line, as two essential and interconnected features of the educational enterprise. The curriculum, he argued, was not an inert body of subject matter—ready to be spoon-fed to students—but in reality represented the accumulated wisdom of the human race. Knowledge, for Dewey, was the outgrowth of people's attempts to solve everyday problems, to come to terms with and to know and understand the world around them. Knowledge was the outgrowth of people's interactions with and interventions in the world. The child, in Dewey's framework, was an intellectually active and personally integrative being striving to make sense of and understand the world. The task before the educator is to psychologize the subject matter—to take the existing knowledge "road maps" and transform them in ways that enable children to become more proficient in their dealings with the world and more aware of the richness and variety that exists in that world. To tie these educational activities to actual problems, to attempt to understand and solve problems that students confronted, was for Dewey a helpful way to structure the curriculum.[1] And so, for Dewey, it was the schools' purpose to bring the child and existing knowledge together in a meaningful fashion.

The graduate of the Dewey school was certainly supposed to be a knowledgeable individual but not someone dressed in the thin knowledge of Hirsch's (1988) cultural literacy garb. Rather, Dewey's educated individual was someone who understands the power of illuminating experience through the manifold lenses of knowledge—who sees the world in the richness, the fullness, and the interconnectedness in which it exists. This richness and fullness was to be accomplished by bringing the child and the curriculum together and by creating a community in which diverse backgrounds could be appreciated and cherished as part of the fabric of the school community.

It is the fabric, the ethos, and this shared sense of the school (or classroom) community that many liberals have underscored. Dewey emphasized that the school and the classroom needed to be miniature communities where students learned to be involved in shared projects, to be guided by shared purposes, and to become responsible community participants. The classroom was not simply a conglomeration of individuals brought together for the recall and memorization of facts, figures, and algorithms. It was seen as a community whose purpose was to find and create shared purposes that would enhance the growth and life of those contained within and connected to it. A progressive curricular agenda would need to attend to the various ways in which collections of individuals can be transformed into communities whose purposes and projects are guided by attempts to connect the student and the curriculum, and to make all students' learning meaningful.

Finally, the liberal heritage underscores the corrective influence of education. Schools are not simply meant to pass on information, skills, and knowledge to students. The school, as Dewey noted and we quoted earlier (see Chapter 3), is not supposed to simply transmit accumulations of the past but must selectively bring forth experiences and understandings that will "make for a better society." Dewey and his liberal successors were certainly not envisioning schools as engines of social transformation, but they did see educational institutions as necessarily involved in the shaping, forming, and guiding of children into the future. Today's progressive agenda has to take seriously the responsibilities of this corrective influence—guiding public education in directions that will sustain all children, directions that will enable all children to be engaged in their learning and to prepare themselves for meaningful labor and worthwhile lives. Within the curricular arena, this view of education highlights one of the questions we raised in the Introduction: knowledge for what? If our education is supposed to have a corrective or transformative effect, we must plan the curricular selections that comprise that education. In making those selections we need to determine what we will include and exclude and examine the logic and connections among what we have included. We need to ask ourselves: What is the purpose, logic, and direction of these curricular selections? While we do not have any simple answers to those questions or an easy calculus with which to answer them, much of our discussion in this chapter will respond to these questions.

The liberal attention to the corrective influence of education through curriculum selection, the concern for a community ethos within the school, and the focus on the child *and* the curriculum provide key guideposts for a progressive curricular agenda. It is certainly one that, even with only this initial outline, looks quite different from the new right's proposals and seems to point to a very different understanding of the kinds of lives we ought to lead. It also differs from much contemporary school practice.

Radical Contributions

> Let the liberals concede that behavior matters and that values matter. And let the conservatives concede that poverty is a cruel and ineffective teacher of virtue and that government can help. Shattered communities do not spontaneously acquire the recently rediscovered "Victorian" values of chastity, diligence and deferred gratification.
>   There is also a much more complex set of causes and effects here than the simple picture of the welfare life as a magnet for promiscuity. Those who peddle that view seem to think that history began in 1964 with LBJ's Great Society. (Kuttner, 1995, p. 5)

Among all the orientations examined in this book, it is only the radical perspective that takes seriously the complexity of cause and effect in social matters. Whereas liberal efforts in education seem to focus on the child, the curriculum, and the classroom, the radical orientation looks outward, beyond the classroom and the school. In fact, one cannot enter and leave the radical arena without coming to terms with analyses of the structural dynamics that contribute to various forms of oppression and underscore the complexity of our social ills. While for some that concern may seem extraneous to the world of curriculum and education, it is a central factor in understanding the forces that affect schools and the children we teach. Radical analyses of these structural dynamics, the radical tradition's concern for participatory and collaborative endeavors, and its desire to reunite thought and action, the head and the heart, are hallmarks of this arena and ones that must be included in our progressive approach to curriculum.

In a democratic society committed to eradicating its discriminatory and repressive features, it can be illuminating to highlight patterned norms, rules, and institutional structures that are discriminatory and repressive. Radical analyses of the structures of class, gender, and racial domination underscore dynamics inimical to a democratic society (Kupfer, 1995). These analyses need not—indeed, must not—be hopelessly abstract or removed from the everyday lives of teachers. Radical analyses of the dynamics of oppression can be quite invaluable in aiding teachers to see the forces that act on our schools, to understand our students and the dynamics that walk with them as they enter the classroom, and to reflect on who we are as teachers and how that affects the experiences and knowledge we offer within schools (Beyer, 1996). Whether we read Jane Roland Martin's (1981) analyses of the extant curriculum as offering a male cognitive perspective, try to understand the class bias present in the class-structured school districts that students attend (Anyon, 1980; Oakes, 1985), or contrast an Afrocentric curriculum (Asante, 1991/92) with the predominant white centered curriculum, radical analyses offer critiques and point to dynamics that few others examine.[2] A progressive agenda committed to the eradication of discrimination and repression, one that is committed to the equality and freedom of its members, cannot do without these critical assessments.

Unfortunately, it is a pervasive feature of schooling and teaching that children become, in some sense, "carriers" of the effects of inequality. They can be harmed by harsh or unfair lives. This situation is compounded by the fact that our curricular expectations and instructional approaches frequently intensify, rather than diminish, the effects of these harsh lives. The following examples should help illuminate this precarious situation. All too often students whose primary language is not English are expected to perform in an academic environment that does little to develop their conceptual understandings in English or in their primary language. In a school setting these students may be "seen" by instructors as lacking in ability. Also, young girls who are taught math in a manner that is highly competitive and in a way that does not recognize their own understandings may soon lose interest. After a while, these young women are said to be uninterested in or unable to perform adequately in that subject. Additionally, poor black students who see the wealth of opportunities and resources available to others but do not find the same avenues open to themselves soon opt for other strategies or life routes (Ogbu, 1987). Frequently these same students are said to lack the essential ingredients for school success. In each of these instances, individual student characteristics have been identified as "the problem." However, radical structural analyses cause one to question highly individualist etiologies of school failure. Radical analyses ask us to examine the social forces that contribute to creating the outcomes that we see. Such an orientation need not excuse individual behavior and responsibility; instead, it places the individual in a larger context and asks us to see a more complicated picture. Individual responsibility and social forces can go hand in hand—but a recognition of the constraining features of racism and poverty lead one to more complex, comprehensive understandings than a picture based solely on an individualistic ontology or a cultural-deficit model.

A sound curricular plan cannot ignore or misrepresent these contexts. If poverty and white supremacy affect the lives students lead, then students need to experience curricula that not only engender hope but give some possibilities for making that hope become manifest in their lives. If educational resources are minimal, a curriculum of struggle for those resources may be an appropriate task. What the radical orientation highlights is that any such education must be an education that is project-based and collaborative. Hope and actual possibilities arise from efforts that are collaborative and engage the participants in an attempt to understand and change their world.

Whether the analysis involves race, class, or gender, each segment of the radical tradition emphasizes collaborative efforts at transformation. Freire's (1974) notion of praxis, the feminist engagement in consciousness raising, and ethnic-centered approaches underscore collective efforts that respond to the dynamics of oppression by those who feel the weight of that oppression. It is implausible and unacceptable to suggest that parents, students, and teachers can ignore those strands that constrain their everyday lives. If a monolingual classroom limits the intellectual development of Spanish-speaking students, then parents and teachers should work together to establish bilingual programs. If inner-city students have to walk through metal detectors to enter the school door so as to be fed a curriculum that fails to provide hope, important skills, or illuminating understandings, transformative efforts are required.

Crucial to these efforts is the understanding that we are talking about children and the future. Hope and realism need to be balanced. It is inexcusable to use students either as place-holders in an economy that demeans them or fodder for political action that adults are either unwilling or unable to accomplish. In an educational setting students' lives need to be nourished so that they can engage and affirm the lives of others around them. An ethic of care needs to guide this effort, along with an understanding of the nature of public schooling. Certainly, at least in our current political situation, a public school curriculum aimed solely at consciousness raising or Freire's problem posing would not thrive. Examining, confronting, and transforming oppressive dynamics will probably only be tolerated and may only be useful if it is part of a "larger" educational effort. Any empowering education and its corresponding curriculum would have to be cognizant of the need to be multicultural, multilingual, and cognitively flexible. An educational and curricular effort for children that responds to the destructive dynamics that fill their lives must care for those children and enable them to master the tools and understandings that will allow them eventually to transform their own and others' lives.

Embedded in the radical call for collaborative educational endeavors to transform the dynamics of oppression is the concern that the educational effort be guided by an ethic of care, love, and attention in an attempt to unite our thoughts and our actions, our heads and our hearts. Not all radical analyses or calls for action are guided by this care and concern for others. Some have even ridiculed it as a lame response to the dynamics that oppress (Reed, 1995). But the ethic of care is a strong strand in most all of the radical analyses that we highlighted. Freire's (1974) transformative educational praxis, Martin's (1992) three Cs of care, concern, and connection, West's (1993) prophetic calls for action, and hooks's (1994) attention to "love as the practice of freedom" are attempts to bring together thought and action in ways that attend with care and attention to those around them. A curriculum that focused solely on the head and did not attend to our connections with others would be an education that diminishes its "participants." To this end Martin (1992) talks of the "schoolhome" as a place where elementary-aged students are engaged in the maintenance of their school building (there are no janitors), work with fellow students and teachers to maintain their building and community, and are involved in a curriculum centered around the activities of journalism and theater. It is toward this general destination that we ought to head.

What is unique about the radical curricular agenda is that many of its proposals combine, in integrative and powerful ways, the main features it highlights. The analytically distinct emphases on structural dynamics of oppression, arenas for collaborative endeavors, and integrative efforts combining the head and the heart, thought and action, can be found in Freire's attention to education as a praxis of problem posing, in the feminist focus on consciousness raising, and in Asante's (1991/92) Afrocentric proposals. We see these distinct radical emphases as central to any progressive curricular reform endeavor, and we view the broader radical approaches as curricular avenues worthy of consideration.

Postmodern Contributions

Although in Chapters 5 and 6 we were not uniformly enthusiastic about the central features of postmodernism, there are some perspectives we view as important—even crucial. Postmodern proponents underscore a skepticism toward universal or broadly generalized claims, they emphasize the social construction of knowledge, and they focus on a concern for the "other." Although we fear that postmodern critics are much too quick to characterize generalized claims as "terroristic" and "authoritarian," we think that a healthy skepticism toward such claims is in order. When the new right ascertains the source of our social ills as behavioral and as rooted in the collapse of traditional values, skepticism is in order. And when the new right claims that character education and a focus on content will solve those "ills," these generalized claims need to be inspected.

The postmodern critique of knowledge and truth as purportedly transcendent assertions about the world is a powerful one. Although we argued that some proponents slide all too easily into an epistemological solipsism, the postmodern view of knowledge emphasizes the social construction and the contextual embeddedness of our understandings of the world and our educational efforts. One curricular consequence of this view is the claim that our current curricular disciplinary divisions are human creations. Other combinations, other lenses, can be created. With this understanding, it seems that different knowledge frameworks and distinct understandings of what constitutes the "basics" in education become possible. Inter- and intradisciplinary curricular orientations receive further legitimation. Project-based and problem-posing educational approaches are also supported. We should note that one need not embrace a postmodern orientation to dismantle or seriously question the existing disciplinary frameworks. Jane Roland Martin (1982), a feminist philosopher who (as far as we know) does not accept the postmodern label, quite effectively criticized the reigning status of our "god-given" subjects and our "immutable basics" in her "Two Dogmas of Curriculum," a paper first developed in the early and mid-1970s. But here we wish to underscore the postmodern view of knowledge as socially constructed.

Certain postmodern theorists also emphasize a concern for the other. Arguing that in the standard curricular canon too many voices and too many peoples have been excluded, postmodern analysts maintain that we need to hear and include the stories of the other in our conversations and in our curricula, as we expand opportunities for interpretation and disruption of the conventional. We need to step into the lives of others in an effort to understand and come to terms with the oppression and exploitation that affect various peoples in our society. These understandings need to be part of the curricula of public schooling. This tenet of postmodernism is shared by those who propose an ethic of care in the feminist tradition, and by other strands in the radical tradition. Any "character" or moral education that does not include a sense of empathy and understanding of others—especially those who have been traditionally excluded—will lack an essential feature of character: a heartfelt care and expressed concern for others.

A progressive curricular agenda emphasizes the corrective and potentially transformative power of education—power that can affect both individuals and the local context in which it occurs. It views schools and classrooms as places that must be personally inviting, intellectually engaging, and morally enriching. The need for students, teachers, and parents to engage in collaborative endeavors focused on meaningful tasks is a central thread in this approach—one that is ever mindful of the need to attend to the "child and the curriculum," the dynamics that oppress, and the voices and the silences of others. The power and direction of this delineation can be appreciated if we compare it to the new right alternative of individual student coverage of subject matter, character indoctrination, and school choice. We need some helpful, albeit loosely formulated, ideals of where to head. This progressive agenda points us in valuable and useful directions. If democracy entails collaborative deliberation within communities concerned with the common good, if it requires that we know and understand the differences and the similarities of an immigrant and colonizing nation, and if it demands a rich and thorough understanding of the social and natural worlds we inhabit, then this progressive agenda marks some progress toward that goal.

Thus far we have discussed progressive guiding principles and have not talked about the contexts of curricular deliberation. In the next section we address the issue of curriculum planning as collaborative deliberation. Subsequently, we outline further, and with greater specificity, directions that a progressive orientation ought to take us.

CURRICULUM PLANNING

Rarely, if ever, do we create something from nothing. And when it comes to the practice of schooling, the community and institutional contexts, the national educational mood, and past curricular practices, all affect what can and will be viewed as defensible curricular offerings and practices. Realistically, our schools' curricula are affected by many "local" factors, including district resources, students, parents, textbooks, teachers, tests, the demands of higher education, and by the larger social forces that have been documented in previous chapters. A school district's financial resources enable or severely constrain the curricular options, the quality of life in the school halls, and the conditions in which teachers and students work and learn (Kozol, 1991). Students, the nominal recipients of the curriculum, eventually "determine" the meaning of the school experience through buying into, ignoring, or rejecting the messages of schooling (Heath, 1983; McNeil, 1988; McQuillan, in press; Ogbu, 1987; Willis, 1977). Parents usually want the curricula offered to enable their children to do well in their adult lives and for schools to be places that care for their children (Goodlad, 1984). Textbooks (especially in secondary education) establish the terrain of what will be "covered" (Apple, 1986; Fitzgerald, 1979). Teachers—given (in)appropriate school conditions—can effectively distance or engage students from the "offerings" (McGinley & Kamberlis, 1992; McGinley, Kamberlis, & Mahoney, in press; McQuillan, 1995). Standardized tests frequently focus the extant curricula on discrete skills and bits of knowledge in a way that does not facilitate learning (*Educational Leadership*, 1989). And higher education directs what is required of students below (Katzman & Hodas, 1995).

Walking into this very real setting with a progressive agenda may seem like a poorly written script for a grade B movie—one that few want to produce, much less work on or eventually watch. But it does not have to be construed this way. Certainly progressive visions and ideals must come to terms with the reality of school stasis and reform, a reality which is neither quintessentially dismal nor unguardedly rosy. And the possibilities for change are obviously mixed. Nevertheless, one guiding principle seems fairly secure: Transformation and change occur when people with real concerns and high stakes want to affect their working situations, the learning contexts, and/or their children's futures. Given the current context of school reform (Toch, 1991), the recent focus on curricular change and standards (American Associaiton for the Advancement of Science, 1989; Committee on High-School Biology Education, 1990; National Commission on Social Sciences in the Schools, 1989; National Research Council, 1989), and the controversies and turmoil concerning canonical knowledge and the Western tradition (Atlas, 1992; H. Bloom, 1994; Gates, 1992), collaborative efforts to affect change appear to be possible.

Curriculum Planning as Shared Deliberation

But where to start? Our materialist inclinations lead us to begin with teachers, parents, and students—with those whose lives are directly affected by the environments in which we learn and work. Teachers, parents, and students are the players who are directly affected by and can impact this drama and thereby affect their own futures. In the past they have helped shape what has come to be known as the public school curriculum (Reese, 1986; Wrigley, 1982). The new right's attempt to create market-aligned choice programs has certainly shown that parents are interested in the process of school reform. Public school choice programs have also highlighted parental, professional, and student involvement in curriculum. For example, in the Boulder Valley School District of Colorado parents, teachers, and community members have created and received funding for a variety of elementary and secondary school programs. These include two elementary programs modeled after the liberal Bank Street approach and Dewey-like curricular efforts, a schoolwide bilingual immersion approach, a core knowledge endeavor modeled along the lines of E. D. Hirsch's (1988) cultural literacy literature, and a Montessori-influenced preschool and elementary school program. At the high school level parents, teachers, and students have pushed for a variety of curricular designs, including an "in-school" International Baccalaureate Program and a new high school modeled along the lines of Theodore Sizer's (1992) essential school reform effort. While Boulder Valley's predominantly white and middle-class population has affected the choices and the options, this example is not an isolated case, and illustrates the variety of options that can be created and implemented in one setting. Other examples exist. Greg Smith (1994), in his edited book *Public Schools That Work*, cites numerous examples of successful public schooling, as does George Wood (1992) in *Schools That Work*. In many of the efforts parents, students, and teachers have been key participants in making the schools work.

Although we think such initiative and momentum cannot be created without support from members of the larger community and active parent involvement, our professional and ethical inclinations point us toward teachers as the central players in the ultimate design, crafting, and implementation of the public school curriculum. Teachers, as a part of their professional role, ought to be curriculum designers. In a certain de facto way they certainly are. But all too often they are allowed to only pay minimum attention to curricular matters, and frequently these efforts are accomplished alone. From our experience working with teachers on curriculum design and our own curriculum deliberation, two factors seem crucial for this endeavor. Curriculum planning is most productive if it is, at least in part, a collaborative affair and if the appropriate time and work conditions are available. Making connections among the student(s), knowledge, and the larger contexts is a large-order task. Even when substantial and clearly articulated curricular frameworks are in place, the planning and deliberative process can be arduous and time-consuming. In this type of endeavor teachers need paid time to perform these tasks. If the work is essential to the educational role and contributes, indeed frames, their efforts with students, it ought to be recognized and compensated. Teachers' curricular work will probably be more productive and the outcomes richer if they are able to work with other teachers and/or concerned educators. Collaboration, the bringing together of individuals with varied abilities, understandings, and skills, usually aids rather than detracts from the planning process. In such collaborative efforts the individuals involved need to share basic values and orientations—that is, they need to agree roughly about the direction they want to pursue and be ready to compromise and make trade-offs as a result of the process. If individuals do not share these basic values, the process will be a tiring and frustrating undertaking—one in which the participants would probably accomplish more by themselves. In our own efforts at designing teacher education curricula, we have been engaged in collaborative deliberations that have been productive and in ones that have stalled. In the productive efforts we have found ourselves with others who share our progressive orientation and in circumstances that foster such ideals. In the stalled efforts we have not been able to come to a reasonable consensus about the goals, purposes, or basic elements of a program. We have seen and experienced similar problems in efforts to redesign and reform curricula at the elementary and secondary levels.

An Emphasis on Context

Thus far what we have specified about curriculum deliberation might fit just as easily into a progressive or a new right educational agenda, at least a new right agenda that recognized teachers' labor and contributions. What makes this notion of curricular deliberation peculiarly progressive, in our sense of the term, is that it is a deliberative process that attempts to balance and integrate an attention to the child, rich understandings of and skillful accomplishments in the world, *and* an awareness of the larger societal dynamics and life contexts in which these children live and to which they may very well return. Whereas Dewey decried the false dichotomy between the child and the curriculum and wanted to bring the two together, we want to add a third element to the design—the social, political, and cultural context.

Dewey understood knowledge to be the outcome of past and present human efforts to deal with and come to terms with the world in which we live. For Dewey, children were beings actively engaged in attempts to understand and become more skillful in the world in which they lived—thus Dewey's two key curriculum design elements. What has been missing (or perhaps inadequately emphasized) in the nominal progressive educational movement, something that George Counts underscored in his talk to the Progressive Education Association, is an articulated direction in which this educational endeavor should head. Early on Counts criticized the progressive movement as lacking a valued direction. Counts (1932) maintained:

> If an educational movement, or any other movement, calls itself progressive, it must have orientation; it must possess direction. The work itself implies moving forward, and moving forward can have little meaning in the absence of clearly defined purposes. . . . Here, I think, we find the fundamental weakness, not only of Progressive Education, but also of American education generally. Like a baby shaking a rattle, we seem to be utterly content with action, provided it is sufficiently vigorous and noisy. . . .
>
> The weakness of Progressive Education thus lies in the fact that it has elaborated no theory of social welfare, unless it be that of anarchy or extreme individualism. In this, of course, it is but reflecting the viewpoint of the members of the liberal-minded upper middle class who send their children to the Progressive schools—persons who are fairly well-off . . . who pride themselves on their open-mindedness and tolerance, who favor in a mild sort of way fairly

> liberal programs of social reconstruction, who are full of good will and humane sentiment . . . who are genuinely distressed at the sight of unwonted forms of cruelty, misery and suffering . . . but who, in spite of all their good qualities, have no deep and abiding loyalties, possess no convictions for which they would sacrifice over-much . . . are rather insensitive to the accepted forms of social injustice, [and] are content to play the role of interested spectator in the drama of human history. (pp. 4–5)

In short, Counts (1932) maintained that the progressive movement needed to "come to grips with life in all of its stark reality, establish an organic relation with the community, [and] develop a realistic and comprehensive theory of welfare" (p. 7). This is what we mean when we write that we need to add to the child–curriculum dualism a third element—the social context. Once we add the societal context to the basic child–curriculum progressive design, we have a more adequate basis for articulating a direction, a direction that would include a conception of a life worth living and an understanding of the dynamics that harm people in an effort to achieve that better life. Part of the movement toward a different social context was articulated in Chapter 6. This context is part and parcel of any student's life and an element in the rich understandings and skillful accomplishments that we call the formal curriculum. Just as Dewey saw the child and the curriculum as integrally interconnected, we construe the child, the curriculum, and the larger context (both the current one and a future one that is possible) as the three essential and interrelated design elements in a defensible outline of curriculum deliberation.

In Chapter 6 we outlined some of the democratic rudiments of the kind of society that we believe is worth living in. Here we place those elements in our progressive curricular framework. Our democratic conception is at odds with the limited notion of freedom, the moral lapses and denials, and the individualism that are central to the new right's ideology. Even the liberal causes and perspectives, with which we are often in sympathy because they lead to reforms of current economic, political, and cultural practices, are not in the end adequate. The sense of the social and natural worlds as malleable, of knowledge as constructed rather than found, as discussed by postmodern writers, is helpful even as their valorization of the other, of difference, and of textuality corrodes a political project that sees transcendent ideas and values as at least possible.

Our vision is guided by a commitment to radical democracy, one that is rooted in attempts to reconceive our social practices and institutions, aimed at structural change, and grounded in populist participation and humility. Approaching our various social contexts with the understandings that (1) collaborative action, moral discussion, and dissent are both expected and valued, and (2) hierarchical structures need to be challenged and replaced with more equitable and empowering arrangements, enables us to engage more fully in the world each day. It is this engagement in communities that encourage genuine participation, moral discourse, and a concern for the common good that can fuel and guide our everyday actions and practices.

We do not, however, currently live in that kind of society. Instead we live in a democratic-capitalist social order in which commodity fetishism, the rule of the market, patriarchy, and white supremacy constrain, distort, and oppress the expression of many individuals' humanity and their ability to act democratically. This affects both adults and children. In our conception of curriculum deliberation—one that attempts to intertwine the child (student), the curriculum, and society—our idealized and realistic understandings of society inform both our views of the child and a sense of what knowledge is most worthwhile. A concrete example should help illustrate what we mean.

In heading toward an education that is democratically empowering and cognizant of the harms and brutish outcomes of our current setting, we need to engage students in a meaningful and challenging education. This is an education that recognizes who the students are, provides knowledge and understandings that will enable them to become skilled adult participants and fully engaged human beings, and readies them for an adult life that may engage neither their skills nor their human capacities. For example, many African American inner-city youth do not find school engaging, challenging, or rewarding. For these students public education tends to provide little substance worthy of engaging. Although many of these students find that their early education offers substance and hope, by high school they have rejected the hope and promise of education. A progressive educational plan for these students needs to understand students, their families, and the community whence they come. It must find ways to instruct students that fit with and build on the patterns and norms of their community, offer knowledge, understandings, and skilled practices that recognize both the students' strengths and the demands of mainstream discourse. As Lisa Delpit (1995) argues, students need to acquire the ability to function in a dominant discourse, though that need not,

> mean that one must reject one's home identity and values, for discourses are not static, but are shaped, however reluctantly, by those who participate within them and by the form of their participation. . . . today's teachers can help economically disenfranchised students and students of color, both to master the dominant discourses and to transform them. (p. 163)

To accomplish this task, Delpit (1995) argues, teachers must "acknowledge and validate students' home language without using it to limit students' potential" (p. 163); "recognize the conflict . . . between students' home discourses and the discourse of the school" (p. 163); and "acknowledge the unfair 'discourse-stacking' that our society engages in" by openly discussing the "injustices of allowing certain people to succeed, based not upon merit but upon which family they were born into, upon which discourse they had access to as children" (p. 165). In this vision and in these suggestions, Delpit brings together the child, the curriculum, and the society.

Multiple Options and Inevitable Trade-Offs

In attempting the task of balancing and integrating attention to the child, forms of knowledge, and the social context, we do not hold that one path or one curricular avenue is the only accepted option. In this complex world and in our progressive orientation, different groups of committed educators and parents could conceivably devise several worthwhile curricular options. There is no one right way, and each path, each chosen direction, will entail compromises and trade-offs. Curricular deliberation is a process that aims at ends, ends that are frequently visionary, tentative, and elusive. They are, as well, frequently reconstructed through the process of deliberation itself. All too often it is difficult to discern if we have reached or gotten closer to those ends. Curriculum deliberation can be a fairly elusive process. And once we are committed to going in a particular curricular direction—say, something akin to a Sizer-like (1992) reform effort—certain compromises and trade-offs are in store. Sizer's (1992) "more-is-less" and interdisciplinary effort must inevitably deemphasize defined disciplinary distinctions and must unavoidably delete what some consider essential. If we make commitments to a secondary effort that highlights the integrity and complexity of the disciplines, the opportunities for disciplinary integration and connection to the child are lessened. Once we attempt an educational project that is focused, like Freire's pedagogy, on social and political contradictions, the emphasis we give to a broad sweep of disciplinary understandings and the attention paid to individual students are diminished. Curriculum planning is akin to the deliberation entailed in many of our life choices—we hope we are headed in a worthwhile direction, and we know as we go that our decisions open some doors and close others. It is helpful if, in this process, we can begin to understand and have some way of appraising what the trade-offs are and what the distinct choices entail.

Curriculum deliberation, as we choose to portray it, is a complex but very rewarding process of interaction and planning. We have experienced, and we have heard others report, the sense of engagement, reward, and accomplishment that comes from deliberating with others and then acting on those plans. And, as we noted earlier, these positive achievements usually come only when the people involved share and can articulate a basic curricular orientation. In the final section, we articulate further some of the conceptions and values that we think need to guide a progressive educational plan. They are, we think, indispensable ones.

A PROGRESSIVE VISION

If curricular decisions depend on a vision of lives worth living and an articulation of the kind of society worth living in, we not only have to begin to articulate that vision but also try to ensure that the curriculum embodies those values, beliefs, and sentiments. Thus far we have delineated a set of guidelines for curriculum deliberation and an understanding of a progressive plan. We have claimed that a progressive curricular plan must view education as transformative; as attending to the child, the available knowledge and understandings, and the social context; and as an endeavor that brings together students and teachers in a collaborative fashion. But we have yet to delineate the broad outlines of what a curriculum could or should cover, what it should embody, and how it should engage students. Although our delineation will be neither highly specific nor complete, there are elements that we think must be included. In fact, we would go so far as to say that a progressive curricular agenda must combine the following broad understandings. It ought to include what Jane Roland Martin (1981) has called the productive and reproductive activities of life—what we shall characterize as the curriculum of the "mother" and the curriculum of the "father." It must also convey the richness of the ways of understanding and viewing the world we inhabit. Whether we construe and frame the curriculum in standard disciplinary, interdisciplinary, or project-based terms, it is crucial that students come to see the rich and manifold ways available to frame, understand, and act in the natural and social worlds. A defensible progressive curriculum would also honor students by encompassing their way of seeing who they are, their understanding of the world around them, and their grasp of the knowledge offered in school. In this curricular orientation teachers would attend to students with care, attention, and connection. A progressive curriculum would also take students' social and political contexts into consideration, doing so in a way that is guided by concerns for democracy and social justice and a vision of a more fair and equitable world.

Gender and the Connundrum of Fuller Lives

Talk of a curriculum sensitive to gender distinctions can be quite problematic. Gender analyses and discussions, like those regarding race, tend to be divisive. Fear of essentialist claims, additional and harmful stereotypes, and further misunderstandings seem to fuel the anxiety that can attend such discussions. But what we propose here is neither unreasonable nor divisive. It is, we think, quite the opposite—an attempt to unify and more fully humanize the curriculum. Basically, we want to maintain that all students need to grow up to be both separate and connected knowers, analytical and synthetic in their attempts to know the natural and social worlds, caring toward people, ideas, and the larger physical world, and sensitive with their heads and their hearts. Mary Belenky, Blythe Clinchy, Nancy Goldberger, and Jill Tarule (1986) have discussed at length the features of separate and connected knowing. Carol Gilligan and Lynn Brown (Gilligan, 1982; Brown & Gilligan, 1992) have analyzed the distinct voices and understandings of girls. Jane Roland Martin (1992) has highlighted the need to emphasize for all students the three Cs of care, concern, and connection. Adrienne Rich (1986) writes passionately of the need to give to young women an education that liberates and empowers them. All of these authors' analyses and proposals seem sound to us, and they do not entail any pernicious essentialism; they do not claim that boys and men "naturally" think and feel this way while girls and women "inevitably" think and feel another way. In its most powerful and benign form, our proposal of gender mix simply requests others to think about curricular avenues that will enable students to grow up to be full, engaged, thoughtful, and caring adults. It is, of course, a path that runs counter to the division of labor that seems to be demanded in some sectors of our economy and in some homes. But it is a vision of a life worth living—not a life forced upon us. Whether one phrases the invitation as an opportunity to learn the curriculum of the mother and father, or terms it as an attempt to encourage both analytical and connected knowers, we think it is an endeavor that needs to be pushed forward.

Some time ago Jane Roland Martin (1981) criticized the existing curriculum as one based on a male cognitive perspective, arguing instead that we needed to bring together both our heads and our hearts, our ideas and our emotions in new curricular designs. We are headed in that direction. It is a direction that is given human embodiment in a recent novel by Anna Quindlen (1994), where she describes the trials of one character, Ellen Gulden, as she attempts to learn empathy, connection, and nurturance after having been raised on a curriculum of analytical rigor and fatherly distinctions. Ellen's trials illuminate our concerns.

In her novel, *One True Thing*, Quindlen (1994), the former *New York Times* columnist, underscores the lessons that can be gained from experiencing the curricula of both the father and mother. In that work the central character, Ellen Gulden, a young, driven, and soon to be successful writer, comes home from New York City to take care of her mother, who is dying of cancer. She comes home begrudgingly at the request of her father, a professor of literature in the small town's liberal arts college. Ellen has been raised on the curriculum of her father, an argumentative, analytical, judgmental approach to the study of literature. She seems compelled to see the world in distinct, clearly delineated categories. Ellen's early years were spent emulating and adoring her father, the father who embellished bedtime stories with linguistic flair and also spent little time engaged with her or her two brothers in activities of their own choosing. When Ellen comes home to care for her mother, Kate Gulden, Ellen hardly knows her. Ellen is acquainted with her mother's artifacts, the objects she has created to make their house a home, and she understands that her mother has been the one who has kept that home together. But it seems that her mother was always the hushed hum of background noise in her years of growing up. Kate Gulden kept home, while Ellen was always leaving home. In part it is a story of what Jane Roland Martin (1992) calls "domesticity repressed," a story of how we have come to denigrate the labor and love required both to maintain a home and to sustain relationships among people. When Ellen thought about her mother she recognized that she was "lucky." It was just that she "rarely considered her at all." For Ellen her mother was like dinner, sustenance her body required, while her father was like dessert.

Caring for her mother takes its toll on Ellen, as it would on anyone, and it brings her into her parents' lives in ways she had not expected. Caring for her mother brings out an edge of anger toward her father. She becomes focused on his infidelities, his aloofness, and his domestic absence and silence. At one point Ellen's mother notes this hostility and asks:

"What has happened between you and your father?"

"What do you mean?"

"You have been very angry with him since you came home."

"Mama, this is not about you. And it's not something we should discuss. I have my own differences with Papa that have nothing to do with you."

"They have to do with me, especially now. He's all you'll have. . . . You and your father will need each other. And you and your brothers. And I hope he can have more of a relationship with the boys, too, if I'm not there to get in the way. But you and he already have such a bond. You're so much alike."

"Please don't say that."

"Why? Because he's not perfect? Because he's not the man you once thought he was?"

"Mama, I can't talk to you about this."

"Ellen," she said, . . . "listen to me because I will only say this once and I shouldn't say it at all. There is nothing you know about your father that I don't know, too. . . . You make concessions when you're married a long time that you don't believe you'll ever make when you're beginning," she said. "You say to yourself when you're young, oh I wouldn't tolerate this or that or the other thing, you say love is the most important thing in the world and there's only one kind of love and it makes you feel different than you feel the rest of the time, like you're lit up. But time goes by and you've slept together a thousand nights and smelled like spit-up when babies are sick and seen your body droop and get soft. And some nights you say to yourself, it's not enough, I won't put up with another minute. And then the next morning you wake up and the kitchen smells like coffee and the children have their hair all brushed and the birds are eating out of the feeder and you look at your husband and he's not the person you used to think he was but he's your life. The house and the children and so much of what you do is built around him and your life, too, your history. If you take him out it's like cutting his face out of all the pictures, there's a big hole and it's ugly. It would ruin everything. It's more than love, it's more important than love. . . . You can be hard, and you can be judgmental, and with those two things alone you can make a mess of your life the likes of which you won't believe. I think of a thousand things I could teach you in the next ten years, and I think of how everything important you learned the first twenty-four you learned from your father and not me, and it hurts my heart, to know how little I've gotten done." (Quindlen, 1994, pp. 168–170)

Ellen's mother recognizes the strengths and weaknesses of her husband's curriculum and she wants, but won't have time, to offer Ellen her own curriculum. It is a curriculum of compassion, of understanding, and of forging and maintaining connections with others. In Kate's generation it was mainly women who mothered and maintained those connections. In Kate's life it was mainly the men who left home to go to work. But we no longer live in Kate Gulden's world. In today's world both men and women enter the realm of public work, and many children have one parent who works long hours only to come home and work again. In today's world too many children live in poverty and in homes where it is simply difficult to maintain those connections. In today's world we risk losing the curriculum of care, connection, and concern. Unlike Ellen, whose opportunities to become acquainted with the curriculum of connection were cut short by her mother's death, today's children are being shortchanged by an economy that has taken care and connection from the home and has not replaced it anywhere else (Martin, 1992).

Talk about the curricula of the mother and father has its dangers and drawbacks. Such talk can idealize, denigrate, and/or essentialize qualities that we associate with both. It can glamorize people in our lives and it can bring to mind imperfections, faults, and failures that are inseparable from our own conceptions and experiences. It can also sound like these features are inherently part of men and women. We do not think they are. But it can also highlight, in an aesthetically powerful way, a direction in which we should head. If we have to choose metaphors, we would rather stick with these than utilize the metaphors of warfare and viruses. A public school curriculum that enabled students to learn from and engage in both separate and connected knowing, that had students involved in maintaining their own classrooms and school facilities, that engaged students in discussions of the ways our market economy commodifies our bodies and ourselves, that required of students that they watch out, care for, and instruct other, younger students, and that engaged both boys and girls in the lessons of analytical thinking and empathetic understanding would, we think, be a powerful force in students' lives and an antidote to some of the significant forces that affect those children. Caring for people and caring for ideas can be embodied in and embraced by a curriculum. A progressive curriculum needs to bring these elements together.

Rich Understandings and Skilled Performances

In a Sunday *New York Times Magazine* cover article on the high-tech magazine *Wired*, the people who run it, the venture capitalists who support it, and the consumers it targets, Paul Keegan (1995) underscored the view of knowledge and education that seems to be gathering support among the high-tech crowd. Calling public schools the "last great bastion of socialist economics," this "new" economic elite maintains that American schools ought to be eliminated, thus freeing up $450 billion and "fueling a high-tech commercial industry that would do a much better job teaching children skills they'll need to be 'knowledge workers' in the new information economy" (Keegan, 1995, p. 88). In his equation, knowledge and education should serve a particular economy—not the students who are in the schools or the democratic society in which the students live (or ought to live). While this elite may view giving skills to future "knowledge workers" as serving the student population, it is, predictably, a very narrow and utilitarian conception. It is a conception, Keegan reminds us, fueled by a social Darwinist understanding, one in which elites basically drive civilization. It seems that some, and we fear all too many, among us have simply never understood or experienced rich and full understandings of the world. If they have had these experiences, then they appear to prescribe them for only a select few. Too many of those who desire to ascend to power view proposals that would enable all children to engage in rich understandings of the world and become skilled practitioners as "outdated." It is a conception of education that is antidemocratic and a view of the curriculum that is insipidly thin.

Very rich and complex views of knowledge, of the disciplines and understandings, are available that can guide and frame our views of the world.

Unfortunately, during the last 80 years arguments have focused on whether the curriculum should be child- or knowledge-centered while, in reality, the push has been toward making the curriculum responsive to the economy. Like Dewey, we think the child–curriculum choice is a false one. What we need to do is develop and utilize the numerous avenues by which the child and the curriculum can be brought together while being ever mindful of the ways in which others will try to reduce those rich understandings to information that will serve an economy. The routes to these rich understandings are truly multiple and include humanist proposals for a liberal arts curriculum that tend to underscore a received view of our world, the more standard progressive formulations that emphasize the child's meaning making, and Freire's (1974) problem-solving approach. All of these avenues, and their various strands, need to be explored. All of the approaches have strengths and carry with them inherent weaknesses.

Michael Oakeshott (see Fuller, 1989), a British political theorist and educational commentator, has written frequently about education as an unrehearsed intellectual adventure and as a passing on of the human inheritance. He, along with (in his earlier days) Paul Hirst (1965), gives credence to and defends what we normally construe as the humanist view of the curriculum. In their formulations, the curriculum we offer students should enable them to frame and makes sense of their experience in the world. The curriculum framework they support is what we have come to call the liberal arts curriculum. Our human inheritance, the standard arts and sciences disciplines [or, as Hirst (1965) terms them, our "forms of knowledge"] are the available lenses that "humanity" has created to make sense of our experience. Hirst (1965) relates:

> To acquire knowledge is to become aware of experience as structured, organized and made meaningful in some quite specific way, and the varieties of human knowledge constitute the highly developed forms in which man has found this possible. To acquire knowledge is to see, to experience the world in a way otherwise unknown, and thereby come to have a mind in a fuller sense. . . . To have a mind basically involves coming to have experience articulated by means of various conceptual schema. (pp. 124–125)

Hirst (1965) goes on to relate that we must not forget

> that the various forms are firmly rooted in that common world of persons and things which we all share, and into this they take back in subtle as well as simple ways the understanding they have achieved. The outcome of a liberal education must therefore not be thought of as producing ever greater disintegration of the mind but rather the growth of ever clearer and finer distinctions in our experience. (p. 137)

Hirst ends his defense of liberal education by calling to mind Michael Oakeshott's elaboration:

> As civilized human beings, we are the inheritors, neither of an inquiry about ourselves and the world, nor of an accumulating body of information, but of a conversation, begun in the primeval forests and extended and made more articulate in the course of centuries. It is a conversation which goes on both in public and within each of ourselves. Of course there is argument and inquiry and information, but wherever these are profitable they are recognized as passages in this conversation, and perhaps they are not the most captivating passages. . . . Conversation is not an enterprise designed to yield an extrinsic profit, a contest where a winner gets a prize, nor is it an activity of exegesis. It is an unrehearsed intellectual adventure. . . . Education, properly speaking is an initiation into the skill and partnership of this conversation in which we learn to recognize voices, to distinguish the proper occasions of utterance, and in which we acquire the intellectual and moral habits appropriate to conversation. And it is this conversation which, in the end, gives place and character to every human activity and utterance. (cited in Hirst, 1965, p. 138)

The liberal education that Hirst and Oakeshott elaborate recognizes past attempts to come to terms with and understand experience. It is a rich and substantial view of knowledge, one that builds upon disciplinary refinements. It is also an approach that must be skeptically inspected, as postmodernists remind us. It is a view that seems to bring with it a commitment to knowledge first and students second. And it is an "initiation" into a particular inheritance, an inheritance that incorporates values and understandings that have been known to create "double binds" for women and barriers for people of color. It is undeniably a rich and valuable orientation, but it is not without its own problems and inherent weaknesses.

In contrast to this discipline-based, liberal arts view, there are others who would have us approach the curriculum through honoring children's thoughtful meanderings. In this framework students are not initiated into forms of knowledge; instead, they would come to understand those forms through grappling with problems, issues, and conundrums that they face. Here the emphasis is on the child, on the child coming to terms—through our inherited understandings—of the world around him or her. Eleanor Duckworth (1987), building on David Hawkins's insight that "you don't want to cover a subject; you want to uncover it" (cited in Duckworth, 1987, p. 7), states:

> That, it seems to me, is what schools should be about. They can help uncover parts of the world that children would not otherwise know how to tackle. Wonderful ideas are built on other wonderful ideas. In Piaget's terms, you

must reach out to the world with your own intellectual tools and grasp it, assimilate it, yourself. All kinds of things are hidden from us—even though they surround us—unless we know how to reach out for them. Schools and teachers can provide materials and questions in ways that suggest things to be done with them; and children in the doing, cannot help being inventive. (p. 7)

For Duckworth, and many others in the liberal tradition, the student's inquiry and wonder lead the educational endeavor and in some significant ways guide the curriculum selection. In Duckworth's approach we cannot cover our knowledge and understanding of the world; rather we enable the child to move capably in these worlds. As Duckworth (1987) states:

Certainly the material world is too diverse and too complex for a child to become familiar with all of it in the course of an elementary school career. The best one can do is to make such knowledge, such familiarity, seem interesting and accessible to the child. That is, one can familiarize children with a few phenomena in such a way as to catch their interest, to let them raise and answer their own questions, to let them realize that their ideas are significant—so that they have the interest, the ability, and the self-confidence to go on by themselves. (p. 8)

The purpose is to encourage, facilitate, and honor students' abilities to have wonderful ideas, to be intellectually engaged.

At the secondary level a variation of this approach has been elaborated by Theodore Sizer, and his Coalition for Essential Schools. Sizer (1992) maintains that the existing curriculum has not engaged students; he has proposed, in its place, an integrated curriculum, smaller student–teacher ratios, and evaluations through exhibitions to create more engaging and motivating educational environments. Arguing that the current high school curriculum is much too fragmented and superficial, Sizer maintains that we need to identify that which is essential and encourage "all students' appropriate and sustained involvement with this most important material. We should insist that they 'make sense' of the cumulative knowledge" (p. 147). He states:

Asking students to display what we have previously told them to memorize, to look up in the dictionary, or to read is limited in purpose. We must expect more: the students must be able to use this knowledge, to acquire the habit of its thoughtful use. . . .

Acquiring the habit of use takes time, which is another powerful reason for us to sharpen and focus the academic program. The teachers can cover material only as fast as each student learns to use it resourcefully. The more that the material makes sense in the world of the student, the stronger and deeper will be his grasp of knowing. Clustering subjects in ways that respect

disciplinary lines and are persuasive as reflections of the real world is necessary. We recommend three such clusters, these to engage all of the students
all of the time, until each student Exhibits successfully for the first-level diploma.
(Sizer, 1992, p. 148)

The clusters that Sizer refers to include math/science, the arts, and his-
tory/philosophy joined together at their core by the tools of inquiry and
expression.

An approach similar to Sizer's is offered by Deborah Meier of the New
York City Central Park East Secondary School. It emphasizes particular
"habits of the mind," habits that she believes cut across disciplinary lines
and professional endeavors. They are

> the question of evidence, or "How do we know what we know?"; the question
> of viewpoint in all its multiplicity, or "Who's speaking?"; the search for con-
> nections and patterns, or "What causes what?"; supposition, or "How might
> things have been different?"; and finally, why any of it matters, or "Who cares?"
> (Meier, 1995, p. 50)

Meier maintains that lawyers, scientists, school administrators, and histori-
ans find these to be the central questions that inform their respective
endeavors. They are also, she claims, the habits that ought to be inculcated
in students and around which the curriculum should be organized.

There are certainly other variations on these curricular frameworks. The
International Baccalaureate program is a variation on Hirst's (1965) forms
of knowledge, and Kieran Egan's (1988, 1990) modes of understanding
("recapitulationist") schema is a modern-day version of John Dewey's notion
of social occupations. Each approach, each variation, carries with it particular strengths and weaknesses. The standard liberal arts approach can be
watered down so that coverage is the key issue and little attention is paid to
the ways it connects with students' lives or concerns or with other distinct
but related disciplinary endeavors. Further, the disciplines are not neutral
lenses on the world. Gender, class, and racial dynamics are and have been
infused into these frameworks in such a way as to diminish many of those
already disenfranchised in our society. The more child-focused approach
has a long history of relegating substantive knowledge and disciplinary
frameworks to the curricular backburners. Attempts to listen to and speak
to children, to create settings that engage them intellectually, and to develop
powerful ways of understanding and interacting with the world are incred-
ibly complex. Efforts to achieve and sustain these sorts of practices can be
quite difficult. But these are the sorts of issues and conundrums any quality education will have to confront, and the direction will certainly affect
the trade-offs faced down the line. But without attention to incorporating

a substantial basis of lenses on and into the world in which we live, a progressive education will lack the power of knowledge. We cannot diminish that power or curtail our students' involvement in it.

This knowledge, whether it be discipline-based and/or student-directed, cannot be left hanging disconnected from the world. Here the notion of praxis and the concern for a project-based curriculum come into play. Forms of knowledge, as lenses, are illuminating for understanding the world, but our understandings should not remain academic, disconnected, or aloof. Freire's (1974) focus on social and political contradictions, as the singular direction for an educational endeavor, cannot lead an entire public school plan. It does, however, have its place. And if we only talk about these contradictions without asking what ought to be done, we have left students and ourselves with only part of an education. Not every lesson or curricular plan must end in some sort of action, but without an integral and regular effort of tying knowledge and action together, we will be purveying a curriculum of thought without action. That is not what we want to continue. Freire's approach is not the only way in which we can encourage thought and action to be united in our schools. Sizer's (1992) reforms emphasize the importance of routine exhibitions, performances in which students are asked to put into practice their knowledge, their understandings, and their growing skills in the world. Whether the exhibition requires students to fill out sample Internal Revenue Service 1040 tax forms, to explore the nature and nuance of a particular emotion through a written essay and another form of expression, or to utilize the disciplines of history, science, and math to analyze features of experience, the expectation is that students use, employ, enact, and interact with the knowledge they have gained. Skilled activities, undertaken at least some of the time in the larger social arena, need to be an integral and essential part of the curriculum.

Attending to Students

While it has been implied in many of the earlier sections that students hold a special place in this progressive formulation, this position needs to be underscored. This special place is not the same as the highest ranking on a scale of importance or a romantic understanding of the uniqueness that makes children special. It is instead a commitment to students that is respectful, honoring, and unwavering. It is somewhat difficult to convey this emphasis without bringing to the foreground all of the outdated baggage that construes an emphasis on the child as unduly "child-centered," epistemologically "unstructured," or lacking in direction and orientation. But such is the terrain on which we find ourselves.

Recognizing students as either children, adolescents, young adults, or adults seems a good place to start. In our view, we have to see our students as more than minds, as more than particular behaviors. We need to understand students as thinking, sentient, and physical human beings. At the university there is a tendency to recognize only the cerebral features of students, and at the elementary level students are sometimes reduced to behaviors and affects. Teachers, and the curriculum they construct, need to recognize the broader rather than narrower view of what it means to be a human being engaged in learning.

An emphasis on the student also honors and respects the student as a striving, wondering, struggling, and engaged individual. Students, 8 or 68 years old, are not always engaged in their present horizon. But the curricula we create need to assume that students can be engaged in the forms of knowledge and experience at hand. Our curricula need to create avenues that will encourage and elicit that engagement, avenues that recognize and honor the strengths that students bring with them to the classroom.

Respect for students can be made manifest in a variety of ways, but one feature that seems essential in an educational setting is an attempt, by the instructor, to see and understand the world from the student's point of view. In the current educational research scene, this can be partially translated into attending to the students' meaning making, making note of what understandings and messages students gain, garner, and create in the classroom. But it seems possible to attend to students' meaning making and at the same time have little respect for them. What is needed, in addition, is a caring attitude toward students. Teachers who care for students, honor and give credence to students' understandings, are not necessarily satisfied with students' achievements or performances. These teachers do not belittle, underestimate, or denigrate students' efforts. Instead they recognize and validate their students and at the same time hold expectations that encourage improvement and insight. To expect more need not denigrate students—such expectations should facilitate, encourage, and anticipate further growth.

Finally, to attend to students means that in a significant and crucial way students are the central element in the educational effort. Curricular efforts ought to be accomplished not for the economy, not for parents, but for students. What that actually means and how it transpires in particular settings can only come about from caring for, attending to, and connecting with the students whom we teach.

The Contexts in Which We Teach

In caring for our students we also need to attend to the contexts in which they have grown up and live. A progressive curriculum needs to take students' social, cultural, and political contexts into consideration, understanding that these contexts inform both their present education and their probable futures. In considering these contexts, we need to be guided by a concern for democratic values and visions of a more fair, equitable, and caring world.

Taking students' present context into consideration is an educational factor that can no longer be ignored. If one of the key curricular goals is to enable students to come to rich understandings of the world and be able to act effectively in that world—and at least some of the time to change it—then we must utilize their present contexts in ways that facilitate the achievement of those goals. Considering students' futures is an effort that brings us to some rather murky and difficult terrain, but one that must be traversed. We do not know our students' futures and we do not want to create curricula based on some forecasted future. But we must recognize students' likely destinations and then guide the educational program with a concern that will enable them to help create, and then participate effectively in, democratic communities. If students grow up poor with few resources, our progressive formulation maintains that their curriculum should enable them to participate effectively in a democratic society. If students grow up in affluent and gated communities, they need to see that wealth is not a by-product of effort alone and that those who are kept out of their communities deserve better. Certainly students should not be spoon-fed visions of justice. But any public and democratic school effort must include a concern about the social dynamics and injustices that harm some more than others. As Deborah Meier (1995) has written:

> The capacity to see the world as others might is central to unsentimental compassion and at the root of both intellectual skepticism and empathy. "Any human being sufficiently motivated can fully possess another culture, no matter how 'alien' it may appear to be," argues noted African-American author and literary critic Henry Louis Gates. "But there is no tolerance without respect—and no respect without knowledge." Such empathetic qualities are precisely the habits of mind that require deliberative cultivation—that is, schooling. If such habits are central to democratic life, our schools must become places that cultivate, consciously and rigorously, these moral and intellectual fundamentals. (p. 63)

CONCLUSION

In the Introduction, we indicated that we would be locating our analysis within what has come to be known as the curriculum field, and we identified six questions as central to the ongoing debates, discussions, and analyses in that field. In concluding this work we would like to return to those questions, briefly identifying and summarizing the responses we have developed. The questions, as we noted earlier, highlight specific concerns, context-dependent issues, and more global aspects of curriculum matters. We will not try to recapitulate each element of our response, but rather summarize succinctly our central convictions. The six questions and our responses follow.

1. *What knowledge and forms of experience are most worthwhile?*

Basically we have maintained that the forms of knowledge and the experiences embodied in the curriculum need to engage students so that they can come to have rich understandings of the world around them—understandings that are affectively informed and practically adept. We have not delineated one particular curricular route, as we think local, democratic deliberation and choice are fundamental elements in the creation of public school curricula, as is a recognition that any curricular direction that accomplishes our three goals will entail inevitable trade-offs.

2. *What is the relationship between the knowledge embodied in the formal curricula of schools and those who are involved in enacting it?*

Students are not the simple recipients of transmitted knowledge but rather active participants in the classroom and educational drama. The knowledge embodied in the curriculum should provide ways to enable students to more fully see, understand, and come to terms with the world around them. We happen to think that interdisciplinary and more strictly delineated disciplinary curricula can facilitate these understandings, but a great deal depends on how capably the knowledge embodied in the curriculum is connected with the student. It is the teacher's task to connect the knowledge embodied in the curriculum with the student and with the context in which this educational interaction occurs.

3. *What types of educational and social relationships are required or desirable in order to facilitate curricular experiences?*

Minimally we have maintained that care, concern, and connection need to characterize these educational relationships, relationships in which the student is central. It is not enough to focus on the cognitive features of students. In an educational relationship we need to care for and with students, as well as nurture and sustain them.

4. *How do larger social, political, and institutional contexts affect the experiences students have with the curriculum?*

In many ways we have claimed that the student and the context need to be seen as interwoven and that teachers must try to understand the ways in which contextual dynamics affect the education we offer all of our students. All too frequently contextual dynamics create obstacles for students and teachers. A great deal more time and attention needs to be paid to these obstacles and to the ways in which students' cultural backgrounds can be gainfully utilized in the classroom.

5. *What are the implicit (and explicit) conceptions of democracy within the curriculum?*

We have argued that the curriculum and the school community must embody and embrace a democratic ethos of care and respect for other individuals, the creation and identification of shared ends, and a respect for and engagement in deliberation. Equally important is a commitment to social justice as we seek to make better worlds with our children.

6. *What are the implicit (and explicit) visions of students' social, political, and economic futures, and how does the curriculum prepare students for those futures?*

All students deserve a future that includes meaningful work in a demo-cratic environment, one that enables individuals to live full, community-oriented, and engaged lives. In today's world only some, in fact very few, students achieve something that approximates that goal. A progressive education would recognize the limited futures envisioned for some students and enlarge and enrich their educational avenues.

While these answers are brief, they are not intended to be cursory. We live in precarious times, times in which public schools are under attack for their public nature. We hope that the attacks can be fended off and that our public schools can be sustained as the progressive institutions we think they could become. All of us deserve such institutions—we should no longer harm or delude ourselves, our own children, or others' children. We need, as Lisa Delpit (1995) maintains, to become more knowledgeable, sophisti-cated, and understanding in educating other people's children. We need to become more attentive to the children and students around us as well as to the world that awaits them.

NOTES

1. Dewey attempted to achieve this integration through a focus on what he called the social occupations. For an elaboration of this attempt see Kliebard (1986).

2. We would add that while some individuals in the academic world diminish the importance of ascertaining the accuracy and reliability of these knowledge claims, we do not. Radical claims about the oppressive dynamics of the world need to be scrutinized and examined. For further elaboration, see Liston (1988).

References

Aiken, W. M. (1942). *The story of the Eight-Year Study*. New York: Harper & Brothers.

Althusser, L. (1971). *Lenin and philosophy*. New York: Monthly Review Press.

American Association for the Advancement of Science. (1989). *Science for all Americans*. Washington, DC: Author.

American Association of University Women (AAUW). (1992). *How schools shortchange girls*. Washington, DC: Author and National Education Association.

Anderson, J. D. (1988). *The education of blacks in the South, 1860–1935*. Chapel Hill: University of North Carolina Press.

Anyon, J. (1980). Social class and the hidden curriculum of work. *Journal of Education, 162*, 67–92.

Apple, M. W. (1979). *Ideology and curriculum*. Boston: Routledge & Kegan Paul.

Apple, M. W. (1985). Old humanists and new curricula: Politics and culture in *The paideia proposal. Curriculum Inquiry, 15*(1), 91–106.

Apple, M. W. (1986). *Teachers and texts: A political economy of class and gender relations in education*. New York: Routledge & Kegan Paul.

Apple, M. W., & Weis, L. (1983). Ideology and practice in schooling: A political and conceptual introduction. In M. W. Apple & L. Weis (Eds.), *Ideology and practice in schooling*. Philadelphia: Temple University Press.

Armstrong, D. M. (1968). *A materialist theory of the mind*. London: Routledge & Kegan Paul.

Asante, M. (1991/92). Afrocentric curriculum. *Educational Leadership, 49*(4), 28–31.

Atlas, J. (1992). *Battle of the books*. New York: Norton.

Baier, K. (1958). *The moral point of view: A rational basis of ethics*. Ithaca, NY: Cornell University Press.

Barber, B. R. (1984). *Strong democracy*. Berkeley: University of California Press.

Barber, B. R. (1992). *An aristocracy of everyone: The politics of education and the future of America*. New York: Ballantine.

Barry, B. (1973). *The liberal theory of justice*. New York: Oxford University Press.

Bartky, S. (1990). *Femininity and domination*. New York: Routledge.

Bastian, A., Fruchter, N., Gittell, M., Greer, C., & Haskins, K. (1985). *Choosing equality: The case for democratic schooling*. Philadelphia: Temple University Press.

Belenky, M., Clinchy, B., Goldberger, N., & Tarule, J. (1986). *Women's ways of knowing*. New York: Basic Books.

Bell, D. (1992). *Faces at the bottom of the well*. New York: Basic Books.

Bellah, R. N., Madsen, R., Sullivan, W. M., Swidler, A., & Tipton, S. M. (1985). *Habits of the heart: Individualism and commitment in American life*. Berkeley: University of California Press.

Bennett, W. (1987). *James Madison High School: A curriculum for American students.* Washington, DC: U.S. Department of Education.

Bennett, W. (1988). Moral literacy and the formation of character. *NASSP Bulletin, 72* (512), 29–34.

Bennett, W. (1989). *Our children and our country: Improving America's schools and affirming the common culture.* New York: Touchstone.

Bennett, W. (1992). *The de-valuing of America: The fight for our culture and children.* New York: Summit.

Berlin, I. (1969). *Four essays on liberty.* New York: Oxford University Press.

Bernstein, R. J. (1983). *Beyond objectivism and relativism: Science, hermeneutics, and praxis.* Philadelphia: University of Pennsylvania Press.

Beyer, L. E. (1982). Ideology, social efficiency, and curriculum inquiry. *Curriculum Inquiry, 12*(3), 305–316.

Beyer, L. E. (1985). Educational reform: The political roots of national risk. *Curriculum Inquiry, 15*(1), 37–56.

Beyer, L. E. (1988a). Can schools further democratic practices? *Theory Into Practice, 27*(4), 262–269.

Beyer, L. E. (1988b). *Knowing and acting: Inquiry, ideology, and educational studies.* London: Falmer.

Beyer, L. E. (1989). *Critical reflection and the culture of schooling: Empowering teachers.* Geelong, Victoria, Australia: Deakin University Press.

Beyer, L. E. (1990). Curriculum deliberation: Value choices and political possibilities. In J. T. Sears & J. D. Marshall (Eds.), *Teaching and thinking about curriculum* (pp. 239–255, 305–307). New York: Teachers College Press.

Beyer, L. E. (1991). Schooling, moral commitment, and the preparation of teachers. *Journal of Teacher Education, 42*(3), 201–210.

Beyer, L. E. (1994). The curriculum, social context, and "political correctness." *Journal of General Education, 43*(1), 1–31.

Beyer, L. E. (1996). *Creating democratic classrooms: The struggle to integrate theory and practice.* New York: Teachers College Press.

Beyer, L. E., & Apple, M. W. (1988). *The curriculum: Problems, politics, and possibilities.* Albany: State University of New York Press.

Beyer, L. E., Feinberg, W., Pagano, J. A., & Whitson, J. A. (1989). *Preparing teachers as professionals: The role of educational studies and other liberal disciplines.* New York: Teachers College Press.

Beyer, L. E., & Liston, D. P. (1992). Discourse or moral action? A critique of postmodernism. *Educational Theory, 42*(4), 371–393.

Beyer, L. E., & Wood, G. H. (1986). Critical inquiry and moral action in education. *Educational Theory, 36*(1), 1–14.

Bleier, R. (1984). *Science and gender: A critique of biology and its theories on women.* New York: Teachers College Press.

Bloom, A. (1987). *The closing of the American mind.* New York: Simon & Schuster.

Bloom, H. (1994). *The Western canon.* New York: Harcourt Brace.

Bobbitt, J. F. (1912). The elimination of waste in education. *The Elementary School Teacher, 12*(6), 259–271.

Bobbitt, J. F. (1913). Some general principles of management applied to the problems of city-school systems. In S. C. Parker (Ed.), *Twelfth yearbook of the National Society for the Study of Education, part I* (pp. 7–96). Chicago: University of Chicago Press.

Bobbitt, J. F. (1918). *The curriculum*. Boston: Houghton Mifflin.

Bobbitt, J. F. (1920). The objectives of secondary education. *The School Review, 28*(10), 738–749.

Bode, B. (1927). *Modern educational theories*. New York: Macmillan.

Bode, B. (1938). *Progressive education at the crossroads*. New York: Newson.

Borrowman, M. L. (1956). *The liberal and technical in teacher education*. New York: Bureau of Publications, Teachers College.

Bowles, S., & Gintis, H. (1976). *Schooling in capitalist America*. New York: Basic Books.

Bowles, S., & Gintis, H. (1987). *Democracy and capitalism: Property, community, and the contradictions of modern social thought*. New York: Basic Books.

Braverman, H. (1974). *Labor and monopoly capital*. New York: Monthly Review Press.

Brenkert, A. (1983). *Marx's ethics of freedom*. London: Routledge and Kegan Paul.

Brody, D. (1980). *Workers in industrial America: Essays on the 20th century struggle*. New York: Oxford University Press.

Brown, L., & Gilligan, C. (1992). *Meeting at the crossroads*. Cambridge, MA: Harvard University Press.

Bryant, C. G. A. (1985). *Positivism in social theory and research*. London: Macmillan.

Burbules, N. C., & Rice, S. (1991). Dialogue across differences: Continuing the conversation. *Harvard Educational Review, 61*(4), 393–416.

Burd, S. (1992, September 30). Humanities chief assails politicization of classrooms. *The Chronicle of Higher Education*, p. A22.

Callahan, R. E. (1962). *Education and the cult of efficiency: A study of the social forces that have shaped the administration of the public schools*. Chicago: University of Chicago Press.

Callinicos, A. (1990). *Against postmodernism: A Marxist critique*. New York: St. Martin's.

Carnegie, A. (1902). *The empire of business*. New York: Doubleday, Page & Co.

Carnoy, M., & Levin, H. (1985). *Schooling and work in the democratic state*. Stanford, CA: Stanford University Press.

Celis, William, 3d. (1993, October 6). Hopeful start for profit-making schools. *New York Times*, pp. A1, B8.

Charters, W. W. (1924). Job analysis and the training of teachers. *Journal of Education Research, 10*, 211–221.

Charters, W. W. (1927). *Curriculum construction*. New York: Macmillan.

Cheney, L. V. (1988). *American memory: A report on the humanities in the nation's public schools*. Washington, DC: U.S. General Accounting Office.

Cheney, L. V. (1992). *Telling the truth: A report on the state of the humanities in higher education*. Washington, DC: National Endowment for the Humanities.

Cherryholmes, C. H. (1988). *Power and criticism: Poststructural investigations in education*. New York: Teachers College Press.

Children's Defense Fund (CDF). (1989). *A vision for America's future*. Washington, DC: Author.

Chodorow, N. (1978). *The reproduction of mothering.* Berkeley: University of California Press.

Clark, B., & Gintis, H. (1978). Rawlsian justice and economic systems. *Philosophy & Public Affairs, 7,* 302–325.

Coleman, P. J. (1989). The world of interventionism, 1880–1940. In R. Eden (Ed.), *The New Deal and its legacy: Critique and reappraisal.* New York: Greenwood.

Committee on High-School Biology Education. (1990). *Fulfilling the promise: Biology in the nation's school.* Washington, DC: National Academy Press.

Counts, G. S. (1932). *Dare the schools build a new social order?* New York: John Day.

Crittenden, P. (1990). *Learning to be moral: Philosophical thoughts about moral development.* Atlantic Highlands, NJ: Humanities Press.

Cuban, L. (1984). *How teachers taught: Constancy and change in American classrooms 1890–1980.* New York: Teachers College Press.

Cubberley, E. (1929). *Public school administration.* Boston: Houghton Mifflin.

Daniels, N. (Ed.). (1975). *Reading Rawls.* New York: Basic Books.

Delpit, L. (1995). *Other's people's children: Cultural conflict in the classroom.* New York: The New Press.

Derrida, J. (1976). *Of grammatology* (Gayatri Chakravorty Spivak, Trans.). Baltimore, MD: The Johns Hopkins University Press.

Derrida, J. (1985, Autumn). Racism's last word. *Critical Inquiry, 12*(1), 290–299.

Derrida, J. (1986, Autumn). But, beyond . . . Open letter to Anne McClintock and Rob Nixon. *Critical Inquiry, 13*(1), 155–170.

Dewey, J. (1916). *Democracy and education: An introduction to the philosophy of education.* New York: Free Press.

Dewey, J. (1935). *Liberalism and social action.* New York: G. P. Putnam's Sons.

Dewey, J. (1938). *Experience and education.* New York: Collier.

Dewey, J. (1956a). *The child and the curriculum.* Chicago: University of Chicago Press. (Original work published 1902)

Dewey, J. (1956b). *The school and society.* Chicago: University of Chicago Press. (Original work published 1900)

Dews, P. (1987). *Logics of disintegration.* New York: Verso.

Duckworth, E. (1987). *"The having of wonderful ideas" and other essays on teaching and learning.* New York: Teachers College Press.

Educational Leadership. (1989). Special issue, "Redirecting assessment." *46*(7).

Edwards, R. (1979). *Contested terrain: The transformation of the workplace in the twentieth century.* New York: Basic Books.

Egan, K. (1988). *Primary understanding.* New York: Routledge.

Egan, K. (1990). *Romantic understanding.* New York: Routledge.

Ellsworth, E. (1989). Why doesn't this feel empowering? Working through the repressive myths of critical pedagogy. *Harvard Educational Review, 59*(3), 297–324.

Elshtain, J. B. (1995). *Democracy on trial.* New York: Basic Books.

Emerson, H. (1913). *The twelve principles of efficiency.* New York: The Engineering Magazine Co.

Faulkner, H. U. (1951). *The decline of laissez-faire, 1897–1917.* New York: Holt, Rinehart & Winston.

Ferguson, A. (1989). *Blood at the root: Motherhood, sexuality and male dominance.* London: Unwin Hyman, Pandora Press.

Feyerabend, P. K. (1978). *Against method: Outline of an anarchistic theory of knowledge.* London: Verso.

Finn, C. (1984). *Against mediocrity: The humanities in America's high schools.* New York: Holmes & Meier.

Finn, C. (1990). Narcissus goes to school. *Commentary, 89*(6), 40–45.

Finn, C. (1991). *We must take charge.* New York: Free Press.

Finney, R. L. (1922). *Causes and cures for the social unrest: An appeal to the middle class.* New York: Macmillan.

Finney, R. L. (1929). *A sociological philosophy of education.* New York: Macmillan.

Foucault, M. (1980). *Power/knowledge: Selected interviews and other writings 1972–1977* (C. Gordon, Ed.). New York: Pantheon.

Fitzgerald, F. (1979). *America revised.* Boston: Atlantic–Little, Brown.

Franklin, B. M. (1982). The social efficiency movement reconsidered: Curriculum change in Minneapolis, 1917–1950. *Curriculum Inquiry, 12*, 9–33.

Franklin, B. M. (1986). *Building the American community: The school curriculum and the search for social control.* London: Falmer.

Franklin, B. M. (1988). Education for an urban America: Ralph Tyler and the curriculum field. In I. Goodson (Ed.), *International perspectives in curriculum history* (pp. 277–296). New York: Routledge, Chapman & Hall.

Freire, P. (1973). *Education for critical consciousness.* New York: Seabury.

Freire, P. (1974). *Pedagogy of the oppressed.* New York: Seabury.

Friedman, B. M. (1989). *Day of reckoning: The consequences of American economic policy.* New York: Vintage.

Friedman, M. (1955). The role of government in education. In R. A. Solo (Ed.), *Economics and the public interest* (pp. 123–144). New Brunswick, NJ: Rutgers University Press.

Friedman, M. (1982). *Capitalism and freedom.* Chicago: University of Chicago Press.

Friedman, M., & Friedman, R. (1980). *Free to choose: A personal statement.* New York: Harcourt Brace Jovanovich.

Fuller, L. (1973). *The morality of law.* New Haven, CT: Yale University Press.

Fuller, T. (Ed.) (1989). *The voice of liberal learning: Michael Oakeshott on education.* New Haven, CT: Yale University Press.

Furniss, N., & Tilton, T. (1977). *The case for the welfare state: From social security to social equality.* Bloomington: Indiana University Press.

Gadamer, H.-G. (1985). *Truth and method.* New York: Crossroad.

Gates, H. L. (1992). *Loose canons: Notes on the culture wars.* New York: Oxford University Press.

Gilligan, C. (1982). *In a different voice.* Cambridge, MA: Harvard University Press.

Giroux, H. (1988). Postmodernism and the discourse of educational criticism. *Journal of Education, 170*(3), 5–30.

Giroux, H., & McLaren, P. (1989). *Critical pedagogy, the state, and cultural struggle.* Albany: State University of New York Press.

Giroux, H. A. (1991). *Postmodernism, feminism, and cultural politics: Redrawing educational boundaries.* Albany: State University of New York Press.

Goodlad, J. (1984). *A place called school*. New York: McGraw-Hill.

Graff, G. (1992). *Beyond the culture wars: How teaching the conflicts can revitalize American education*. New York: Norton.

Greenberg, E. S. (1985). *Capitalism and the American political ideal*. Armonk, NY: Sharpe.

Gutmann, A. (1987). *Democratic education*. Princeton, NJ: Princeton University Press.

Haber, S. (1964). *Efficiency and uplift: Scientific management in the progressive era, 1890–1920*. Chicago: University of Chicago Press.

Hacker, A. (1992). *Two nations*. New York: Ballantine.

Harding, S. (1986). *The science question in feminism*. Ithaca, NY: Cornell University Press.

Harvey, D. (1989). *The condition of postmodernity*. Cambridge, MA: Blackwell.

Hayek, F. A. von. (1976). *Law, legislation, and liberty* (Vol. 2). London: Routledge.

Heath, S. B. (1983). *Ways with words: Language, life, and work in communities and classrooms*. New York: Cambridge University Press.

Held, D. (1987). *Models of democracy*. Stanford, CA: Stanford University Press.

Hirsch, E. D. (1983). Cultural literacy. *The American Scholar, 52*(2), 159–169.

Hirsch, E. D. (1987/88). Restoring cultural literacy in the early grades. *Educational Leadership, 45*(4), 63–70.

Hirsch, E. D. (1988). *Cultural literacy: What every American needs to know*. New York: Vintage.

Hirst, P. (1965). Liberal education and the nature of knowledge. In R. D. Archambault (Ed.), *Philosophical analysis of education* (pp.113–138). New York: Humanities Press.

Hobbes, T. (1958). *Leviathan, parts I and II*. Indianapolis, IN: Bobbs-Merrill. (Original work published 1651)

Hochschild, J. (1984). *The new American dilemma: Liberal democracy and school desegregation*. New Haven, CT: Yale University Press.

Holland, D., & Eisenhart, M. (1990). *Educated in romance*. Chicago: University of Chicago Press.

hooks, b. (1989). *Talking back*. Boston: South End Press.

hooks, b. (1994). *Outlaw culture*. New York: Routledge.

Ichilov, O. (1990). Dimension and role patterns of citizenship in democracy. In O. Ichilov (Ed.), *Political socialization, citizenship education, and democracy* (pp. 11–24). New York: Teachers College Press.

Ise, J. (1961). *Our national park policy: A critical history*. Baltimore: The Johns Hopkins Press.

Jackson, P. W. (1968). *Life in classrooms*. New York: Teachers College Press.

Jameson, F. (1984). Postmodernism, or the cultural logic of late capitalism. *New Left Review, 146*, 53–92.

Kaestle, C. (1973). *The evolution of an urban school system: New York City, 1750–1850*. Cambridge, MA: Harvard University Press.

Karier, C. (1975). *Shaping the American educational state: 1900 to the present*. New York: Free Press.

Katzman, J., & Hodas, S. (1995). *Class action*. New York: Villard.

Kaufman, P. W. (1984). *Women teachers on the frontier*. New Haven, CT: Yale University Press.

Keegan, P. (1995, May 21). The digerati. *New York Times Sunday Magazine*, pp. 38–44, 86–88.

Keller, E. F. (1985). *Reflections on gender and science*. New Haven, CT: Yale University Press.

Keller, P. (1982). *Getting at the core: Curricular reform at Harvard*. Cambridge, MA: Harvard University Press.

Kilpatrick, W. H. (1918). The Project Method. *Teachers College Record, 19*(4), 319–335.

Kilpatrick, W., Bode, B., Dewey, J., Childs, J., Raup, R. B., Hullfish, G., & Thayer, V. T. (1933). *The educational frontier*. New York: D. Appleton-Century.

King, W. I. (1915). *The wealth and income of the people of the United States*. New York: Macmillan.

Kiziltan, M. U., Bain, W. J., & Canizares, A. M. (1990). Postmodern conditions: Rethinking public education. *Educational Theory, 40*(3), 351–369.

Kliebard, H. M. (1975a). Bureaucracy and curriculum theory. In W. Pinar (Ed.), *Curriculum theorizing: The reconceptualists* (pp. 51–69). Berkeley, CA: McCutchan.

Kliebard, H. M. (1975b). Persistent curriculum issues in historical perspective. In W. Pinar (Ed.), *Curriculum theorizing: The reconceptualists* (pp. 39–50). Berkeley: McCutchan.

Kliebard, H. M. (1977). The Tyler rationale. In A. A. Bellack & H. M. Kliebard (Eds.), *Curriculum and evaluation* (pp. 56–67). Berkeley, CA: McCutchan.

Kliebard, H. M. (1982). Education at the turn of the century: A crucible for curriculum change. *Educational Researcher, 11*(1), 16–24.

Kliebard, H. M. (1986). *The struggle for the American curriculum, 1893–1958*. New York: Routledge & Kegan Paul.

Koerner, K. F. (1985). *Liberalism and its critics*. London: Croom Helm.

Kozol, J. (1991). *Savage inequalities: Children in America's schools*. New York: Crown.

Kuhn, T. S. (1970). *The structure of scientific revolutions* (2nd ed.). Chicago: University of Chicago Press.

Kuhn, T. S. (1977). *The essential tension: Selected studies in scientific tradition and change*. Chicago: University of Chicago Press.

Kupfer, A. M. (1995, July). Conflict resolution of "convict revolution"?: The problematics of critical pedagogy in the classroom. *Urban Education, 30*(2), 219–239.

Kuttner, R. (1995, May 8–14). Punishing the poor. *Washington Post National Weekly Edition*, p. 5.

Laidler, H. W. (1931). *Concentration of control in American industry*. New York: Crowell.

Larrabee, M. (1993). *An ethic of care*. New York: Routledge.

Lasch, C. (1984). *The minimal self: Psychic survival in troubled times*. New York: Norton.

Lather, P. (1991). *Getting smart: Feminist research and pedagogy with/in the postmodern*. New York: Routledge.

Leach, M. S. (1992). Can we talk? A response to Burbules and Rice. *Harvard Educational Review, 62*(2), 257–263.

Lee, G. C. (1961). *Crusade against ignorance: Thomas Jefferson on education.* New York: Teachers College Press.

Levin, H. M. (1990). "Political socialization for workplace democracy." In O. Ichilov (Ed.), *Political socialization, citizenship education, and democracy* (pp. 158–176). New York: Teachers College Press.

Levine, R. F. (1988). *Class struggle and the New Deal: Industrial labor, industrial capital, and the state.* Lawrence: University Press of Kansas.

Liston, D. P. (1988). *Capitalist schools: Explanation and ethics in radical studies of schooling.* New York: Routledge.

Liston, D. P., & Zeichner, K. M. (1987). Reflective teacher education and moral deliberation. *Journal of Teacher Education, 38*(6), 2–8.

Liston, D. P., & Zeichner, K. M. (1991). *Teacher education and the social conditions of schooling.* New York: Routledge.

Locke, J. (1960). *Two treatises of government* (P. Laslett, Ed.). New York: New American Library. (Original work published 1690)

Luke, C., & Gore, J. (1992). *Feminisms and critical pedagogy.* New York: Routledge.

Lukes, S. (1973). *Individualism.* New York: Harper & Row.

Lyotard, J.-F. (1984). *The postmodern condition: A report on knowledge.* Minneapolis: University of Minnesota Press.

Lyotard, J.-F. (1985). Defining the postmodern. ICA Documents 4.

Macdonald, J. B. (1975). Curriculum and human interests. In W. Pinar (Ed.), *Curriculum theorizing: The reconceptualists* (pp. 283–294). Berkeley: McCutchan.

MacIntyre, A. (1984). *After virtue: A study in moral theory.* Notre Dame, IN: University of Notre Dame Press.

MacKinnon, C. (1989). *Toward a feminist theory of the state.* Cambridge, MA: Harvard University Press.

Mansbridge, J. J. (1983). *Beyond adversary democracy.* Chicago: University of Chicago Press.

Martin, J. R. (1981). The ideal of the educated person. *Educational Theory, 31*(3), 97–109.

Martin, J. R. (1982). Two dogmas of curriculum. *Synthese, 51,* 5–20.

Martin, J. R. (1985). *Reclaiming a conversation: The ideal of the educated woman.* New Haven, CT: Yale University Press.

Martin, J. R. (1992). *The schoolhome.* Cambridge, MA: Harvard University Press.

Martin, J. R. (1994). *Changing the educational landscape.* New York: Routledge.

Marvin, F. S. (1937). *Compte, the founder of sociology.* New York: Wiley.

Marx, K. (1848/1948). *Manifesto of the Communist Party.* New York: International Publishers.

Mattingly, P. H. (1975). *The classless profession: American schoolmen in the nineteenth century.* New York: New York University Press.

McClintock, A., & Nixon, R. (1986, Autumn). No names apart: The separation of word and history in Derrida's "le dernier mot du racisme." *Critical Inquiry, 13*(1), 140–154.

McClure, S. S. (1914). *My autobiography.* New York: Frederick A. Stokes.

McGinley, W., & Kamberelis, G. (1992). Transformative functions of children's writing. *Language Arts, 69,* 330–338.

McGinley, W., Kamberelis, G., & Mahoney, T. (in press). Just only stories. In

T. Rogers & A. Soter (Eds.), *Reading across cultures*. New York: Teachers College Press.

McHale, B. (1987). *Postmodernist fiction*. New York: Methuen.

McNeil, L. (1988). *Contradictions of control*. New York: Routledge.

McQuillan, P. (1995, April). *"Knowing" and empowerment; or student empowerment gone good*. Paper presented at the annual meeting of the American Educational Research Association, San Francisco.

McQuillan, P. (in press). *"There is no excuse": Educational opportunity in an urban American high school*. Buffalo: State University of New York Press.

Meier, D. (1995). *The power of their ideas*. Boston: Beacon Press.

Mill, J. S. (1956). *On liberty*. Indianapolis: Bobbs-Merrill. (Original work published 1859)

Mises, L. von (1956). *The anti-capitalistic mentality*. New York: Van Nostrand.

Mooney, C. J. (1990). Academic group fighting the "politically correct left" gains momentum. *Chronicle of Higher Education, 37*(15), A1, A13, A16.

Mooney, C. J. (1991). Scholars decry campus hostility to Western culture at a time when more nations embrace its values. *Chronicle of Higher Education, 37*(20), pp. A15–A16.

Muelder, H. R. (1984). *Missionaries and muckrakers: The first hundred years of Knox College*. Urbana: University of Illinois Press.

Myrdal, G. (1944). *An American dilemma*. New York: Harper & Brothers.

Nasaw, D. (1979). *Schooled to order: A social history of public schooling in the United States*. New York: Oxford University Press.

National Commission on Excellence in Education. (1983). *A nation at risk: The imperative for educational reform*. Washington, DC: U.S. Government Printing Office.

National Commission on Social Studies in the Schools. (1989). *Charting a course: Social studies for the 21st century*. Washington, DC: Author.

National Research Council. (1989). *Everybody counts: A report on the future of mathematics education*. Washington, DC: National Academy Press.

Neill, A. S. (1977). *Summerhill: A radical approach to child rearing*. New York: Pocket Books.

Nicholson, C. (1989). Postmodernism, feminism, and education: The need for solidarity. *Educational Theory, 39*(3), 197–205.

Noble, D. (1977). *America by design: Science, technology, and the rise of corporate capitalism*. New York: Knopf.

Noble, D. (1984). *Forces of production: A social history of industrial automation*. New York: Knopf.

Noddings, N. (1984). *Caring: A feminine approach to ethics and moral education*. Berkeley: University of California Press.

Noddings, N. (1992). *The challenge to care in schools*. New York: Teachers College Press.

Novak, M. (1982). *The spirit of democratic capitalism*. New York: Simon & Schuster.

Nozick, R. (1974). *Anarchy, state, and utopia*. New York: Basic Books.

Oakes, J. (1985). *Keeping track: How schools structure inequality*. New Haven, CT: Yale University Press.

O'Conor, A. (1993/94). Who gets called queer in school? Lesbian, gay and bisexual teenagers, homophobia and high school. *The High School Journal*, 77(1&2), 7–12.

Ogbu, J. U. (1987). Variability in minority school performance: A problem in search of an explanation. *Anthropology and Education Quarterly*, *18*, 312–334.

Ogbu, J. U. (1990). Minority education in comparative perspective. *The Journal of Negro Education*, *59*, 45–57.

Ogbu, J., & Matute-Bianchi, M. (1986). Understanding sociocultural factors: Knowledge, identity, and school adjustment. In California Bilingual Education Office, *Beyond language: Social and cultural factors in schooling language minority students* (pp. 73–142). Los Angeles: California State University, Evaluation, Dissemination and Assessment Center.

Okin, S. (1989). *Justice, gender and the family*. New York: Basic Books.

Olson, J. S. (1988). *Saving capitalism: The reconstruction finance corporation and the New Deal, 1933–1940*. Princeton, NJ: Princeton University Press.

Pagano, J. A. (1990). *Exiles and communities: Teaching in the patriarchal wilderness*. Albany: State University of New York Press.

Paley, V. G. (1984). *Girls and boys*. Chicago: University of Chicago Press.

Paley, V. G. (1989). *White teacher*. Cambridge: Harvard University Press.

Palmer, B. (1990). *Descent into discourse*. Philadelphia: Temple University Press.

Pinar, W. F. (1988). *Contemporary curriculum discourses*. Scottsdale, AZ: Gorsuch Scarisbrick.

Plant, R. (1991). *Modern political thought*. Cambridge, MA: Blackwell.

Quindlen, A. (1994). *One true thing*. New York: Random House.

Ravitch, D. (1983). *The troubled crusade: American education 1945–1980*. New York: Basic Books.

Ravitch, D. (1990). Multiculturalism: E pluribus plures. *The American Scholar*, *59*(3), 337–356.

Ravitch, D., & Finn, C. (1987). *What do our 17-year olds know?* New York: Harper & Row.

Rawls, J. (1971). *A theory of justice*. Cambridge, MA: Harvard University Press.

Reed, A. (1995, April 11). What are the drums saying, Booker? The current crisis of the black intellectual. *Village Voice*, pp. 31–36.

Reese, W. (1986). *Power and the promise of school reform*. Boston: Routledge & Kegan Paul.

Rich, A. (1985). Taking women students seriously. In M. Culley & C. Portuges (Eds.), *Gendered subjects* (pp. 21–28). New York: Routledge & Kegan Paul.

Rich, A. (1986). *Of woman born*. New York: Norton.

Rockford school offers cash-for-grades program. (1992, September 29). *Chicago Tribune*, p. 3.

Roehrs, C. (1994). *Radical curriculum theories: Examining changes in perspective*. Unpublished manuscript.

Ropke, W. (1960). *A humane economy*: The social framework of the free market. Chicago: Henry Regnery.

Rorty, R. (1979). *Philosophy and the mirror of nature*. Princeton, NJ: Princeton University Press.

Rorty, R. (1989). *Contingency, irony, and solidarity*. New York: Cambridge University Press.

Ross, E. W., Cornett, J. W., and McCutcheon, G. (1992). *Teacher personal theorizing: Connecting curriculum practice, theory, and research*. Albany: State University of New York Press.

Rothman, R. (1992). Despite recession's impact, Tampa High on school-to-work link. *Education Week, 11*(23), 1, 16–17.

Rubin, L. B. (1976). *Worlds of pain: Life in the working class family*. New York: Basic Books.

Rubin, L. B. (1994). *Families on the fault line: America's working class speaks about the family, the economy, race, and ethnicity*. New York: HarperCollins.

Saussure, F. de (1966). *Course in general linguistics*. New York: McGraw-Hill.

Schubert, W. H. (1986). *Curriculum: Perspective, paradigm, and possibility*. New York: Macmillan.

Searle, J. (1990, December 6). The storm over the university. *New York Review of Books*, pp. 34–42.

Sears, J. T., & Marshall, D. (1990). *Teaching and thinking about curriculum*. New York: Teachers College Press.

Selden, S. (1988). Biological determinism and the normal school curriculum: Helen Putnam and the NEA Committee on Racial Well-Being, 1910–1922. In W. F. Pinar (Ed.), *Contemporary curriculum discourses* (pp. 50–65). Scottsdale, AZ: Gorsuch Scarisbrick.

Seligman, E. R. A. (1910). Introduction. In A. Smith, *An inquiry into the nature and causes of the wealth of nations, Volume 1* (pp. vii–xvi). New York: Dutton.

Selznick, P. (1992). *The moral commonwealth: Social theory and the promise of community*. Berkeley: University of California Press.

Shor, I. (1986). *Culture wars: School and society in the conservative restoration 1969–1984*. Boston: Routledge & Kegan Paul.

Shor, I. (1987). *Freire for the classroom*. Portsmouth, NH: Heinemann.

Sinclair, U. (1906). *The jungle*. New York: Grosset & Dunlap.

Sirotnik, K. A. (1983). What you see is what you get: Consistency, persistency, and mediocrity in classrooms. *Harvard Educational Review, 53*, 16–31.

Sizer, T. (1992). *Horace's school: Redesigning the American high school*. New York: Houghton Mifflin.

Smith, A. (1804). *The theory of moral sentiments*, Volumes 1 & 2. London: T. Cadell & W. Davies.

Smith, A. (1969). *The theory of moral sentiments*. New Rochelle, NY: Arlington House. (Original work published 1759)

Smith, A. (1910a). *An inquiry into the nature and causes of the wealth of nations* (Vol. 1). New York: Dutton. (Original work published 1776)

Smith, A. (1910b). *An inquiry into the nature and causes of the wealth of nations* (Vol. 2). New York: Dutton. (Original work published 1776)

Smith, E. R., & Tyler, R. W. (1942). *Appraising and recording student progress*. New York: Harper & Brothers.

Smith, G. (Ed.) (1994). *Public schools that work*. New York: Routledge.

Snedden, D. (1921). *Sociological determination of objectives in education*. Philadelphia: Lippincott.

Stanic, G. M. A. (1988). A historical perspective on justifying the teaching of mathematics. In I. Goodson (Ed.), *International perspectives in curriculum history* (pp. 209–227). New York: Routledge, Chapman & Hall.

Strike, K. A. (1982). *Educational policy and the just society*. Urbana: University of Illinois Press.

Taylor, C. (1992). *Multiculturalism and the politics of recognition*. Princeton, NJ: Princeton University Press.

Taylor, F. W. (1911). *The principles of scientific management*. New York and London: Harper & Brothers.

Teitelbaum, K. N. (1988). Contestation and curriculum: The efforts of American Socialists, 1900–1920. In L. E. Beyer & M. W. Apple (Eds.), *The curriculum: Problems, politics, and possibilities* (pp. 32–55). Albany: State University of New York Press.

Thorndike, E. L. (1935). *The psychology of wants, interests, and attitudes*. New York: Appleton-Century Crofts.

Toch, T. (1991). *In the name of excellence: The struggle to reform the nation's schools, why it's failing, and what should be done*. New York: Oxford University Press.

Tocqueville, A. de (1900). *Democracy in America* (H. Reeve, Trans.). New York: Collier. (Original work published 1838)

Toulmin, S. (1972). *Human understanding*. Princeton, NJ: Princeton University Press.

Twentieth Century Fund. (1983). *Making the grade: Report of the twentieth century fund task force on federal elementary and secondary education policy*. New York: Author.

Tyack, D. (1974). *The one best system: A history of American urban education*. Cambridge, MA: Harvard University Press.

Tyler, R. W. (1949). *Basic principles of curriculum and instruction*. Chicago: University of Chicago Press.

Unger, R. M. (1975). *Knowledge and politics*. New York: Free Press.

Unks, G. (1995). *The gay teen*. New York: Routledge.

U.S. Department of the Interior. (1991). *The national parks: Shaping the system*. Washington, DC: U.S. Department of the Interior.

Vallance, E. (1977). Hiding the hidden curriculum: An interpretation of the language of justification in nineteenth-century educational reform. In A. Bellack & H. M. Kliebard (Eds.), *Curriculum and evaluation* (pp. 590–607). Berkeley: McCutchan.

Van Biema, D. (1995, June 26). Militias: The message from Mark. *Time*, pp. 56–62.

Violas, P. (1978). *The training of the urban working class: A history of 20th century American education*. Chicago: Rand McNally.

Waks, L. J. (1995, April). *The character of contemporary life: An analysis of "post order" theories*. Paper presented at the annual meeting of the American Educational Research Association, San Francisco.

Walsh, M. (1992a). "Turning lives around" is the goal of Burger King–school partnerships. *Education Week, 11*(32), 1, 15.

Walsh, M. (1992b). Yale president's move is touted as a 'coup' for the Edison Project. *Education Week, 11*(37), 1, 18.

Welch, S. (1991). An ethic of solidarity and difference. In H. A. Giroux (Ed.), *Postmodernism, feminism, and cultural politics: Redrawing educational boundaries* (pp. 83–99). Albany: State University of New York Press.

Wellman, D. (1977). *Portraits of white racism*. New York: Oxford University Press.

West, C. (1991). *The ethical dimensions of Marxist thought*. New York: Monthly Review Press.

West, C. (1993). *Race matters*. Boston: Beacon.

White, S. K. (1992). *Political theory and postmodernism*. New York: Cambridge University Press.

Whitson, J. A. (1990, October). *Curriculum as* Bildung: *Implications for critical curriculum inquiry*. Paper presented at the Twelfth Conference on Curriculum Theory and Classroom Practice, Dayton, Ohio.

Will, G. (1995, April 23). Seeking social reward equality may not be the right approach. *Sunday Herald-Times* (Bloomington/Bedford, IN), p. A12.

Williams, R. (1961). *The long revolution*. New York: Columbia University Press.

Willis, P. (1977). *Learning to labor: How working class kids get working class jobs*. Westmead, England: Gower Publishing Co.

Wilson, H. S. (1970). *McClure's magazine and the muckrakers*. Princeton, NJ: Princeton University Press.

Wilson, W. J. (1990). *The truly disadvantaged: The inner city, the underclass, and public policy*. Chicago: University of Chicago Press.

Winch, P. (1958). *The idea of a social science and its relation to philosophy*. London: Routledge & Kegan Paul.

Wirth, A. G. (1983). *Productive work in industry and schools: Becoming persons again*. Lanham, MD: University Press of America.

Wolff, R. P. (1977). *Understanding Rawls: A reconstruction and critique of "A theory of justice."* Princeton, NJ: Princeton University Press.

Wollstonecraft, M. (1982). *Vindication of the rights of woman*. Harmondsworth, UK: Penguin.

Wood, G. H. (1990). "Introduction" to "Breaking Barriers," a thematic issue of *Democracy and Education*, 5(2), 4.

Wood, G. H. (1992). *Schools that work*. New York: NAL–Dutton.

Workers' pay drops sharply despite rise in firms' profits. (1995, June 23). *Chicago Tribune*, p. 11.

Wright, E. (1985). *Classes*. London: Verso.

Wrigley, J. (1982). *Class politics and public schools: Chicago, 1900–1950*. New Brunswick, NJ: Rutgers University Press.

Wynne, E. (1985/86). The great tradition in education: Transmitting moral values. *Educational Leadership, 43*(4), 4–9.

Wynne, E. (1987). Students and schools. In K. Ryan & G. McLean (Eds.), *Character development in schools and beyond*. New York: Praeger.

Wynne, E., & Ryan, K. (1993). *Reclaiming our schools*. New York: Macmillan.

Young, E. F. (1901). *Isolation in the school*. Chicago: University of Chicago Press.

Index

NAMES

Aiken, W. M., 24
Althusser, L., 110
Anderson, J. D., 9
Anyon, J., 108, 195
Apple, M. W., xi, xii, xiv, 13–
15, 104, 106, 111, 155, 199
Armstrong, D. M., 6
Asante, M.K., 130, 195, 197
Atlas, J., 200

Baier, K., 54
Bain, W. J., 138
Barber, B. R., 83, 160, 168,
169, 175
Barry, B., 79
Bartky, S., 115, 118–120
Bastian, A., 181
Belenky, M., 207
Bell, D., 123, 125–126, 129–130
Bellah, R.N., 46–47, 54, 175
Bennett, William, xii, xiii, xx,
29–34, 36–38, 40, 44, 57, 95,
162, 166, 189
Berlin, I., 58
Bernstein, R. J., 143
Beyer, L. E., xi, xiv, 2, 5, 18, 22,
23, 27, 144, 155, 156, 156
n. 1, 157 n. 6, 169, 195
Bleier, R., 143
Bloom, Allan, xii, xiii, 48, 52
Bloom, H., 200
Bobbitt, J. Franklin, 19, 20, 28, 84
Bode, Boyde, 83, 98
Borrowman, M. L., 7
Bowles, Samuel, 104, 106, 108,
111, 158, 164–165, 176, 180,
185, 187
Brandeis, Louis, 10
Braverman, H., 10
Brenkert, A., 102
Brody, D., 71
Brown, Lynn, 207
Bryant, C. G. A., 139

Burbules, N. C., 157 n. 5
Burd, S., 63
Bush, George, 35

Callahan, R. E., 1, 8, 10, 11, 17
Callinicos, A., 146–147, 151, 152
Calvin, John, 46
Canizares, A. M., 138
Carnegie, Andrew, 8–9
Carnoy, Martin, 104, 110
Celis, William, 64 n. 1
Charters, W. W., 19, 21, 84
Cheney, Lynne V., xii, 63
Cherryholmes, C. H., 169
Childs, John, 98
Chodorow, Nancy, 115–118,
121
Clark, B., 79
Clinchy, Blythe, 207
Coleman, P. J., 65
Counts, George S., 202–203
Crittenden, P., 172
Cuban, L., 24
Cubberley, Ellwood, 19, 84

Daniels, N., 79
Delpit, Lisa, 204–205, 219
Derrida, J., 141, 151, 154, 157
n. 4, 157 n. 7
Dewey, John, 27, 66–68, 72,
74–78, 83, 87–90, 93, 96, 98,
137, 164, 181, 186, 192–193,
202, 203, 211, 214
Dews, P., 135, 147–148
Duckworth, Eleanor, 212–213

Edwards, R., 10, 72
Egan, Kieran, 214
Eisenhart, Margaret, 115
Ellsworth, Elizabeth, 144–146,
182
Elshtain, Jean Bethke, 169,
179–181, 183

Emerson, Harrison, 10
Engels, Friedrich, 136

Faulkner, H. U., 97 n. 2
Feinberg, W., 2, 156
Ferguson, Ann, 115, 118–119
Feyerabend, P. K., 143, 169
Finn, Chester, xii, xiii, xx, 29–
31, 33, 40, 95, 162, 189
Finney, Ross L., 15, 19
Fitzgerald, F., 199
Foucault, M., 136–137, 143,
146–148, 154, 169
Franklin, Barry M., xi, xii, 6, 23,
25, 26
Franklin, Benjamin, 7, 46
Freire, Paulo, 108, 112–113,
181–182, 196, 197, 205, 211,
215
Friedman, B. M., 184
Friedman, Milton, 39, 43–44,
50, 51, 53–54, 56, 57, 59, 60,
64 n. 2, 64 n. 3, 91–92, 94,
165
Friedman, Rose, 43–44, 50, 51,
60, 64 n. 3
Fruchter, N., 181
Fuller, L., 102
Fuller, T., 211
Furniss, N., 73

Gadamer, H.-G., 169
Gates, H. L., 200
Gillan, John, 139
Gilligan, Carol, 115–117, 207
Gingrich, Newt, 159
Gintis, Herbert, 79, 104, 106,
108, 111, 158, 164–165, 176,
180, 185, 187
Giroux, H. A., xiv, 133, 137,
140
Gittell, M., 181
Goldberger, Nancy, 207

Smith, Greg, 201
Snedden, David, 19
Stanic, G. M. A., 20
Strike, K. A., 86, 87, 96
Sullivan, W. M., 54
Swidler, A., 54

Tarule, Jill, 207
Taylor, Charles, 182
Taylor, Frederick Winslow, 10–12, 18, 71
Teitelbaum, K. N., 23
Thayer, V. T., 98
Thorndike, Edward L., 6
Tilton, T., 73
Tipton, S. M., 54
Toch, T., 200
Tocqueville, Alexis de, 7, 51, 64 n. 3
Toulmin, S., 138–139

Tyack, David, 2
Tyler, Ralph W., 24–28

Unger, R. M., 74, 75, 83
Unks, G., 131–132 n. 1

Vallance, E., 3, 45
Van Biema, D., 142
Vanderlip, Frank A., 1
Violas, P., 3

Waks, L. J., 135
Walsh, M., 40, 41
Weis, Lois, xi, 106
Welch, S., 144, 183
Wellman, David, 124, 126
West, Cornell, 104, 124, 128, 129, 172, 179, 181, 197
White, Stephen K., 133, 143
Whitson, J. A., 2, 156, 169

Whittle, Chris, 40
Will, George, 59
Williams, R., 143, 179
Willis, Paul, 111, 199
Wilson, H. S., 65
Wilson, W. J., 103
Winch, P., 143
Wirth, A. G., 186
Wolff, R. P., 79
Wollstonecraft, Mary, 97 n. 5
Wood, George H., 90, 157 n. 6, 201
Wright, E., 132 n. 2
Wrigley, J., 200
Wynne, Edward, 29, 36–38, 44, 162–163, 166, 168

Young, Ella Flagg, 22

Zeichner, K. M., 144, 156

SUBJECTS

Adopt-A-School programs, 41
Affinity groups, 145–146
African Americans. *See also* Multiculturalism; Race; Racism
    and civil rights, 125–126, 129–130
    lack of engagement in schooling, 204
    poverty of, 31, 99, 128
    responses to racial repression, 129–130
    women, 31, 123–124, 163, 165, 168
Afrocentric curriculum, 130, 195, 197
American Association for the Advancement of Science, 200
American Association of University Women (AAUW), 99–101, 103
American Educational Research Association (AERA), 28
American Sociological Society, 139
Assembly lines, 11, 89, 107
Assertive Discipline, 137–138
Association of Artists of the World against Apartheid, 151–152

Banking model of education, 108
Basic Principles of Curriculum and Instruction (Tyler), 24–25, 28
Boulder Valley School District (Colorado), 200–201
Bourgeoisie (capitalist class), 55, 105–106, 108–109

Capitalism
    advantages of, 44–45
    alienation in, 71, 106–109, 119–120, 179, 183, 186

classes in, 55, 68–72, 99, 105–109, 164
cultural manifestations of, 172–174
democratic, 55–56
ideology of, 110–111
individualism in, 46–48, 77
laissez-faire, 68, 74, 82, 172, 178, 185
larger enterprises in, 70–71, 72
production methods of, 7–8, 55, 69–73, 105, 176
and public schools, 26, 40–41, 104–112
racial hostility and economic domination in, 125
and scientific management, 10–12, 17, 18, 21, 25, 71
welfare state in, 109, 179, 184
Capitalism and Freedom (Friedman), 60
Capital punishment, 173–174
Care, concern, and connection (three Cs), 197, 207, 218
Central Park East Secondary School (New York City), 214
Character, and the new right, 31–32, 36–38, 46, 162, 164–165, 198
Child and the Curriculum, The (Dewey), 192
Children's Defense Fund (CDF), 99, 100
Civil rights, 125–126, 129–130
Classical liberalism, 42–52, 167, 176
    competition in, 44
    consciousness in, 67–68, 74–75
    critique of, 66–73, 180
    democracy and, 83, 90
    free markets in, 43–46, 50, 65, 91–92

About the Authors

Landon E. Beyer is Associate Professor and Director of Teacher Education at Indiana University, Bloomington. His interests include curriculum theory and development, alternative approaches to the preparation of teachers, the arts and aesthetic education, and the social foundations of education. He has published widely in scholarly journals on these and related topics. He is editor of *Creating Democratic Classrooms: The Struggle to Integrate Theory and Practice* (Teachers College Press, 1996), and senior editor (with Michael W. Apple) of *The Curriculum: Problems, Politics, and Possibilities*, second edition (State University of New York Press, in press).

Daniel P. Liston is Associate Professor of Education at the University of Colorado at Boulder. His interests include curriculum theory, radical educational analyses, and teacher education. He has published in numerous scholarly journals and is the author of *Capitalist Schools: Explanation and Ethics in Radical Studies of Schooling* (Routledge, 1988), co-author (with Kenneth Zeichner) of *Teacher Education and the Social Conditions of Schooling* (Routledge, 1991), and co-editor (with Kenneth Zeichner) of a series entitled *Reflective Teaching* (Lawrence Erlbaum, in press).